Kronik

FROM EMPIRE TO REPUBLIC
The Social History of the Ottoman Empire and the Birth of Modern Turkey

—

HALİL İNALCIK

KRONIK BOOKS: 561
History: 8

CHIEF EDITOR
Adem Koçal

EDITOR
Ahmet Yaşar

COVER DESIGN
Kutan Ural

COLORIZE COVER PHOTO
Yiğit Alp Kırık

First Printing, The Isis Press, 1995
Second Printing, Kronik Kitap, 2024, Istanbul

ISBN
978-625-6228-14-6

KRONİK BOOKS
Şakayıklı Sk. N°8, Levent
Istanbul - 34327 - Turkiye
Phone: +90 (212) 2431323
Fax: +90 (212) 2431328
kronik@kronikkitap.com

Republic of Turkey
Ministry of Culture and Tourism
Certificate Number
34569

www.kronikkitap.com
kronikkitap

PRINT AND COVER
Optimum Basım
Tevfikbey Mah. Dr. Ali Demir Cad. No: 51/1
34295 K. Çekmece / İstanbul
Telefon: (0212) 463 71 25
Matbaa Sertifika No: 41707

HALİL İNALCIK

FROM EMPIRE TO REPUBLIC

The Social History *of the* Ottoman Empire *and the* Birth *of* Modern Turkey

Kronik

HALİL İNALCIK

World-renowned Turkish historian Halil İnalcık, who was dubbed the "Şeyhü'l-Müverrihin" (sheikh of historians), was born in Istanbul, 1916. İnalcık taught the history of Ottoman Empire and Turkey at the Universities of Ankara (1942-1972), Chicago (1972-1986), Princeton (1967), Harvard (1992) and Bilkent (1994-2016). İnalcık was a member and president of many Turkish, American, British and Serbian Academies, and had been the recipient of several honorary doctorates. İnalcık gave various seminars and conferences in Turkey and abroad and published numerous books and articles on Ottoman and Turkish history. İnalcık passed away at the age of 100 in Ankara in 2016.

His books published in English by Kronik Kitap

The Ottoman Empire and Europe: The Ottoman Empire and Its Place in European History

The Ottoman Empire: Sultan, Society and Economy

CONTENTS

PREFACE

In this volume, I have collected some papers dating between 1962 and 1992, and mostly dealing with Ottoman social history and the emergence of modern Turkey. In No. II, "On the Social Structure of the Ottoman Empire: Paradigms and Research", published for the first time here, an attempt is made to review critically the principal theories on the Ottoman political-social system. The following paper discusses the *çift-ḫāne* system, which represents the organization of the Ottoman rural society on the basis of a particular agrarian-fiscal system. No. IV deals with circumstances of the long struggle for the conquest of Northern Albania by the Ottomans with a description of its demographic consequences as revealed in the Ottoman censuses of 1467 and 1519.

Ottoman archive collections on religious organizations are described in No. V, with a special examination of the sees of the Greek Orthodox Church on the basis of a register of *Peskopos Mukataası* of the period 1641-1651. No. VI is a paper read at a 1992 conference on Sephardic Jews, and examines the particular circumstances which induced the Ottoman government both to extend its protection to the Sephardic Jews expelled by the Spanish government in 1492, and to grant them settlement rights in the Empire.

The following four articles, Nos. VII-X attempt to study the Ottoman impact on Europe and Europe's influence on the Ottoman Turks, culminating in the emergence of the secular Turkish Republic under the leadership of Kemal Atatürk.

In republishing these papers here in one volume, no attempt has been made to revise or modify them except to add a few necessary footnotes, bringing to the attention of the reader some important references and new publications. While in the original of some of the articles, terms are rendered in transcription alphabet, in others modern Turkish spelling is used. No alteration has been made to this in the present publication. Although some of these papers were first published two or three decades ago, we thought they may contain points still of interest to the specialist as well as to the general reader.

Halil İNALCIK

I

THE RISE OF OTTOMAN HISTORIOGRAPHY

There appear to have been good reasons why Ottoman historiography first produced its general works early in the fifteenth century after the collapse of Bāyezīd's empire and then upon the death of Meḥemmed the Conqueror at the end of the same century. Th. Seif has already pointed out that various *Tevārīkh-i āl-i ʿOsmān* were written towards the end of the fifteenth century as a result of the Ottoman consciousness of having established a great empire. The attempt to correlate the phases of Ottoman historiography with the development of Ottoman history itself can shed new light upon various problems.*

I

With the first serious studies on Ottoman sources after the First World War it was thought that the oldest accounts of Ottoman history must be a *menāqibnāme* by Yakhshī Faqīh and Aḥmedī's chapter on the Ottomans in his *Iskendernāme.* Yakhshī Faqīh's work, the *Menāqib-i āl-i ʿOsmān,* which deals with the period up to the time of Bāyezīd the Thunderbolt, is mentioned only by ʿĀshıqpasha-zāde (Ashpz.). He had met Yakhshī Faqīh in Geyve in 1413. The latter had been granted land by Meḥemmed I whom he seems to have supported in his struggle for the Sultanate. The bitter criticism in

* In this article the transcription system of *Encyclopaedia of Islam*, 2d edition, is followed with the exceptions: č > ç, dj > j and ḳ > q.

Ashpz. against Chandarlı 'Alī Pasha who sided with Emīr Süleymān apparently comes from Yakhshī Faqīh. It seems that he composed his work under Meḥemmed I. Fr. Giese rightly pointed out that for the first century of Ottoman history Ashpz. and the anonymous *Tevārīkh-i āl-i 'Osmān* must have used a common source which appears to be Yakhshī Faqīh. Giese further suggested that this source can be reconstructed from these and Neshrī who, Giese thought, had included a good text of Ashpz. When Uruj's chronicle was discovered, it was immediately seen that it is connected with the same source. Fr. Babinger, its editor, was of the opinion that it was composed in the Conqueror's time and the anonymous *Tevārīkh* was nothing but a new version of it. But in the first place the history of Uruj was dedicated to Bāyezīd II as is seen in the introduction of the Manisa manuscript.

Secondly, Uruj and the anonymous *Tevārīkh* are independent versions of the original source in Ashpz. (compare, for instance, the battle of Qoyun-hisari in three texts). Their relationship on the basis of a common source can be established from the emergence of 'Osmān Ghāzī up to the suppression of Muṣṭafā, the rebellious brother of Murād II in 1422. Now it seems that the common source was Yakhshī Faqīh's work with a continuation to 1422. Let us have a closer look at our chronicles.

In the first chapters the following theme is common to the three sources: An Oghuz group immigrated into Anatolia under Süleymān-shāh who was drowned in the Euphrates. His son Ertoghrul and his brothers moved back to Sürmeli-Çuqur. (Three brothers are named in Neshrī and Kemāl Pashz., and only two in Ashpz., Uruj, and the anonymous *Tevārīkh*). 'Alā' al-Dīn, the Seljuqid ruler, granted to Ertoghrul and his followers the area of Sögüd-Tomaliç-daghı and Ermeni-beli. This theme is enlarged in Uruj and the anonymous *Tevārīkh* with additions from different sources, but from Tursun Faqīh's *khuṭba* in the name of 'Osmān Ghāzī onwards our three texts agree much more closely. Here only the anonymous *Tevārīkh* contains an original account of the fight at

Yalak-ova between ʻOsmān's forces and the emperor's army which was sent to relieve Nicaea.[1] Incidentally, it is this battle not that of Qoyun-ḥiṣārı that agrees with the account of the battle at Baphaeon described by Pachymeres. Baphaeon is mistakenly associated with Qoyun-ḥiṣārı by Hammer and by all who wrote after him. There is a version of the same account in Neshrī which is linked with ʻOsmān's receiving the symbols of princely power as a reward for this success. ʻOsmān's victory over the forces sent by 'the *tekvur* of Konstantinople' under his son in Uruj may be another variant of the same account. It would have been most surprising if there had been no mention in the Ottoman sources of this event which induced Pachymeres to mention ʻOsmān in his history for the first time. In fact it is mentioned by Uruj and the anonymous *Tevārīkh* but it is not mentioned by Ashpz.

The famous story of the dragon and the dervish in connection with the siege of Nicaea is found only in the anonymous *Tevārīkh* and is a widely scattered folk-tale which is also found in the *Saltuqnāme.* Uruj inserted a story about Bābā Ilyās citing his source as the *Menāqibnāme* by Elvān Chelebi. Besides these additions from *menāqibnāme*s Uruj and the anonymous *Tevārīkh* give two accounts of the battle of Maritza against the Serbs, one corresponding to that of Ashpz. the other completely different. Uruj's account of the battle against Mirčea in 1395 is completely original and agrees with what we now know from a Turkish document about it.[2] No mention is made of this important event in Ashpz. while a second account of it is found in the Bodleian pseudo Rūhī, Neshrī and Bihishtī apparently from the same source. On the other hand Ashpz. has whole chapters which Uruj and the anonymous *Tevārīkh* lack altogether, such as those on Orkhan's operations in the Sakarya

1 Now see H. İnalcık, "Osmān Ghāzī's Siege of Nicaea and the Battle of Bapheus," *The Ottoman Emirate*, Elizabeth Zachariadou, ed., Rethymnon 1993, 77-98.

2 See *Proceedings of the Tenth International Congress of the Byzantinists* (Istanbul, 1957), 220-2.

valley. Ashpz.'s further additions from his oral sources are not included, of course, in the other two texts. Relating to Bāyezīd I's time we find a greater number of additions. Only the anonymous *Tevārīkh*. contains a detailed account of Timur's capture of Sivas and his treatment of Bāyezīd in captivity as well as the stories about Sulṭan Aḥmed the Jelayirid. These stories are repeated by 'Ālī[3] nearly two hundred years later who said he obtained them from Hamzavī. On the other hand, in the anonymous *Tevārīkh* the verse portions of these stories appear to come from the same source. It is safe to say that the important additions on this period in the anonymous *Tevārīkh* must have come from a separate source.

The statement on Bāyezīd's treatment of the corrupt *qāḍīs* and the clown is found jointly in our three texts with the difference that the anonymous *Tevārīkh* and Uruj reproduce the original source more fully. In general the anonymous *Tevārīkh* is more detailed in the parts criticising the administration than the other sources.

Uruj and Ashpz. make the same mistakes when they spell the name of the battlefield of Marj Dābiq as *Majnūn Ṭabaq* while the anonymous *Tevārīkh* gives the correct form. I think this is another indication that Uruj cannot be considered as a source for the anonymous *Tevārīkh*.

To sum up Ashpz., Uruj and the anonymous *Tevārīkh* use each in his own fashion a common source from the emergence of 'Osmān up to 1422. In general Ashpz.'s version is the most detailed, although Uruj appears to give in a few places a fuller treatment of the original text. All three of them add to the common source new information from different sources such as oral traditions and *menāqibnāmes*. However, the anonymous *Tevārīkh must* have also used a rhymed work from 1402 up to 1424, probably Hamzavī's. For this reason all these texts must be considered as separate sources. Kemāl Pashz. and Neshrī both of which may be connected with the Ashpz. source group should be considered also separate versions because even in the statements obviously from the common source

3 Vol. V, 94.

both of them contain details which cannot be found in any other. On the other hand individual copies of all these chronicles may be as important as different texts because their authors made revisions at various dates with additions or abridgements. For example, the Cambridge manuscript of Urujs concludes with the events in 899 H. But according to the introduction in the Manisa manuscript this copy is a revision, which brings the events up to 906 H. and in it we find detailed additions, for instance on the tribes in the Çukur-ova which came with Süleymān-shāh, allegedly grandfather of 'Os̲mān. This addition was made apparently in view of the current struggle against the Mamluks to get the upper hand in this region. There is no doubt that Ashpz. also made such new revisions with continuations. Therefore, Professor Wittek's theory of a more detailed Ashpz. text than those we possess today is still valid even when we recognize many additions made by Nes̲h̲rī in Ashpz.'s text as coming from Rūḥī's source and the calendars.

Here is a summary of what we have said on the earliest texts connected with the so-called Yak̲h̲s̲h̲ī Faqīh. (see the genealogy of the texts in I, p. 29 below).

It is to be observed that the first compilation originated in the period of struggle for the existence of the Ottoman state after the fateful defeat in 1402. One can easily see in this historical account the effort to explain the disaster as God's punishment for the sins committed under Bāyezīd I. He and his *vezīr* 'Alī Pasha are accused of encroaching upon the *S̲h̲erī'at (S̲h̲arī'a)* and introducing innovations in the government. When the chronicle describes 'Os̲mān G̲h̲āzī as having no gold and silver in his possession at his death and as rejecting new taxation on dealings in the bazaar as a violation of the *S̲h̲erī'at.* our source appears to intend to criticize his own period by setting the first Ottoman ruler as an ideal example. The emphasis put on the respect shown by the first Ottoman rulers for the dervishes by granting them generous plots of land can also be interpreted as a denunciation of Bāyezīd I's policy of abolishing the right on the *mulk* and *waqf* lands. Thus, this work on the first century of Ottoman history bears the marks of the great disappointment at the collapse of Bāyezīd's empire. The Ottomans then felt the need to have a general outlook on their historical existence and at the same time sought a historical basis for their future claims. The soft and conciliatory policy of Meḥemmed I and Murād II in contrast to Bāyezīd's impetuous government seems also to be reflected in these reactionary views. Timur's successors regarded any new action on the part of the Ottomans altering the situation set up by Timur in Central Anatolia as a violation of the status quo, and sent threatening words to Murād II on account of his operations against the Karamanids. What is more, the Timurids were trying to keep the Ottomans as their vassal, at least legally. Now what we find in the Ottoman chronicles as well as in Murād's letter to Shāhrukh is that in order to continue their *ghazā* obligations in Rumeli the Ottomans claimed, as leaders of the *ghazā,* that they had to repulse the Karamanid attacks from the rear.[4] The genealogies in the chronicles which link them to the Oghuz tradition seem to have been forged simply to make the Ottomans appear the equals of the Khāns in the East, so that they could escape the vassalage of the Timurids and claim supremacy over the Turkish principalities in Anatolia. Bāyezīd I had already claimed the title of *Sulṭān al-Rūm* which would make him the heir of the Seljuqids over all Anatolia. Our chronicle put these words in the mouth of 'Osmān: 'If Allah gave the Seljuqid Sultan the Sultanate, the same Allah gave me the Khanate by reason of *ghazā*. If he says that he is of the Seljuqid house I say I descend from Gökālp.'[5] Yazıjı-zāde of the time of Murād II added similar statements in his *Tārīkh-i āl-i Seljuq* which later were taken over by Rūḥī or his source. Another tradition in our chronicle made 'Osmān the legal heir of the last Seljuqid Sultan. That all these claims were added in the sources in the period after Bāyezīd I is well demonstrated by Professor Wittek.

4 Ferīdūn, *Munsheāt' us-Selāṭīn*, I, Istanbul 1274 H., 193-196.

5 Ashpz. Giese ed., 20.

In brief, our original source is shaped under the strong influence of the ideas current in the Ottoman state in the first decades of the fifteenth century, and thus represents a particular outlook on Ottoman history which the future historians, Ottoman or Western, found ready for their use without understanding much of its true meaning. The compiler of this chronicle appears to have used as his material *menāqibnāme*s and *ghazavātnāmes* written on individual events and persons.

After 1422, however, Ashpz. on the one hand and the anonymous *Tevārīkh* and Uruj on the other follow completely different sources. Ashpz. often adds his own personal experiences and oral information to the *menāqibnāme*s which he says he summarized in his work. At the end of Murād II's reign he says: "I, 'Āshiqī Dervīsh Aḥmed, have seen and known all the *ghazās* that this Sultan made as well as the circumstances which occurred to him and his utterances and actions, but I wrote them in summary in this *menāqibnāme*." As for the anonymous *Tevārīkh*. and Uruj they follow essentially a common source from 1422 to 1484. Significantly enough Uruj gives two different accounts of Mustafa's rebellion in 1422, the first of them is apparently the same as in the anonymous *Tevārīkh*. and Ashpz. The anonymous *Tevārīkh* shifts to the new source with the usual formula of '*Rāvīler shöyle eydürler kim*', on the events after 1422. The common source of Uruj and the anonymous *Tevārīkh* for the period after this date seems to be the calendars which we shall deal with presently. But let us first examine *nıenāqibnāmes,* apparently original sources of Ottoman historiography in the first period.

The origin of this religio-heroic literature was sought on the one hand in the popular Turkish epics, on the other in the Islamic tradition of *maghāzī siyar,* and *menāqib-i evliyā* literature. F. Köprülü suggested that the achievements of the Anatolian Turks in the Rumeli *ghazā* areas gave birth to a third cycle of these popular epics after those represented by *Battālnāmes* and *Dānishmendnāmes.* In his opinion the third cycle is exemplified by the *Saltuqnāme* which is a collection of the popular *menāqib,* religio-epic tales, the *g͟hazā* and islamizing activities of the famous saint San Saltuq in Rumeli.

In Ashpz., the anonymous *Tevārīk͟h.* and Uruj we find actually two kinds of *menāqibnāme*; one consists of typical folk-tales as in the case of 'Os̲mān Ghāzī's dream about the future of his house, and Murād I's miraculous deeds; the other consists of *menāqibnāmes* or *g͟hazavātnāme*s of real historical information. The typical examples of the latter are the detailed accounts of the first battle of Kossovo and of Mehemmed I's activities between 1402 and 1415 in the Bodleian pseudo-Rūḥī and Nes͟hrī. The story of the capture of Bursa in Ashpz. can be considered as the same type of *menāqibnāme.* As an original example of this type we now possess a separate *G͟hazavātnāme. G͟hazavāt-i Murād K͟hān* on the battle of Varna in 1444. Though a *menāqibnāme* of a later period this detailed book gives a good idea of this kind of *menāqibnāme*s. The epic of G͟hāzī Umur in Enverī's *Düstürnāme* can be also classified as belonging to this type of *menāqibnāme* or *g͟hazavātnāme.* Incidentally, our texts use both terms indiscriminately, a fact which is quite normal if we consider that in the Ottoman frontier lands dervishes and *g͟hāzīs* often became identical. In any case, written about individual events or persons, about sultans or famous frontier *begs,* these historical *menāqibnāme*s appear in general to give detailed and quite reliable historical information.

In a society imbued with the *g͟hāzī* spirit *menāqibnāme*s were usually intended to be read aloud in public gathering, in the army or in the bazaars where we find, as one *qāḍī* record of Bursa reports, merchants equipping soldiers at their own expense. Reflecting popular feelings in simple language, the genre of *menāqibnāme* survived in many *g͟hazavātnāme*s as well as in such popular works as Ashpz. and the anonymous *Tevārīk͟h* in the following centuries. Actually Ashpz. addresses his listeners, 'Hey g͟hāzīler' and concludes as follows: 'Whoever reads or listens to these *menāqib* of the house of 'Os̲mān and sends prayers for their souls, may God grant him heavenly bliss.'

As for the calendars which became the main source of Uruj and the anonymous *Tevārīkh* and which were found in astrological works entitled *jedāvil al-taqvīm, jedvel al-ikhtiyārāt* or *aḥkām ve ikhtiyārāt.* they belong to an early branch of Muslim astronomy. As a basis for their predictions of the future, astrologers of the early centuries of Islam included in their works chronological lists on important events, political or natural. Referring to the scheme proposed by the Ikhwān al-Ṣafā for astrological works in the tenth century, Fr. Rosenthal considers them to be very close to an annalistic history. It seems that the Anatolian Turks were interested in this *'ilm* quite early. We have an original copy of Zayn al-Münejjim b. Süleyman al-Konevī's *Jedvel al-ikhtiyārāt* written in Sīvās late in the summer 1371 which contains a chronological list on the Sejuqids and the Ilkhanids. The subsequent notes made on the cover of the manuscript referring to such events as the meeting of Bāyezīd Beg, Tāj al-Dīn Beg and Ḥāji Shād-geldi on Chal-dagh on 6 Muharrem 780, are very interesting because they show how astrologers recorded their chronological data on the spot. The significance of the numerous Ottoman works on *aḥkām ve ikhtiyārāt* many of which contain chronological lists has been realized only recently.[6] The oldest Ottoman works that have survived belong to the years of 849 and 851 H. and are obviously based on earlier works. It seems that at the beginning of each new year a calendar with *aḥkām ve ikhtiyārāt* was drawn up for the Sultan's use. In fact there exists another calendar for the year of 856 H. in which the chronological lists in the above-mentioned texts were summarized. Thus, the *münejjims* in the court can be regarded as the first *vaq'anuvīs.*

Now let me give you an example of how Uruj and the anonymous *Tevārīkh* drew their information from these calendars. In the calendar of 849 H. we read as follows: "It is four years since the castle and the city of Novabiri and some of its territory were taken from the unbelievers by Shihāb al-Dīn Pasha, Beglerbegi of Rumeli, and some places by Ishaq Beg, Beg of Uj-eli, in the time of

6 See my *Fatih Devri Üzerinde Tetkikler ve Vesikalar*, (Ankara, 1954), i.

Murad Khan." In the anonymous *Tevārīkh* we read: "It was in the year of 843 H. that Sultan Murad fell upon Belgrade but could not take it and then came back and conquered the castle of Novaberda and Shihāb al-Dīn Pasha, Beglerbegi of Rumeli, and Isḥāq Beg, Beg of Uj, conquered some of its territory." And in Uruj is as follows : "In the year of 843 H. Shihāb al-Dīn Pasha took the castle of Novaberda and its territory on this side, Isḥāq Beg, *beg* of Uj, was along with him." Lastly Neshrī gives the same record this way: "In the year of 844 the castle of Novabiri with some provinces of the unbelievers were taken by Shihāb al-Dīn and some castles by Isḥāq Beg, *beg* of Uj." It is noticed that Uruj copies out its source fairly well but the anonymous *Tevārīkh* leaves the honour of the capture of Novobrdo for the Sultan. The calendars must have used a chronicle for the first Ottoman rulers since it is unlikely that any calendar was written in this early period. In fact the calendars give very little information until the last years of Murād I. The chronicle that they may have used seems to be the same as that used by Karamānī Meḥemmed in 1480. Important contemporary events were usually related in some detail as was the case with the battle of Varna in the calendar of 849 H. This statement of one page is reduced to a few lines in the calendar of 856 H. But it is to be noted that Uruj's description of this battle is much more detailed than even that of the *taqvīm* of 849. Apparently Uruj as well as the anonymous *Tevārīkh* made use of *ghazavātnāme*s for the great events such as the battles of Varna or Kossovo and one can see breaks in the chronological records of *taqvīm*s whenever *ghazavātnāme*s are used. Our texts contain peculiarly abundant records taken from *taqvīms* concerning earthquakes, astronomical phenomena, fires and pests. The calendars, the anonymous *Tevārīkh* and especially Uruj are incomparably better in chronology than later compilations such as Neshrī. One important characteristic of Uruj is that he gives the names of pashas in the Dīvān every time there is a change. For instance, that Mehemmed Pasha was the first vizier in 832 is reported only in Uruj, a fact also confirmed by his *vaqfiyyes.* For these details the Manisa and Paris manuscripts of Uruj are better than those published by Babinger. Also Uruj is much more detailed in its chronological parts up to the first years of Bāyezīd II than the anonymous. It is most likely that the latter used a *taqvīm* or *taqvīms* of recent date with the data much summarized. For the first period of Bāyazīd II's reign up to 891 H. the anonymous *Tevārīkh* appears to use a more detailed *taqvīm* than Uruj, while from 891 onwards they both follow one *taqvīm* which contains the precise dates for all the important events. We hope that a systematic investigation in our library collections may bring to light the original calendars used by Uruj and the anonymous *Tevārīkh.* (See the genealogy of the texts: I and II, p. 29 below)

II

It was thought that, along with Yakhshī Faqīh, Aḥmedī's *Dāsitān-i Tevārīkh-i Mulūk-i āl-i 'Osmān* in his *Iskendernāme* was the second oldest account for the first century of Ottoman history, and we know that this *Dasitan* was dedicated to Süleymān I (1403-10). Here we shall try to show that Aḥmedī's source is the same one as that used by Shükrullāh. Karamānī Meḥemmed Pasha, Meḥemmed Konevī, pseudo-Rūḥī, Sarıja Kemāl and Neshrī. Rūḥī and Neshrī reproduce the information more completely than the others. Thus, these texts altogether represent a second group of sources as distinct from the group of Ashpz., Uruj, and the anonymous *Tevārīkh.* Neshrī tried to unite these two different groups selecting the statement on a given event from one of these sources and arranging his selection chronologically, apparently without making any important change in the statement itself. But the Bodleian manuscript of pseudo-Rūḥī seems to copy out the statements without insertions or omissions such as are made by Neshrī. so that it contains the original source more completely. For example, in the chapter *Ḥikāyet-i Murūr-i Süleymān Pasha ilā Rumeli* Neshrī follows the common sources with pseudo-Rūḥī up to '*Karası vilāyeti timariydi, hemen feth olundughu gibi ana vermishdi*' and then with the word *al-qiṣṣa* he changes over to the Ashpz. text.

In this section the remainder of the account given by Rūḥī is left out by Neshrī, but in one place he adds with the expression '*derler ki*' the names of the two castles conquered by Süleyman Pasha as *Ödküklük* and *Eksamilye* as alternatives to the names *Jimbini* and *Aya Shilonya* given by Ashpz. But in their statement from the common source Neshrī gives a more detailed text than the Bodleian pseudo-Rūḥī. We find *Ödküklük* and *Eskamilye* in Shükrullāh. Meḥemmed Qonevī, Sarıja Kemâl, Qaramānī Meḥemmed, but not in Aḥmedī, whose work, though the oldest, is the shortest recension of the common source. In this second group of sources which differ from each other only by their additions or omissions, there is a completely different tradition about the origin of the Ottomans and their immigration into Anatolia. Characteristic points in this tradition are as follows: Akhlat is mentioned as the first settlement area of an Oghuz group of 340 immigrant families; the genealogy is recorded as Ertoghrul, son of Gündüz-Alp, son of Gök Alp, son of Sarquq-Alp, son of Qopuk-Alp. This group had finally settled down in Qarajadagh near Ankara. 'Alā' al-Dīn, the Seljuqid ruler, came to Sulṭān-öyügü and made Ertoghrul a *ghāzī* chief there. The pseudo-Rūḥī seems to combine this tradition with that of Ashpz., while Neshrī mostly gives both traditions side by side. Rūḥī also adds the interesting account of Yazıjızāde of the election of 'Osmān by the Oghuz tribes in the *Uj* (frontier zone) as well as of the general conditions in Anatolia at that time. In Karamānī we find Akhlat and the Kopuk- Alp genealogy but no figure; in the *Selāṭīnnāme* by Sarıja Kemāl only the number of the immigrants as 1340. Aḥmedī, the earliest version of the source, contains only the statement on 'Alā'al-Dīn as in all the other texts.

To show the degree of their relationship to the original source the following example is interesting. Aḥmedī mentions a certain Sheykh Efendi without giving his name. Shükrullāh gives the name as Ramazān, but Rūḥī, Sarıja Kemâl, and Neshrī make it clear that Sheykh Ramazān was appointed *qāḍī'asker* by Bāyezīd I. On the biography of Ramazân *Shaqā'iq-i Nu'māniyye* takes over the same information from them. The punishment of the corrupt *qāḍī*s by Bāyezīd I is mentioned by Aḥmedī, Shükrullāh and Rūḥī; an account is also given by the Ashpz. group but from another source.

We can conclude that Aḥmedī's source was used by others separately and more fully. This source must have come down to the conquest of Malatya in 1399. Now it is clear that we have various versions of it made in the fifteenth century: Aḥmedī towards 1410. Shükrullāh in 1456-59, Karamānī Meḥemmed and Meḥemmed Qonevī towards 1480, Rūḥī, Neshrī, and Sarıja Kemāl around 1490. As a separate and apparently older source than that contained in the first group of chronicles, it is undoubtedly most important for a critical study of the first century of Ottoman history. For example, we can now state positively that in Bāyezīd I's time there was a radical reform of the *qāḍīs,* an event which in the form in which it occurs in the Ashpz.-Yakhshī Faqīh tradition has the appearance of a legend. The archaic character of the Aḥmedī-Rūḥī tradition is shown by its emphasis on the *ghazā,* its more modest genealogy for the Ottoman house, the eminent place devoted to Süleymān Pasha, brother of Murād I, and the fact that it mentions such names as Sinān Pasha and *qāḍī asker* Sheykh Ramazān who were unknown to Ashpz.

It appears that Shükrullāh. Rūḥī, and Neshrī used a text which had copied Aḥmedī's source more faithfully than Aḥmedī himself and had continued it up to the end of Meḥemmed I's time. In fact, Shükrullāh. Rūḥī, and Neshrī are closely related to each other up to 1421. The section covering the period 1399 to 1420 in these texts shows again a completely different character from the Ashpz.-Uruj tradition. It deals with the uprising of the Ṣūfis in Qaraburun, the disorders in the Amasya and Tokat region caused by the Qarakoyunlu intervention, the fortification of the three castles of Saqçi, Yeni-Sale and Yergögi on the Danube, and the capture of Severin. The first group of chronicles lack these points completely.

Rūḥī makes two long additions to his source, one concerning Murad's expedition into Karaman-eli and the battle of Kossovo, the other concerning Meḥemmed I's struggle for supremacy during the period of civil war. As we have said these must have been taken from two different *menāqibnāme*s. We find these additions in Neshrī too, the first one with more detail than Rūḥī and the second identical in both texts.

For Mūrād II's time Rūḥī is an independent source with original data except for the second reign of this sultan from 1446 to 1451 where he appears to use the same source as Ashpz. Probably this was a separate *menāqibnāme.* This is the only part where the two texts agree. Ashpz. gives the common source in more detail except on Meḥemmed II's expedition into Qaramān-eli in 1451. The demonstration of the Janissaries against the Sultan during this expedition is related only by Rūḥī. Shükrullāh gives a very superficial outline of Murād II's time and Meḥemmed Konevī seems simply to copy it. For the reign of Meḥemmed the Conqueror, Qonevī appears to use a calendar which makes him very close to Uruj and the anonymous *Tevārīkh.* That Karamānī did not use Shükrullāh directly as a source can be seen by comparing their treatment of the reign of Murād II. For the conqueror's time Karamānī seems to have made use of a calendar. As for Rūḥī he gives an original text on the reigns of Meḥemmed II and Bāyezīd II up to the conquest of Aqqerman and Kili in 1484 (he distinguishes two expeditions of the Conqueror into Serbia in 1454 and 1455, mentions the wounding of Mahmud Pasha during the expedition against Trebizond and the dispatch of Aḥmed Bikrījī by Uzun Ḥasan to make peace). (See the Genealogy of the Texts: III, p. 29 below).

A completely original work on the Conqueror's reign is Tursun Beg's *Tārīkh-i Ebu'l-Feth* which is based on his own personal experience. As for the *Shāhnāmes* written under the Conqueror we shall deal with these later.

III

Tārīkh-khwāns, history-readers and popular poets reading *menāqibnāmes* were present in the courts of the Seljuqid Sultans and Turkmen *begs* in Anatolia. The Ottomans continued the tradition. It seems that historical works in the form of *ghazavātnāme*s were written to be read aloud to the Sultan in his retreat to satisfy his pride and literary taste.

As the time went by the court and upper classes were interested in more sophisticated types of *menāqibnāmes* and *g͟hazavātnāmes.* written in high literary style and mostly in Persian. Aḥmedī's *Dāsitān* in Turkish can be regarded as one of the first examples of it. Around 1456 Kās͟hifī, a Persian poet, wrote his *G͟hazavātnāme-i Rūm,* a versified work in Persian glorifying the Conqueror's *g͟hazās.* It was dedicated to the sultan; as a historical source it contains quite a lot of original information. Under Meḥemmed II this kind of literature which is shown under the general name of *s͟hāhnāme* seems to have flourished. A number of Persian poets who then invaded the Ottoman capital were in keen competition not only with the Ottoman writers but also with each other to attract the Sultan's favours. Following Kās͟hifī, Ḥamīdī, Mu'ālī. S͟hehdī are the names which have survived as the authors of such works during this period. In Laṭīfī's *Tez̲kire* it reads: "Thirty poets were granted salaries and yearly pensions (by the Conqueror) who were putting in rhyme his history or writing poems in his praise." Mu'ālī's *K͟hünkārnāme* was discovered recently at the Topkapı-Sarayı, but Ḥamīdī's and S͟hehdī's works are missing. It is safe to say that *s͟hāhnāme*-writing as an early type of court historiography was established in the middle of the fifteenth century. Its main function was to glorify in a high literary form the exploits of the reigning Sultan; but occasionally *s͟hāhnāme* writers composed also general histories of the Ottoman house. For their own time they produced generally original works based on first-hand information. Still linked with the old *menāqibnāme* tradition special *g͟hazavātnāmes* were composed for famous chiefs of *g͟hazā. G͟hazavātnāme-i Mik͟hāl-og͟hlu 'Alī Beg* by Sūzī Çelebī was recently published by A. S. Levend. *G͟hazavāt-i Dāvūd Pas͟ha* by K͟hayr al-Dīn Çelebī, no copy of which has been found, was actually borrowed by Kemāl Pasha-zāde in his *Tevārīk͟h* at the end of the seventh volume. The genre of the old popular *menāqibnāmes* seemed also to continue in the court on the one hand with the *qiṣṣa-khẉāns* who were ranked below the *shāhnāme*-writers, and on the other hand with the appointment of *münshīs* who were famous stylists to compose *Tevārīkh-i āl-i ʿOsmān* on the model of fashionable Persian historiography. Under Bâyezid II who desired that the history of his house be written in Turkish, we find written in the *shāhnāme* style Qivāmī's *Fetḥnāme* on the Conqueror's *ghazā*s, Kemāl's *Selāṭinnāme,* a general history of the Ottomans, the *Quṭbnāme* by Firdevsī on the naval expedition for Mytilene, and the *ghazavātnāme* by Ṣafāyī on the exploits of Kemāl Re'īs. Qivāmī's work was recently published by Fr. Babinger and the manuscript copies of others are now known.[7] In the following centuries the genre of *shāhnāme* continued with numerous works some of which had real artistic value in calligraphy, miniature and illumination. It is to be noted that some of the *shāhnāme*-writers were versed not only in these but in astrology too. *Sūrnāmes* describing royal wedding festivities can be considered as a branch of *shāhnāme* genre.

IV

Was it just a coincidence that many of the general histories of the Ottoman house were composed in Bāyezīd II's time and that most of them concluded with the events of 1484-85? Ashpz., Rūḥī, the first composition of the anonymous *Tevārīkh,* the Menzel manuscript of Neshrī, Meḥemmed Konevī, Qivāmī, Sarıja Kemāl, Tursun Beg end their work with the events of 1484 or 1485. For this unusual activity in producing compilations on the general history of the Ottomans at that time the first and foremost reason was no doubt Bāyezīd II's desire to see such works written and the '*ulemā*' of his time responded to it. Bāyezīd II then wanted to use this means for shaping public opinion in his favour. Bāyezīd represented a reactionary policy in all political, social, and legal fields in contrast to the Conqueror, while Jem Sulṭān, still alive, was regarded as the symbol of the previous régime. In all the above-mentioned works

7 See A. S. Levend, *Gazavatnameler*, (Ankara, 1956).

Bāyezīd is demonstrated primarily as a just and law-abiding ruler with the mission of consolidating the large conquests which his predecessor had made (see especially the introductions in Tursun Beg, Kemāl Pshz., and Idrīs). Gedik Aḥmed who was an idol of the Janissaries and had seized actually all the power in the state was executed in 1482 and his father-in-law Isḥāq Pasha was dismissed from the grand vizierate the following year. The Janissaries became restless and Gedik Ahmed's previous opposition to the policy of concessions to Christendom was shared naturally by all the *gh̲āzī* elements. It was under these conditions that Dāvūd Pasha, famous for his *gh̲āzā* achievements in Bosnia, was chosen as grand vizier and the Sultan felt bound to lead the army himself into Moldavia where the Conqueror had previously failed. In order to influence public opinion the victory won there should have been propagated as widely as possible. Commenting on the victory in Moldavia Meḥemmed Konevī said emphatically as follows: "None of his ancestors was able to take these two strongholds", and Tursun Beg emphasizes that Sultan Meḥemmed was not able to lay siege to Kili.[8] If the Ashpz. text is read in the light of Bāyezīd's reactionary policy its polemical character would become evident throughout. It can be added that in Nes̲h̲rī Gedik Ahmed is blamed for his ill advice to Bāyezīd during the battle of Otluq-beli in 1473, while Ibrāhīm C̲h̲andarlı is praised for his efforts, all this being simply an addition to the original source by Nes̲h̲rī himself. Also Dāvūd Pasha's role in the Conqueror's time is often exaggerated in most of these works. A careful study of their introduction is revealing indeed. In pseudo-Rūḥī we read: "Sultan Bāyezīd said: 'Histories of the prophets are regarded as the best and most preferable, and thus the '*Ulemā*' prefer to write this kind of histories, but the history of the Ottoman Sultans who are the most distinguished and honourable among others has not yet been the subject of a compilation written in a language for everybody's profit. It is desirable that it should have been.' This statement of the Sultan made me decide to collect the

8 *TOEM* edition, 186.

histories [of the Ottomans] in Turkish which are circulating in the Ottoman dominions." Neshrī makes a similar statement in his preface: "I found that many works are written on the other '*ilms* but that those on history still remain scattered especially in Turkish." Sultan Bāyezīd's insistence on such a history in a Turkish simple enough to be understood by everybody is significant.

The works written in the first years of Bāyezīd and directly connected with the victory in Moldavia are most important for Ottoman historiography, because it was these compilations that became the basis of all that is written later on the first two centuries of the Ottoman history and their original sources are now mostly unavailable for us. Ashpz. obviously made several revisions of his wok with continuations and the one seems to have been made in 1484-85. Meḥemmed Konev! started writing under Meḥemmed the Conqueror and completed his work under Bāyezīd II. An official record testifies that Mevlānā Rūḥī was given awards by Bāyezīd towards 1503. Sarıja Kemâl completed his *Selāṭinnāme* in June 1490. As to Neshrī's work, Professor Taeschner finds in view of the Menzel manuscript, 1485 as *terminus post quem* and 1495 as *terminus ante quem* for the date of its composition. Statements in Bihishtī. Uruj, and the anonymous *Tevārīkh* are clear enough to show that all are written under Bāyezīd II.

An attempt has been made in the preceding pages to find out what kind of sources were used in the main compilations, and we concluded that in their greatest part Ashpz. on the one hand, Rūḥī on the other, give us two different traditions in their most detailed form. Neshrī is, indeed, the oldest compilation which seeks to combine the two traditions from Ashpz. and pseudo-Rūḥī. But it is again a question whether Neshrī used a source common to Rūḥī or a detailed copy of Rūḥī, because Neshrī relates the same accounts as in Rūḥī but often with more details even on the events as late as 1484. It is to be recalled that Neshrī also utilized calendars which were a source for Uruj, the anonymous *Tevārīkh*, and Konevī, too. Now it is possible to draw a list showing which parts in Neshrī come from which sources. He appears to add very little personal information.

Not only did reaction to the Conqueror's policies characterize the compilations made under Bāyezīd II, but also the consciousness of having established a universal Muslim empire in competition for supremacy with the Mamluk and Persian states in the East required a new evaluation of Ottoman history at that time. In the previous outlines of world history, for example in Shükrullāh's and Enverī's works, Ottoman history occupied a modest place as a continuation of Islamic history, and the Ottoman Sultans were presented as *ghāzīn* on the frontiers of the Muslim world. But now Bāyezīd II claimed to be *Ashraf al-Salāṭīn,* the most distinguished and honoured of the Muslim rulers, and one of these compilers (Ruhi) said that except for the Prophet himself and his four immediate successors no other Muslim ruler had more achievements than the Ottoman sultans. It must be remembered that it was then that the Ottomans had entered a long war against the Mamluks for south Anatolia and wished to show themselves superior to their opponents in every respect. The Ottomans still emphasized their *ghazā* mission but claimed that it had the most significant place in Islam. Around 1502 Kemāl Pasha-zāde said in the introduction of his work: "The Sultan remarked that if the histories and stories and anecdotes were not written down and thus the glories and the achievements of the great rulers were not perpetuated for the ages to come, they would be forgotten. He, therefore, asked that his achievements and those of his ancestors should be recorded. And in order to be useful for the distinguished as well as for ordinary people it should be composed in a clear style in Turkish and I was appointed by him to do this."

About the same time Idrīs Bidlīsī, a famous Persian *münshī,* was ordered by the Sultan to write a great history in Persian worthy of the Ottoman house. Idrīs himself relates it as follows: "Sulṭān Bāyezīd ordered that a history of this great dynasty from its beginning in the year of 710 up to the present year of 908 should be written in a style favoured by the distinguished as well as by ordinary people with the correction and elucidation of the accounts concerning this dynasty. It is true that there are in Turkish a number of works on the subject but their stories lack elegance in style and truth on the events."

The *Shaqā'iq*[9] makes it clear that the *qāḍī'asker* Mu'ayyad-zāde had suggested to Bāyezīd II that as Molla Idris was asked to write a history of the Ottoman house in Persian, it was suitable or perhaps necessary to have a work in Turkish on the same subject and this could be accomplished only if Mevlānā Kemāl Pshz. agreed to do it. It is clear that unsatisfied with the current histories of his house, Bāyezīd II gave orders to two great *müshīs* of his time, Idris in Persian, Ibn Kemāl in Turkish, to write this history again. They tackled the task in a similar plan devoting a separate book to each Ottoman Sultan. With his most elaborate work, *Hasht Bihisht*, Idrīs composed Ottoman history in the most sophisticated form of Persian historiography. Later Khoja Sa'd al-Dīn took this work as a model for his *Tāj al-Tevārīkh* in Turkish, which became a classic. It seems that Idris followed mainly the Rūḥī tradition. We find in Idrīs some of the personal accounts of Tursun Beg, too. Idrīs gives some original information on the events concerning central and eastern Anatolia. The description of the Ottoman court and government in a separate chapter gives this work a unique place among Ottoman chronicles. The Turkish counterpart of *Hasht Bihisht* is Ibn Kemāl's *Tevārīkh-i āli-'Osmān,* the largest and the most important compilation in this period. It is also an important literary work reflecting the desire to create a high Turkish prose competing with Persian. Ibn Kemâl apparently used a detailed copy of Neshrī and added Karamānī's account for the first period. For the Conqueror's time he followed principally Tursun Beg and Neshrī, and there are indications that he is also familiar with Rūḥī or his source and a detailed copy of Uruj like the Paris or Manisa manuscripts. As was said above, his work contains here Khayr al-Dīn Çelebī's *Ghazavāt-i Dāvūd Pasha*- Moreover Ibn Kemāl added many important details from his personal knowledge as well as from contacts with others. He shows great skill in selecting his sources on individual events and utilizing them. He can be regarded as the greatest of all the Ottoman historians including Khoja Sa'd al-Dīn, 'Ālī, Na'īmā, and Jevdet Pasha.

9 Turkish translation by Mejdī, *Hadā'iq al-Shaqā'iq*, Istanbul 1269 H., 384.

GENEALOGY OF THE TEXTS

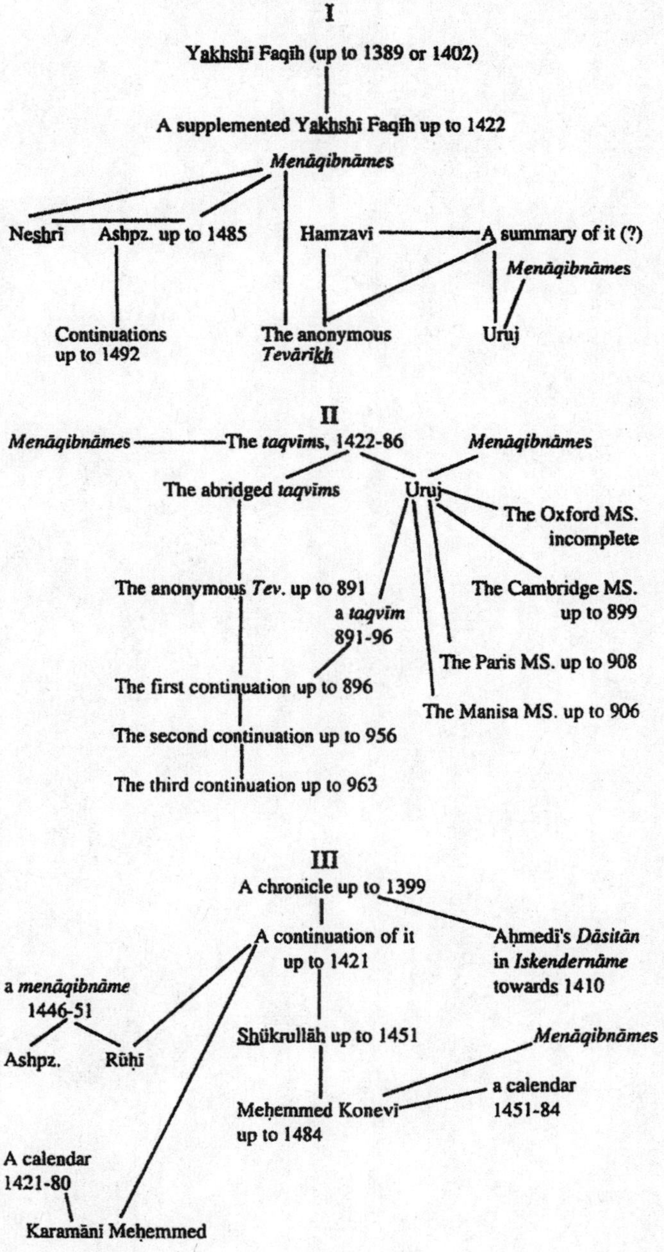

II

ON THE SOCIAL STRUCTURE OF THE OTTOMAN EMPIRE: PARADIGMS AND RESEARCH

In this paper an attempt will be made to review the principal typological efforts that have been applied to Ottoman social history up to the present.

From the point of view of methodology, researchers on Ottoman history can essentially be divided into two groups. In the first group are those who have chosen a definite theoretical model and sought to interpret the findings of Ottoman empirical historians according to that model. In the second group are historians who take as a subject of research the topics suggested in Karl Marx, or Max Weber or, less frequently, other models and proceed to examine them in the light of historical sources. As the first group pressed the debate over whether Ottoman society represented a feudal mode of production (FMP) or Asiatic mode of production (AMP) or a patrimonial state historians began to do empirical research on such topics as landholding and agrarian relations, socio-economic integration between town and countryside, population pressure, impact of the price revolution on the Ottoman empire and its place in the capitalist world economy. One cannot but agree that both approaches have helped us to better approach and understand Ottoman society and to formulate our questions clearly.

Marxist social historians, seek to apply their model, which can be described in the words of Hindess and Hirst[1] as one in which, a

1 Barry Hindess and Paul Q. Hirst, *Pre-capitalist Modes of Production*, (London: Routledge and Kegan Paul, 1975), 183.

distinct mode of appropriation of the surplus-product presupposes a distinct structure of relations of production. A distinct structure of relations of production presupposes a set of forces of production which corresponds to the conditions of the labour process it establishes. What forms did society's ideological-legal superstructure take, within what kind of dependence on that basic foundation? And, how did the whole social structure, as an integrated totality or global structure coalesced of all its elements, come into being? According to Marxist theorists, we will be able to understand and explain social formation only when we can answer these questions.

Social Formation Question in Turkish Thought

In the nineteenth century modernization was regarded by Ottoman thinkers as westernization, thus a cultural problem, a value-system problem in general. However, in the nascent Turkish press of the 1860's, journalist-intellectuals (Namık Kemal, Ziya Paşa and others), who approached social problems in the Turkish society complained bitterly that westernization and open-door trade policies were destroying both the Ottoman handicrafts and Ottoman cultural values.[2] Later on, Ziya Gökalp, the founder of the science of sociology in Turkey, analyzing social problems entirely as a socio-cultural problem, introduced Emile Durkheim's positivist-collectivist methodology and his view of social structure as an organic totality.[3]

Atatürk, while imposing radical reforms in the name of the national will and constitution, drove home the idea that he represented "the Turkish nation's conscience."[4] However, a fundamental change began to occur in the Republican period, with the 1930 world economic crisis.

---

2 Şerif Mardin, *The Genesis of Young Ottoman Thought, A Study in Modernization of Turkish Political Ideas*, (Princeton: P.U.P., 1962), 252-38.

3 *Turkish Nationalism and Western Civilization*, *Selected Essays of Ziya Gökalp*, trans. and ed. by Niyazi Berkes, (London: G. Allen and Unwin, 1958), 97-183.

4 *Atatürk' ten Düşünceler*, ed. E. Z. Karal, 3rd edition (Ankara: İş Bankası Kültür Yayınları, 1969), 42-43.

Then debates started about failures in the economic field, widespread poverty and backwardness, the socio-economic structure and the dynamics of change. Ottoman social structure was seen as the origin of Republican Turkey's problems. On the one hand, serious empirical research on the Turkish-Islamic era's social and economic institutions began (especially under the direction of Fuad Köprülü and Ömer Lûtfi Barkan),[5] while on the other, by claiming to spur political action for the completion of "the socio-economic phase of the Atatürk revolution," a group of intellectuals adhering to the Marxist theory (Ş. S. Aydemir, İ. Hüsrev and others) applied for the first time modes of production and social formation theory to the problems of Ottoman-Turkish society.[6] Ottoman-Turkish social structure came to be characterized as a stagnant village economy with a primitive division of labor. According to İsmail Hüsrev,[7] "this was a social order of a ruling class, of feudals who through force laid claim to extensive lands and exploited the rural manpower."

Hüsrev was the first Turkish writer to emphasize the need to rescue Ottoman history from being mere tales of the "sultans' adventures" and instead "to investigate the social aspects of the Ottoman history independently and within its own special conditions."[8] According to Hüsrev,[9] in the Ottoman system there was a class which appropriated "the surplus product" by force. Within this class it was the *sipahis* with *timars,* the men of religion with *wakfs* and the Sultan and his men that appropriated the

5 For a bibliography of M. F. Köprülü, see *Fuad Köprülü Armağanı / Mélanges Fuad Köprülü*, (Istanbul, 1953), XXVII-L; for Ö. L. Barkan see 41-45 below.

6 For the so-called *Kadro* movement, see Ş. S. Aydemir, *İnkılap ve Kadro*, (Ankara: Bilgi Y., 1968); K. Karpat, *Turkey's Politics, the Transition to a Multi-Party System*, (Princeton, P. U. P., 1959); for the earlier period, see Mete Tuncay, *Türkiye'de Sol Akımlar, 1908-1925*, (Ankara, 1967); A. Cerrahoğlu, *Türkiye'de Sosyalizmin Tarihine Katkı*, 5 vols., (Istanbul, 1975).

7 *Türkiye'de Köy İktisadiyatı*, (Ankara: Kadro II, 1934), 153.

8 *Op.cit.*, 152.

9 *Op.cit.*, 152-172.

peasants' surplus product.[10] Socio-economic relations in Ottoman society, he argued, were based on a system of force and legal bonds.[11]

These views have persisted up to the present time as fundamental concepts among Marxist interpreters of Ottoman regime in Turkey. Marx and Engels' placement of the Ottoman Empire within a vaguely defined category of "eastern" or "Asiatic" empires goes back to the 18th-century Enlightenment philosophy.[12] In fact they based their theories about the Ottoman Empire on a very restricted – and extremely biased – information.[13] Within the last thirty years, particularly as a result of research on land and population surveys in the Ottoman archives, it has become possible to have a more solid picture of Ottoman social structure. After İsmail Hüsrev, those who have studied Ottoman social structure within the framework of Marxist theory have sought to apply somewhat modified forms of AMP or FMP models by relying on the results of the empirical research. Also, since the model of "feudal exploitation" – that is, the usurpation of the peasant class' surplus product through force and violence – dovetails so well with the Balkan nationalist history tradition, this paradigm has been taken up by Balkan historians since World War II.

Marxist Paradigm in the Balkan Historiography

A. The Feudal Mode of Production Theory

In the FMP, the common criterion of feudalism for all Marxist theorists is "the appropriation of the surplus product" of the peasants, through extra- economic means, by a dominant military-political class. Some

---

10 *Ibid.*, 159.

11 *Ibid.*, 187-188; for the Turkish writers after İ. Hüsrev, see M. A. Şevki, *Osmanlı Tarihinin Sosyal Bilimle Açıklanması*, (Istanbul: Elif, 1960); *Türkiye'de Sosyal Bilim Araştırmalarının Gelişimi*, ed. S. Atauz, (Ankara: Türk Sosyal Bilimler Derneği, 1986), in particular, 195-232 (B. Akşit).

12 See, Perry Anderson, *Lineages of the Absolutist State*, (London: NLB, 1974), 461-472.

13 See K. Marx, *The Eastern Question*, eds. E. M. Aveling and E. Aveling, reprint, (New York: A. M. Kelley, 1969), ch. IV.

historians, while remaining faithful to this criterion, tend to consider "Ottoman feudalism" as a *sui generis* type among a number of varieties of feudalism. They conceive of the formation of Ottoman feudalism in the following manner: Türkmen tribes, headed by individual chieftains, gathered under the leadership of a *bey,* military leader, and initiated the conquests. The tribes who settled on the conquered lands established a kind of communal ownership, and thus, from the point of view of social structure, as Marx and Engels thought, were at a level of feudalism similar to that of Germanic tribes after their conquest of Roman lands. Western society is believed to have passed to a "progressive," classical, feudalism after the eleventh century with the emergence of the socio-economic order of the manor based on seigneurial ownership of the land. In contrast, the Ottomans blocked this development by replacing communal ownership of land with state ownership.

In Balkan historiography, in general, the feudal nature of the Ottoman regime had been traditionally, if confusingly, discussed in terms of western feudalism. According to the Bulgarian Ottomanist Bistra Cvetkova[14], for example, the Ottoman regime was "le régime

14 "L'évolution du régime féodal turc de la fin du XVIe jusqu'au milieu du XVIIIe siècle". *Études Historiques*, I (Sofia, 1960); *idem*, "Changements intervenus dans la condition de la population des terres bulgares depuis la fin du XVIe siècle jusqu'au milieu du XVIIIe siècle", *Études Historiques*, V (Sofia, 1970); for a bibliography of Bulgarian historiography on Ottoman period, see, N. Todorov, "Les études balkaniques en Bulgarie", *Études Historiques*, V (Sofia: 1970), 658,668, note 77; also, B. Cvetkova, "Sources et travaux de l'orientalisme bulgare". *Annales, ESC*, no. 6 (1963), 1158-1182; *Études Balkaniques*, a quarterly published by the Institute of Balkan Studies, Bulgarian Academy of Sciences, since 1964 on the economic history of south-eastern Europe in general, see *Bibliographie d'Études Balkaniques* (Sofia: Institut d'Études Balkaniques, since 1968); J. R. Lampe and M. R. Jackson, "An Appraisal of Recent Balkan Economic Historiography", *East European Quarterly*, 2 (1975), 197-240; J. R. Lampe and M. R. Jackson, *Balkan Economic History, 1550- 1950*, (Bloomington: Indiana Univ. Press, 1982), 21-49; *Balkanistica, A Journal of Southeast European Studies*, IV (Columbus, 1977-1978), bibliographic contributions by K. E. Naylor and E- G. Walters, J. M. Halpern and R. A. Wagner, J. R. Lampe and S. V. Papacosma; for a general

féodal turc", *timars* were "domaines seigneuriaux", *khassa çiftliks* were "biens privés", *khass* possessors were "grands feudataires", palace favorites were "l'aristocratie du palais", and the land they possessed "la grande propriété foncière", and "l'exploitation inhumaine des féodaux" opened the way to "soulèvements paysans".

However, after the second World War, in eastern European socialist countries Marx' feudal mode of production theory has been in general the model for interpreting Ottoman socio-economic structure. Vera P. Mutafčieva,[15] another Bulgarian Ottomanist, has been widely followed in these countries. Mutafčieva stresses that the seigneur, unlike the Ottoman *timar* holder, exercised direct and absolute control over land and labor, and further that the *sipahi's khassa* land is not comparable to the western 'réserve'.

There are points for Marxist social formation theory in as much as they often serve criteria for determining the "progressiveness' or "regressiveness" of a feudal system.

According to Mutafčieva,[16] Ottoman feudalism is actually a composite consisting of an "advanced" feudalism, which the Ottomans found in the Balkan states at the time they invaded

discussion of the question of the socio-economic structure of the Balkan peoples under Ottoman rule also see N. Todorov, *La ville balkanique aux XVe-XIXe siècles, développement socioéconomique et démographique*, (Bucharest: AIESEE, 1980), 12-55, 187-315.

15 De l'exploitation féodale dans les terres de population bulgare sous la domination turque aux XVe et XVIe siècles," *Études Historiques*, I, (Sofia: 1960), 145-170; *idem*, "Agrarian Relations under Turkish Domination in Bulgarian Territories Down to the Middle of the Seventeenth Century", *Istoričeski Pregled*, VII, 2, 158-192 (in Bulgarian); *idem.*, *Agrarian Relations in the Ottoman Empire, XV-XVIth centuries*, (Sofia, 1962), (I used the unpublished Turkish translation preserved in the Turkish Historical Society Library (Ankara); *idem*, *Le Vakif–un aspect de la structure socio-économique de l'empire ottoman (XVe-XVIIe s.)*, (Sofia: Comité de la Culture, 1981), a collection of articles published in 1962-1982; also see. N. Todorov, *op. cit.*, 168 note 7; V. Mutafčieva and Str. Dimitrov, "Agrarverhältnisse im osmanischen Reiche im XV-XVI. Jahrhundert", *Ier Congrès International des Études Balkaniques et Sud-Est Européennes*, Sofia: 969, Actes III: Histoire, 689-702.

16 *Agrarian Relations*, Turkish Irans., 52; cf. *Le Vakıf*, 24.

them, and their own "primitive" feudalism.[17] The Ottomans' pre-invasion feudalism can be characterized as "primitive," Mutafčieva contends, inasmuch as the Ottoman invasion fits the recurring pattern of Eurasian pastoral nomads invading settled societies. Before the invasion, she observes, local feudal lords in the Balkans had succeeded in weakening the centralized state system by establishing their own control over agricultural land and peasants. The Ottomans, however, interrupted that trend. When Turkish nomads established their domination over Balkan society, they rose to the level of a central administration and transformed the native feudal lords into *timar* holders under the control of a powerful state. In order to achieve this control, the conquerors had at the outset declared all agricultural land to be state property. The state was thus immediately in a position to implement the *timar* system, thereby ensuring the dependency of all feudatories. Under this regime, the typical Ottoman "feudal class" was made up of *timar*-holders with restricted control over land and peasant labor.

Actually, Mutafčieva, taking the Marxist theory of feudal rent on land as her point of departure, sees the state which collects "rent" as a tax, the soldiers who held *timars,* and finally, 'the great feudals" who gained control of freehold and *wakf* lands, as parts of the same feudal structure. All shared "the rent-tax" at various levels in the system. Anyone who appropriated "rent," whether by state assigment or by right of conquest, was a feudal lord.[18] The state was "feudalism personified".

17 For the emergence of the landed aristocracy in Byzantium and the Balkans see G. Ostrogorsky, *Pour l'histoire de la féodalité byzantine*, Brussels 1954; Ostrogorsky attempted to establish parallelism between western and eastern feudalisms; for a criticism of this theory see P. Lemerle, "Esquisse pour une histoire agraire de Byzance," *Revue Historique*, vol. 219 (1958).

18 Following B. Djurdjev's erroneous interpretation of a passage in the law-book of Mehmed the Conqueror, Mutafčieva claimed (*Agrarian Relations*, 6-7; "De l'exploitation féodale", 156) that there was "a seven day feudal labor rent" in the Ottoman regime. This was simply a confusion of the "seven services" in the passage, cf. comments on *çift-resmi*, below; also see a recent Bulgarian

It is difficult to reconcile Mutafčieva's hypothesis with the actual findings of the empirical research. The thesis common to all east European Marxist historians – the socio-economic retrogression under Ottoman centralist power – has to be re-examined. It is highly questionable that pre-Ottoman Byzantine and Balkan feudals can be compared to the landlords of so-called "advanced feudalism" who reorganized their estates for a market economy. Even among the Hungarian nobility large landowners were foreign to such economic concerns before the seventeenth century.[19]

Studies based on archival documents show that the Ottomans incorporated into the *timar* system many of the local feudal lords who had transformed state lands into their own private property under previous decentralized states.

An early Ottoman register of Albanian *timar*-holders[20] in 1432 provides perhaps the most reliable evidence of these local feudals. It shows that by 1432 56 out of 335 timars in Ottoman Albania belonged to members of the pre- Ottoman military class, with some of them controlling many villages.[21] Isa beg, and his father, the famous Albanian seigneur Pavlo Kurtik (Kurtić), or Iskender Beg (the famous Skanderbeg Kastriota) were among these feudal lords.

---

study on pre-Ottoman and Ottoman feudalism by H. Matanov, "Problems of the State Structures in the South-West Balkan Lands During the Second Half of the 14th Century," *Études Balkaniques*, vol. 21-1 (1984), 116-125; C. Asdracha, "From the Byzantine *Paroikoi* to the *Vasalli Angararii:* The Case of the Fiefs of Corfu" *Études Balkaniques*, XXII/1 (1986), 114-122.

19 See below: Hungarian Historiography.

20 *Sûret-i Defter-i Sancak-i Arvanid*, ed. H. İnalcık, (Ankara: Türk Tarih Kurumu, 1954); H. İnalcık, "Timariotes chrétiens en Albanie au XVe siècle d'après un registre de timars ottomanes", *Mitteilungen des Österreichischen Staatsarchivs* IV (1952), 118-138.

21 It appears that Islamicization was not a requirement for membership in the Ottoman military class. Although many local seigneurs adopted Islam as Ottoman timar-holders in the second or third generation, they evidently did so as a result of social factors, see, H. İnalcık "Ottoman Methods of Conquest", *Studia Islamica*, II (1954), 115-120; see also note 26 below.

On the other hand Mutafčieva rejects the notion of a compact feudal class in Ottoman society. Instead, she says that within the feudal class there "was the highest possible differentiation." As a result of the conflict of interests this led to a genuine "social struggle" within the ruling class.

The real feudal lord in the Ottoman society, she believes, was not the *sipahi* with a small *timar,* but the holder of large *timars, mulks* and *wakfs*, who had taken over incomparably greater sources of income. Ottoman great feudatories, Mutafčieva adds, included members of the ruling dynasty, *ghazi* frontier begs, high dignitaries and descendants of the early Ottoman aristocracy. The petty timar-holders who had small incomes and were called on in return for heavy military service were locked in a struggle with the great feudatories or the state. Great feudatories were instinctively worked to tighten and expand their control over state lands. They sought to obtain grants of ownership from the Sultan by bureaucratic means by utilizing legal loopholes. Lands which were transformed by these means into freehold private property rapidly acquired the status of *wakf* land, becoming virtually exempt from state control. When the quantity of such land became too large, or reached a point which hindered the performance of essential state functions, powerful sultans attempted broad reforms to convert it back to state land. The reform carried out by Sultan Mehmed the Conqueror provides[22] the best example of the struggle between the state and the great feudals who were trying to convert lands into their own private property and *wakf.* The lasting opposition of the great "feudals", the holders of *wakf* and *mulk* property, is attested to by the widespread political reaction in the time of Mehmed's successor.

We agree with Mutafčeva that these developments did occur as far as actual control of the sources of revenue was concerned. However, perhaps except for the lands whose ownership was granted by the Sultan (*temlik*), other types of title to land and revenue did

22 Cf. my "L'Empire Ottoman", 85-87 and "Mehmed II", *İslâm Ansiklopedisi*, VII (1957), 506-535.

not necessarily entail absolute hereditary rights to the land. Even *temliks* did not guarantee a kind of family patrimony unless they were converted into religious endowments *(wakf)*.

Mutafčieva's contribution to Ottoman social history is her focus on the *wakf* institution as a socio-economic entity and its fundamental place in the Ottoman socio-economic structure.[23] However, her argument that the large *wakfs* established as family *wakfs* (i. e. those controlled by the founder's descendants) formed a kind of *feudal landed property* free from the state's control, is not convincing.

Mutafčieva herself is well aware that in the classical age the state itself encouraged the establishment of *wakfs* since they provided basic public works and services such as the construction of mosque complexes, urban water systems, schools, caravanserais, bazaar complexes and the like. In his capacity as administrator the descendant of the wakf founder was permitted only ten percent of the *wakf* revenues and was closely supervisioned by the government and the local *cadi.* Any surplus revenues (*zawā'id)* were frequently taken by the government. It requires imagination to see the descendants of the *wakf* founders as "great Ottoman feudals" in possession of large patrimonies free from state control. Actually, these "gentlemen" *(çelebi)* lived in cities and were, at best, urban notables.

Other areas of crucial importance as far as structural change is concerned have to do with what developments in the very cell of agrarian production, i.e., peasant family-farm, and in the peasants' relations with the landowner, occured when land was converted to *wakf.* These areas, so important for Marxist theory, have not been dealt with by Mutafčieva and others who use the feudal mode of production theory. In general until the eighteenth century, the basic form of agricultural production based on family-farm (see *çift-hane* system, *infra*) seems to have remained unchanged in villages which passed under *wakjs.* Growth in the size of *wakf* villages and better protection against abuses of local authorities, did not bring about structural changes in the organization of production itself.

23 Vera Moutaftchieva, *Le Vakıf un aspect de la structure socio-économique de l'empire Ottoman* (XVe-XVIIe s.) (Sofia: Comité de la Culture, 1981).

1. Yugoslav Historiography

Yugoslav historiography also traditionally defines Ottoman social structure as a feudal system.[24] The Ottoman conquest, it is believed, did away with a nascent feudalism based on private ownership, which was expandine in the Yugoslav lands. However, in the post World War II period, among the Balkan nations, it was first the Yugoslav-Bosnian scholars who had the opportunity of utilizing the Ottoman archives in Istanbul. They produced a number of solid studies on Ottoman institutions and socio-economic history. Among them, Branislav Djurdjev and Nedim Filipović focused their investigations on "Ottoman feudalism", and in particular on the internal dynamics of the "feudal class" each of whose component groups, they believe, strove to maximize its share of surplus-product from the peasantry. Filipović[25] put special emphasis on the distinct character of the developments in Bosnia- Herzegovina. His point of departure was the long controversy over the origins of big farms and landlordism which had caused terrible eruptions in the region during the nineteenth century.

In an effort to legitimize the big landowners' rights, the old school claimed that these landowners inherited *çiftlik* lands from pre-Ottoman times. Filipović and his colleagues were able to demonstrate that big *çiftliks* and landlordism in Bosnia-Herzegovina

24 For Yugoslav historiography on Ottoman period see, *Ten Years of Yugoslav Historiography 1945- 1955*, (Beograd: Yugoslavija, 1955), 256; *Historiographie yougoslave, 1955-1965*, (Beograd; Fédération des Sociétés Historiques de Yougoslavie, 1965), 115-142 (Ottoman period); *Bibliographia Historico-Occonomica lugoslaviae*, (Zagreb: Komisi Ekonomsk Historiju Yugoslavije, 1978); the main reviews publishing studies on Ottoman period: *Godišnjak, Istoriskog Društva Bosne i Hercegovine*, Sarajevo: Filozofski fakultet; *Prilozi za Orientalnu Filologiju i Istoriju Yugoslavenskih Naroda pod Turskom vladavinom*, Sarajevo: Orientalni Institut; *Balcanica*, a review published by the Académie Serbe des Sciences et des Arts (since 1970).

25 "Some Characteristics in the Development of the System of Timar in Bosnia-Hercegovina," *Pregled*, II and V (Sarajevo: 1953) (in Serbian), Turkish trans.: *Istanbul Üniversitesi, İktisat Fakültesi Mecmuası.* XV (1953-1954), 154-188.

resulted from the dissolution of the Ottoman *miri* (state owned) land and *timar* system. He agrees that following the conquest, the Ottoman state had allowed the members of the pre-Ottoman nobility to become part of the Ottoman "military" class. But this occurred with the important change that their freehold landed properties were converted to *timars* under the universal Ottoman principle of state ownership of agricultural lands. In our study on Christian timar-holders we had already supplied irrefutable evidence of this Ottoman policy;[26] but, contrary to the thesis of Filipović and other Balkan social historians, we tried to show that even in the pre-Ottoman Balkans when the "great men" in the provinces and the church had asserted control over the sources of revenue, the ultimate principle of the state's *dominium eminens* on land was never forgotten and was re-established under the strong centralist rule of the Ottomans.

Having made this point, we agree with Filipović that the pre-Ottoman feudatories in Bosnia-Herzegovina were incorporated, and over time completely assimilated, into the Ottoman regime. When the process was completed, "peasants considered this group as one capable of collecting the rural revenue *(hasil* or surplus-product) exclusively through the sultan's favor".[27] Down to the 1560's the Ottoman classical *miri* land and *timar* regime functioned well, and in this period, Filipović asserts, Bosnia-Herzegovina, did not evince features distinct from the rest of the empire.

Later on, because of the keen competition for *timar* and the precariousness of tenure, native Bosnian *timar*-holders demanded that the government recognize hereditary rights on *timars* and the extension of these rights not only to sons but also to brothers and, later on, to other relatives.

---

26 "Stefan Duşan'dan Osmanlı İmparatorluğuna: XV. Asırda Rumeli'de Hristiyan Sipahiler ve Menşeleri", *Fuad Köprülü Armağanı/Mélanges Fuad Köprülü*, (Istanbul, 1953), 207-248, trans. into Serbian by N. Filipović, "Od Stefana Duš ana do Osmankog Čarstva", *Priloz za Orijentalni Filologiju: Istorija*, 3-4 (1952-1953), 23-54.

27 Filipović, *op. cit.*, 166.

Timars or *ziamets* thus became rather like family landholdings, and their possessors hereditary landlords over a peasantry reduced to actual 'servage'. To illustrate the process leading to the big landlords of the nineteenth century, Filipović adds[28] that the government had to make such concessions in view of the necessity of reinforcing these frontier soldiery against growing external military pressure. Such concessions were already introduced under Ahmed I (1603-1617) and were consolidated towards the middle of the seventeenth century. At that point the members of the families of consolidated (*odjaklık*) *timars* formed a *real social* class, a kind of landed nobility.

According to Filipović, however, the rise of this new class and the fact that the peasant tenants were reduced to the status of 'serfs' were due to another on-going process, namely the *çiftlik*-building movement, particularly as it developed in the area in the eighteenth and nineteenth centuries. In fact, this process, which was wholly socio-economic in nature, prevailed in the period with the military as well as with tax farmers, usurers and the like in the formation of a new Ottoman social class of upstarts. With the participation of towns-folk and their "usury and merchant capital" the movement soon acquired its widespread socio-economic character. Already, family *timars* were subject to sales and transfers as if they were landed properties.

In brief, the formation of the consolidated *çiftliks* and their rapid spread in Bosnia in the eighteenth century occurred, Filipović says, as a result of the dissolution of the original *timar* regime. Vacant *timar* lands then became concentrated, mostly by covert and illegal devices, in the hands of either a rising class of provincial upstarts or big *timar*-holders (*zaims* or *kapetans).* The latter using the same devices, enlarged and consolidated their original military *çiftliks.*[29] The state's widespread application of the tax farm system to extract public revenue provided the principal means for this process.

Although Filipović supports his conclusions with Ottoman documentary materials several points, however, are not completely

28 *Ibid.*. 180-181.

29 *Ibid.*. 174-175, 184-185.

clear. He faults the rigid character of the Ottoman agrarian system responsible for its failure to respond to society's new needs as they arose.[30] However, he does not offer an explanation of why the system was too inflexible to change or develop. He does not pay attention to basic organization of production, i.e., the peasant *çift-hane* system, and the state's firm policy to maintain it.

Also, although special conditions in the Bosnia-Herzegovina frontier region were to some extent responsible for the peculiar character of the landholding regime in later centuries, the extension of inheritance rights over the *timars,* the key factor in the process, must be explained as a direct result of the revolutionary liberalizing policy on land possession rights of the Ottoman government after 1695.

2. Hungarian Historiography

In order to test the theory of the pre-conquest advanced feudalism it may be particularly useful to examine Hungary and the Balkan countries, notably Wallachia, Moldavia and Transylvania which kept their internal autonomy, and to some extent, followed their own socio-economic evolution.

After the second World War, Hungarian historiography[31] also followed the Marxist theory of FMP in its approach to Ottoman history.

30 *Ibid.*, 170-171.

31 Major studies in Western languages on the Ottoman period in Hungary have been published in *Acta Orientalia Academiae Scientiarum Hungaricae*, Budapest; for studies in Hungarian see, Z. Kakuk, *Hungarian Turcology: 1945-1974, Bibliography*, (Budapest, 1981), 139-164; Marxist interpretation of the Hungarian social history is summarized with useful bibliography by Laszlo Makkai, "La Noblesse de la Hongrie historique à l'époque du féodalisme tardif (1526-1760)"; *idem, Noblesse Française, Noblesse Hongroise, XVI*^{e}*-XIX*^{e} *siècles*, Akademiai Kiadó, Budapest; *idem*, "Agrarian Landscapes of Historical Hungary in Feudal Times", *Studia Historica*, 140 (Budapest, 1980), 1-18; *idem*, "Die Hauptzüge der wirtschaftlich - sozialen Entwicklung Ungarns im 15.-17. Jh.", *La Renaissance et la Réformation en Pologne et en Hongrie*, (Budapest, 1963), 27-46; *Histoire de la Hongrie des origines à nos jours*, ed. E. Pamlényi, (Budapest, 1974), chapter V, 145-207 (L. Makkai); Zs. P. Pach, "The Development of

Hungarian historians, too, speak of two kinds of feudalism before and after the Ottoman conquest. Thus, they contend that Hungarian feudalism, which was developing in the direction of an advanced type of feudalism, was swept aside and replaced by the Ottomans' "primitive" or "regressive" form of feudalism.[32] Using this framework, Hungarian historians nevertheless did undertake some important analytical studies based on archival research.

In the period 1526-1541, after the Ottoman conquest, Hungary was divided into three parts, the regions under Ottoman domination, Habsburg-controlled Hungary, and the Transylvanian principality all of which had been quite well researched by Hungarian historians.

Hungarian "advanced feudalism", they assert, developed in the regions under the Habsburg rule. There, local magnates, the "great feudal lords", achieved full autonomy vis-à-vis the central authorities. The economic and social autonomy of the nobles, however, was based completely on "feudal privilege", rather than independent economic functions.[33] In the middle of the seventeenth century, ninety percent of the villages and towns was owned by twelve thousand nobles, and within this group, fewer than one hundred magnate families owned as much as a third of the agricultural land. The lesser nobility was dependent on the preeminent hundred.

Feudal Rent in Hungary in the Fifteenth Century", *The Economic History Review*, 2d series, vol. XIX, no. 1 (1966), 1-13; *idem*, "Production et productivité agricoles en Hongrie à l'époque du féodalisme tardif (1500-1850)", *Nouvelles Etudes Historiques* (Budapest: Akademiai Kiadó, 1965), 581-638; *idem*, *Die Ungarische Agrarenlwicklung im 16.-17. Jahrh*, Akademiai Kiadé, Budapest 1964; *Compte Rendu*, *Le IVe Congrès International d'Histoire Économique*, *1968*, published in *Acta Historica Academiae Scientiarum Hungaricae*, 15 (1969), 29-50; *Nouvelles Études Historiques*, 2 vols. (Budapest: Akademiai Kiadó, 1965): *Themes*, *Eighth International Economie History Congress*, (Budapest, 1982), (Large Estates and Small Holdings, Protoindustrialization, Technical Change), Akademiai Kiadó, Budapest, 1982.

32 For their interpretation of feudalism see "compte rendu"; and *Themes* mentioned in note 31.

33 Makkai, "La noblesse", 164: "Rien ne fut plus loin de ces seigneurs terriens, produisant en régie propre, que l'esprit capitaliste d'investissement pour le profit".

In the sixteenth century, relations between the nobles and the peasants working the land were completely founded on "feudal privilege". During this period, production for the market was not yet a matter of discussion; likewise, production on the seigneur's *reserve* land reflected the traditional form of peasant exploitation (wheat cultivation was standard).

It should be emphasized that the "big estate", before the Ottoman conquest, was not a large scale consolidated type of farm. As in the Ottoman *çift-hane* system, agricultural activity consisted of small peasant operations. Likewise, "the demesne fields retained in the lord's occupation were very small in proportion to the vast mass of holdings of tenants".[34] As in the Ottoman *çift- hane* system, tenant obligations were imposed upon the peasant family as a unit. Since labor service was relatively limited, however, the giving of traditional food gifts on holidays assumed correspondingly greater significance. It is worth noting that these gifts (primarily chickens, bread and cheese), and the gifts appropriated by the *timar*-possessing *sipahis* under the term *'ādet* in the Balkans, were identical. The grain tax, remitted to the lord in a defined amount per household, was also a widespread traditional tax in the Balkans.[35]

According to Hungarian historians, in the seventeenth century, "second serfdom", reflecting the lords' more rigorous exploitation of peasant labor, finally became dominant.[36] It was, however, not until the second half of the eighteenth century that landlords fell under

34 Pach, "The Development...", 4; I believe Pach understood best the nature of the basic traditional agrarian system and its continuity in Hungary based on small peasant family-farms.

35 See my, "*Yük (Himl)* in Ottoman Silk Trade, Mining, and Agriculture", *Turcica*, XVI (1984), 147-151. In the Byzantine Empire the delivery of chicken and wine three times a year to the *pronoia*-holder existed under the name *kaviskia* which was converted to cash in later times.

36 Makkai, "Die Hauptzüge...", 37-46; *idem*, "Neo-Serfdom, Its Origin and Nature in East Central Europe", *Slavic Review*, (1975), 225-238; L. Makkai and V. Zimányi, "Structure de production, structure de consommation", *Demanda e consum*, Firenze 1978.

the influence of the changing conditions of the world market, with the result that the feudal structure underwent a fundamental change in the direction of capitalist agriculture.

Transylvanian Feudal Lords, Peasants and Ottoman Challenge

The well-studied region of Transylvania offers an interesting case of the so-called "feudal society in transition" and the social background of the Ottoman conquest.

In contrast to the pattern of development of feudalism in Habsburg Hungary, feudalism in the Ottoman-controlled Transylvanian principality, according to L. Makkai,[37] developed quite differently. Here, one third of the lands was under state ownership, and the peasant was not a serf, but a 'free' peasant under the direct rule of the prince.

In summary, Makkai asserts, here we can speak of "une structure sociale archaïque", belonging to the phase of primitive feudalism. The prince's control over the nobility was much greater than in the Habsburg region. In Transylvania we do not see nobles of the magnate type, with control over wide areas of land. Foreign trade was also monopolized by the prince.

The Romanian historian Stefan Pasco,[38] however, stresses the enserfment of the peasantry by the big landowners in Transylvania and an acute class conflict derived from excessive feudal demands which the Ottoman threat aggravated. He asserts that the intensification of feudal control through enserfment and the usurpation of land from peasant communities started quite early and led to violent conflicts before Ottoman domination.

In the first half of the fifteenth century conditions of servage had worsened so much that eventually a terrible peasant rebellion broke out in 1437-38. The developments concomitant to enserfment were

37 Makkai, "La noblesse...", 167-168; *idem*, *Histoire de Transylvanie*, (Paris-Budapest, 1976), chapter X and XVII.

38 La *révolte populaire de Transylvanie des années 1437-1438*, (Bucarest: Académie de la République Populaire Roumaine, 1964), 14-33.

expansion in trade and urban growth, and increases in agricultural and monetary rent and labor services. The threat of an Ottoman invasion which was imminent in the 1430's, resulted in an increase, first temporary, then permanent, in impositions required from the serfs.

The extra war contribution was fixed at one gold florin per peasant household in the meeting of the Diet in 1397 (Nicopolis, 1396). This was in addition to the heavy load of various taxes and feudal dues and services already rendered by the serfs to the landlord.[39]

The conflict for a greater share of peasant rent between different groups, military and ecclesiastical, within the "feudal class", or between the state and the feudal groups, Pasco suggests, was a manifestation of active class contradiction. The peasant flight to neighboring lands was an avoidable aspect of these conditions. Also, the activities of *Haidouk* bands which dated back to this period, Pasco adds, was the sign of the social disruptions in the countryside.

The war preparations in the face of the Ottoman menace in 1437, signalled a peasant uprising, first in the region of Bobal in northern Transylvania. In the first phase of the revolt small nobles made common cause with the peasantry. The express goal of the rebellion, Pasco says, was clearly anti-feudal. The rebels wanted the abolition of the new dues and services, termination of the conditions of servage, and restoration of the old "liberties".

Later, in the same year, the nobility united under a pact directed against both the Turks and peasants. The provisions of the agreement, made after the second confrontation in September 1537, included the following interesting points:[40] The serf or peasant had to pay the lord *one florin annually for each plough drawn by eight oxen, half a florin for that drawn by four, and twenty five dinars for that drawn by two oxen or horses.* A serf without cattle who had other possessions or small livestock corresponding in value to a plough was also to pay one florin. A serf who had possessions worth less than a plough was to pay less than a florin and a serf with no possessions earning his

39 *Ibid.*, 37-43.

40 *Ibid.*, 84.

livelihood by wage work, twelve dinars. Personal labor service was fixed at one day a year. Serfs were to perform extra labor services for the care of pond or repair work on the lord's mill. A serf could leave the land only with his lord's consent. As will be seen below, the assessment method of dues based on peasant labor force and plough-animal power is typical of the hearth-land taxation in the Byzantine and Ottoman empires.[41]

The third phase of rebellion which started in November became widespread and had as its decisive goal the abolition of servage, a goal which the Ottomans were promising to the peasants in the Balkans. This time, the center of confrontation was the city of Cluj. There, the peasants were crushed in the final clash of January 1438. With the king, Sigismund, dead as of 1437, the Ottomans believed it was the right moment to strike.

In 1438, under Sultan Murad II himself the Sultan's troops reached as far as Sibiu, the capital, while Ottoman raiders overran the land for six weeks.[42]

It is no mere coincidence that protests against feudal innovations or aggravation of customary dues and labor services were rampant through the Balkans during the Ottoman conquests. The Hungarian historian, E. Frances,[43] a Marxists interpreter of later Byzantine history, finds the popular uprisings in the Byzantine empire and Bulgaria in the fourteenth-century Balkans before the Ottomans took over also to be similar in nature.

In the third region, that Ottoman controlled, according to Makkai[44], the Ottomans did away with nobility. The majority of the

41 Cf. "Çift-Ḫāne System and Peasant Taxation", in this volume.

42 See H. İnalcık, "Byzantium and the Origins of the Crisis of 1444 in the Light of Turkish Sources", *Actes du XIIe Congrès International d'Études Byzantines, Ochrida 1961* (Belgrade, 1964), 159,164.

43 "La féodalité byzantine et la conquête turque", *Studia et Acta Orientalia*, IV (1962), 69-90; *idem*, "Quelques aspects de la politique de Jean Cantacuzène", *Rivista di Studi Bizantini e Neoellenici*, V (1968), 167-176; *idem*, "La féodalité et les villes byzantines aux XIIIe et XIVe siècles", *Byzantinoslavica*, XVI (1955), 76-96.

44 L. Makkai, "La noblesse...", 166.

nobles fled to Habsburg Hungary or to Transylvania. However, they did not give up their feudal rights over the serfs, but attempted to collect taxes from them as before. Thus, in the Ottoman region, as a result of this double taxation, the circumstances of the peasantry worsened. After a lenghty struggle, the Ottoman administration recognized the necessity of reaching a compromise in this matter.

In 1541, the Ottomans established a system of direct administration in Hungary, that is, they reorganized the country under the *timar* system.[45] Thus, the land and the peasantry fell under the direct authority of the central administration. Central control was established through detailed population and taxation surveys (*tahrir*), the foundation of the system. By translating these registers into Hungarian and analyzing them, Hungarian Ottomanists L. Fekete, Gy. Káldi-Nagy, G. David and others[46] have provided valuable assistance in elucidating the socio-economic conditions and administration under the Ottomans. Through such work, it has become possible to put aside some old biases of Hungarian historiography.

However, Káldy-Nagy,[47] the authoritative historian of the Ottoman period, subscribed in his interpretation to the main thesis of east European Marxist historiography and asserted that in 1541, with the establishment of the direct Ottoman rule in Hungary the land under cultivation was declared to be "domains of the treasury" which "abolished the feudal system prevailing up to that time; all the estates of the former feudal lords became the property of the Ottoman treasury. Thus, Ottoman conquest brought about "a retrogression in agricultural production," and consequently "a return to extensive animal breeding."[48] According to Káldy-Nagy,[49] the

45 Gy. Káldy-Nagy, "The effect of the *Timar*-system on Agricultural Production in Hungary", *Studia Turcica* (Budapest, 1971), 241-248.

46 For a complete list for their works see, Kakuk, *op. cit.*, and *Türkologischer Anzeiger, Turcology Annual* (Vienna: Institut fur Orientalistik, I975-).

47 Gy. Káldy-Nagy, "The Effect...", 241-248.

48 *Ibid*,, 246.

49 *Ibid*,, 248.; cf. other studies of the same author: "Rural and Urban Life in the Age of Sultan Suleiman", *Acta Orienlalia*, XXXII (1978), 285-319; "Macht

negative effect of the Ottoman occupation was due to the fact that high-ranking *timar* (*khass*) holders "did not engage in farming and commodity production," and timar-holders were merely interested in the income from it, not in the land development." "Agricultural development", the Hungarian orientalist argues, "was retarded by the *timar*- system which nipped in the bud the beginnings of the large scale agricultural production in Hungary.... The *timar*-system ... maintained both economic and social development, as late as the seventeenth century, at the stage of early feudalism not in Hungary, but in the whole territory under Turkish rule".

Káldy-Nagy's conclusion is based on an exclusive type of lands, namely *khass* lands whose holders were primarily interested in deriving the highest cash income and, therefore, shifted from grain cultivation to stock breeding. During this particular period, European demand was growing and cattle prices were constantly going up. Also, the example of *mulk/wakf* is unrepresentative because it is established[50] that in such lands stock breeding for distant market was given more attention than in ordinary agricultural lands chiefly as a result of labor shortage.

It is clear from Ottoman surveys[51] that the Ottoman reorganization made no revolutionary changes in the ordinary village production unit as it existed in Hungary or the Balkans. In Hungary, *çift-hane* corresponded to *kapu* "gate", or peasant household. One *florin* gold piece per household, a pre-conquest royal tax was called *kapu-resmi/*

und Immobiliarvermögen eines türkischen Beglerbegs im 16. Jahrhundert", *Acta Orienlalia*, XXV (1972), 441-450; "The First Centuries of the Ottoman Military Organization", *Acta Orientalia*, XXXI (1977), 147-183; "The Administration of the *Sanjaq* Registrations in Hungary", *Acta Orientalia*, XXI (1968), 181-223; E. Vass, "Quatre documents ottomans concernant la contribution d'une *puszta* hongroise au XVIIe siècle". *Acta Orienlalia*, XXVIII (1974), 253-262; G. David, "Some Aspects of 16th Century Depopulation in the *Sanjaq* of Simontornya", *Ada Orientalia*, XXVIII (1974), 63-74.

50 H. İnalcık, "Capital Formation in the Ottoman Empire", *The Journal of Economic History*, XIX (1969), 129-130.

51 In particular see, *Kanuni Devri Budin Tahrir Defteri*, ed., Gy. Káldy-Nagy, (Ankara: DTC Fakültesi, 1971).

gate-tax in early Ottoman regulations (Buda, Hatvan, Estergon and Novigrad, all of Suleyman I's time).[52] It was re-named as *ispendje* (from Serbian *jupanitsa)* in later regulations (Uyuar, of Murad III's time).[53] In both cases, this tax was paid directly to *sipahis* in two instalments. In fact, before the Ottoman conquest in Hungary, in the second half of the fifteenth century, there seems to have been a general trend toward conversion of labor services and taxes in kind into cash payments.[54] It is important to note that one *florin* of gate-tax, assessed as cash payment in exchange for labor services, corresponded to the *çift-resmi* or *ispence* collected as the cash equivalent of seven particular services in the Ottoman system.[55] Thus, by continuing and generalizing the gate-tax for all of Hungary the Ottomans appear to have actually completed "the evolution in the feudal relations" which had started before their arrival.

Although the displacement of the old Hungarian nobility by the Ottoman *timar* and *khass* holders can be characterized as a revolutionary change the traditional estate which was then broken up had continued its production mode on the same production unit, the peasant family-farm. When discussing the "big farm" and the "small farm", the key point must be the actual organization of production unit, not the size of the landholder's estate. As in the Byzantine empire and in the Balkans similarly in pre-Ottoman Hungary also, the estates which were gathered in the hands of great feudal lords were, in fact, not organized as large consolidated production units. Obviously, the dominant form of operation on these lands was in general based on small peasant families; the

52 Barkan, *XV. ve XVI ıncı Asırlarda Osmanlı İmparatorluğunda Ziraî Ekonominin Hukukî ve Malî Esasları*, Istanbul 1943, 301-303.

53 *Ibid.*, 313-1, 316-1.

54 Pach, *op. cit*,, 5.

55 For the identification of *ispence* and *çift-resmi*, see my "Osmanlılarda Raiyyet Rüsûmu", *Belleten* XXIII (1959), 575-610; Ottoman law-makers themselves identified the gate-tax with the *ispence*, see reference given in note 48c, on *ispendj* also see D. Bojanić, "De la nature et l'origine de l'ispendje", *WZKM, Festschrift Paul Wittek*, volume LXVIII, 9-30.

"reserve" land controlled directly by the Hungarian feudal lords consisted not of actual sown Fields, but of lands which needed no continious or extensive labor, such as vineyards and pastures.[56]

3. Romanian Historiography[57]

Combining archival research with anthropological field work Henri Stahl[58] who tried to establish a "morphogenèse" of agrarian society in Romanian lands deserves a special place in our review. His investigations of peasant economy and social conditions are of particular interest for the questions under discussion. First, Stahl rejects the general view held by the old Romanian school of

56 Pach, *op. cit.*, 3.6.

57 Results of the Romanian research on the socio-economic structure of Wallachia and Moldavia under the Ottoman suzerainty are presented in western languages mainly in the following publications: For The International Congress of the Historical Sciences, Romanian Academy published a series of studies in western languages under the title, *Nouvelles Études d'Histoire*; also, *Contributions Roumaines au* Ve *Congrès International d'Histoire Économique*, (Leningrad, 1970, Bucharest, 1971); in general see, V. Candea, *Les Études du Sud-Est Européen en Roumanie*, (Bucharest 1986); since the foundation of the International Association of South-East European Studies in 1963, an institute has been established, which publishes the *Revue des Études du Sud-Est Européennes* (Bucharest, since 1963); specialized studies published in *Studia et Acta Orientalia* (Bucharest, first issue 1959) by the Société des Sciences Historiques et Philologiques de Roumanie: section d'Études Orientales; for translations of Ottoman documents, a new series is established: *Documente Turcesti privind Istoria Romanici*, vol. I: 1455-1774, ed. M. A. Mehmed, (Bucharest: Academy, 1976); *Revue Roumaine d'Histoire* contains important articles on Romano-Ottoman history; Romanian scholars outside Romania publish the *Revue des Études Roumaines* (Paris, since 1953); for a general bibliography see, *Bibliografia istorica a Romanici, 1969-1974*, and following volumes; recently important sources on Moldavian social-economic history have been published in *Moddăva in epoce feudalismulni*, vol. I (1961), and *Documente slavo-moldvenesti din veacurile, XV-XVI* (1978).

58 Henri Stahl, *Les anciennes communautés villageoises roumaines, asservissement et pénétration capitaliste*, (Bucharest and Paris: Académie de la République Socialiste de Roumanie, 1969); *idem*, "Paysage et peuplement rural en Roumanie", *Nouvelles Études d'Histoire*, vol. III (Bucharest, 1965), 71-85.

historians that the Romanian feudal system had the same nature as western feudalism. Romanian feudalism, he suggests,[59] actually followed a course of development of its own under quite different conditions and circumstances. Basically following Marx and Engels, who theorized that villages with communal land ownership came into being after the German invasions and settlement of the Roman territories, Stahl suggests[60] that Romanian free "village communities" go back to the settlement of Dacian tribes with their egalitarian field arrangements.

Stahl finds a further reorganization of such communities when they later submitted to pastoral nomads coming from the eastern steppes.[61] Subsequent to the collapse of Roman domination in 271 A. D., these communities subject to pastoral nomads evolved into small "states organized under military chiefs". However, these chiefs, later called *knez,* cannot be compared to a western type feudal lord in terms of his control of land and peasant labor. Stahl insists that the use of western terminology in these circumstances is simply misleading. Originally elected by the village community, village chieftains dependent on the nomad state performed the function of local agent for the collection of tribute for the conqueror. They were transformed into hereditary lords deriving their authority from the khan. In their new role they were called *boyar,* a term of Turkic origin, and formed a "feudal class".[62]

59 Les *anciennes communautés...*, 26, 185-186.

60 *Ibid.*, 36.

61 *Ibid.*, 36, 39-45, 244-245; Stahl agrees with A. A. Tschuprow in the definition of the free communal village which constitutes "un ensemble de... ménages, détenteurs d'un territoire, liés entre eux par des relations de telle nature, que l'ensemble a le droit de s'immiscer, selon des règles précises, dans l'activité économique et les droits juridiques de chaque ménage en particulier." But Stahl adds that such a village may fall under the domination of a feudal lord, who can appropriate for himself the rights of the village assembly and the village still remains as a communal one; this is because its organization of production does not change; such a change occurs only when this community comes into contact with a more advanced exchange economy.

62 *Ibid.*, 42-44.

While such a change was almost completed in Moldavia, in Wallachia free "village communities" continued their existence under traditional chiefs. In the east, in Moldavia, Stahl points out,[63] villages had indeed quite a different origin and development after the Turkic-Tatar domination. Invasions of pastoral nomads from the east, especially the Tatars, also caused large scale depopulation resulting in totally deserted villages. When these lands were reconquered by the Romanian voyvodes during the fourteenth century it was the voyvode himself who was responsible for the colonization and recreation of village settlements. Under these conditions, land was always considered to belong to the voyvode and purely feudal relationships based on land control developed. However, new villages were still organized, as in Wallachia, in the form of "free" village communities, the only difference being a closer dependence of peasants on boyars. Similar conditions of dependence would be established in the old villages of Wallachia when, in the sixteenth century, boyars were able, under quite different circumstances, to impose enserfment on their villagers.[64]

After the second World War, Romanian historiography in general asserted that Ottoman suzerainty played a vital role in furthering "feudalism" in Romanian territories. Ottoman "exploitation" of populations in Wallachia and Moldavia, it is argued, was carried out in two ways; first by subjecting them to tribute payment through the voyvodes and second, by establishing a monopolistic predatory system on its economy. It has been calculated that in the period 1538-1600 alone, the Sultan extracted 13 to 15 million gold pieces from the Romanian principalities.[65] Economic dependence

63 *Ibid.*,164-169, 187.

64 *Ibid.*, 19-24, 159-189.

65 Mihai Maxime, "Le statut de la Moldavie et de la Valachie à l'égard de la Porte ottomane dans la seconde moitié du XVIe siècle," *Nouvelles Études d'Histoire*, vol. VI/1 (Bucharest, 1980), 239, note; *idem*, "Les obligations économiques de la Moldavie et de la Valachie envers l'Empire Ottoman et le caractère de la tribut roumaine," *Actes du IIe. Congrès International des Études du Sud-Est Européen* (Athens, 1970); cf. Ion Matei, "Quelques problèmes concernant le régime de la domination ottomane dans les pays roumains" *RESEE*, X-I (1972), 65-81; XI-I (1973), 81-95.

and "exploitation", it is argued, was realized in its visible form through the obligation to provide the giant Istanbul market and the Ottoman palace and army with meat, wheat, salt, fats, horses and cattle at prices fixed by the Porte. It is true that Istanbul, then the largest city in Europe, survived by these shipments by sea, the only low cost transportation for these bulky commodities. Romanian historiography lays emphasis on the exploitative character of such an exchange system as part of Ottoman despotism. But we immediately add on the basis of the evidence which Ottoman archival material provides that at a time when western capitalism did not yet penetrate these regions immense amounts of capital were pumped into Romanian lands through the ever increasing demand for foodstuffs and raw materials for the Ottoman center.

In later periods, one can speak of two competing markets, Ottoman and European each of which played a dominant part successively. It is the historian's task to find out when and how these two systems came to compete[66] and when the Ottoman monopolistic system was considered as "unjust exploitation". At any rate, the total abolition of the Ottoman monopoly system in 1829 was welcomed in Romanian lands as a milestone on the path to independence.

Stahl recognizes the fundamental role of Ottoman economic dependence in shaping "feudal" structure in the Romanian countryside.[67]

66 Stahl, 208-211; C. C. Giurescu, "Despre Caracter relatilor dintre romani şi turci", *Probleme controverate in istoriografia română* (Bucharest, 1977), 120-121, believes that "the value of the products shipped to Istanbul, the Balkans and the Middle East exceeded by far that of the exports to Austria, Poland, Italy and other countries." The Ottoman-Romanian trade balance was in favor of Romania during the 16th-18th centuries; increasing trade, particularly in livestock to European countries from Hungary and Romania, however, is believed to have important effects --capital accumulation, expansion on money economy and concentration of land in fewer hands, see Zs. Pach. "Die ungarische Agrarentwicklung im 16.-17. Jahrhundert; P. Cemovodeanu, "England and the Question of Free Trade in the Black Sea in the 17th Century", *Revue Roumaine d'Histoire*, VI- 2 (1967), 15-22; A. Lapadatu, *Über die Genesis der rumanischen Agrargesellschaft des 18. Jahrhunderts*, (Berlin, Rome, Munich, 1978).

67 *Op. cit.*, 179, 187.

'The boyars' complete control of the "village communities", he suggests, occurred under the impact of the Ottoman market, particularly during the sixteenth century. In order to produce more for this ever growing market, the boyars now, Stahl asserts,[68] "captured the village communities' indivisible lands to convert into private economic exploitations", which precipitated the transformation of the Wallachian state into an "aristocratic, feudal oligarchy". The voyvode now became a tool in the hands of the boyars and "submitted to the terrorist injunctions of the Turks who began to introduce a new form of exploitation of the country reminiscent of the ancient predatory state of the steppe nomads". These new conditions, Stahl points out, deeply and adversely affected relations on the land and acted to consolidate servage in the Romanian countryside. In the early fifteenth century the Wallachian voyvode still represented a strong centralist power and could transfer land possession rights from one boyar to another, although such grants were limited to his own reign (this was actually the rule in the Ottoman home provinces). But during the sixteenth century, parallel to the establishment of the boyars' full control over land and peasant labor, the voyvode's authority began to weaken. By the turn of the century Romanian lands were already counted among those east European countries where the so-called "second serfdom" had become prevalent.[69] Already in the period

68 *Ibid.*, 179.

69 *Ibid.*, 159-188, 247-250; the use of this loose term for the specific developments in the Balkans is misleading in most cases, see H. İnalcık, "The Emergence of Big Farms, *çiftliks:* State, Landlords and Tenants", *Contributions à l'histoire économique et sociale de l'empire Ottoman*, Collection *Turcica*, III, (Louvain: Peelers, 1984), 105-126; B. McGowan, *Economic Life in Ottoman Europe: Taxation, Trade and the Struggle for Land, 1600-1800*, (Cambridge: CUP, 1981), 121-170; Andrei Otetea, "Le second asservissement des paysans roumains (1746-1821)", *Nouvelles Études d'Histoire*, (Bucharest, 1955), 299. On "second serfdom" or "refeodalisation", see papers presented and debates at the *Fifth International Congress of Economic History*, 1970 Leningrad, section V: "Les formes de propriété dans le système féodal et les origines du capitalisme"; and *Contributions roumaines*, (Bucharest, 1971), 129-134 (P. Cemovodeanu and S. Goldenberg).

1450-1550, Stahl points out, the Wallachian boyars' hereditary rights on the land in opposition to the rights of the state were extended and consolidated by the recognition of female rights of inheritance and the partition of landed property among heirs. In Moldavia, the same process was in operation through the sale of villages by the voyvode, who claimed that he needed extra money to pay the Ottoman tribute.

Stahl also stresses an extremely interesting phenomenon in connection with these developments, namely the flight of peasants from their homeland to the Ottoman side of the Danube.[70] There, the Ottoman *çift-hane* system prevailed while enserfment of the peasant was in full swing on the other side. But also, during this period of disorder (1593-1600) the Ottoman military class tried to take advantage of the new situation. They sought the fugitive labor and created privately owned farms for themselves as the following case illustrates.

In 1597, following the war against Michael the Brave, Alexander, the new voyvode of Wallachia complained to the Sultan that "most of the peasants abandoning their homes took refuge in the (uncultivated) harvest plots and the farms in the possession of Ottoman officials such as *müteferrika, çavuş, sipahi* and *yeniçeri* in the Ottoman territory beyond the Danube from Ibrail to Vidin".[71] Taking the fugitive peasants under their protection, these officials forbade the voyvode's men to collect poll-tax *(djizya)* and other taxes from them. The voyvode insisted that these peasants be sent back to their homes in Wallachia. Otherwise, he warned, taxes owed to the Sultan could not be realized. The Ottoman government admitted that "a few thousand peasants" had come over and settled in such farms. What is more, the boyars complained that many Muslims, including *çavuçes* and garrison commanders, turned some villages in the Wallachian territory into privately possessed farms (*çiftlik*) and settled Wallachian peasants on them. Under their protection these peasants resisted the payment of taxes. Since the Ottoman

70 Op. *cit.*, 229.

71 Başvekâlet Archives, Istanbul, *Mühimme Defteri*, no. 33, document 18.

treasury was losing revenue and the Ottoman government did not want to violate the autonomy of Wallachia, the Sultan ordered the dismantling of the recently created farms in Wallachia and the return of the peasants to their homes. The Sultan's decree, however, is not clear as to whether those peasants who had settled in Ottoman territory were also to return home.

Following the Marxist theory of feudal evolution, the analyses of Romanian historians still have to clarify several key questions. The real conditions of the Romanian peasant in the period prior to the "enserfment", the "enserfment" itself, the true nature of the collectivistic village communities, and the nature of the boyars' control over land and peasant labor are, I believe, still open questions. Perhaps originally, the peasants' status was not so diffeent from that of the Byzantine *paroikos* or Ottoman *reaya* on the other side of the Danube. The voyvode's right to make land transfers and to put restrictions on partition and possession of the land is reminiscent of the regime that prevailed in both the Byzantine and Ottoman empires. Also it is interesting to note that state ownership of land was an established fact in Moldavia as far as villages inherited from the Tatar period (*ocoale*) were concerned. It can be argued that the so-called "village communities", which Henri Stahl contends were the original form of the Romanian village, might in most cases be no more than a post-Roman village type in which independent peasant families maintained family-farms in their possession as production units while the village itself had communal rights on unused land, pastures, water resources and so on. Stahl bases his hypothesis on observations of a number of modern villages in a particular district where the periodic distribution of land among the peasant families take place. This may be a special case specific to the area.

As for the status of the peasant, rather than being categorized simply as "free" or "enserfed" (*asservi*) it should be defined in terms of peasant dependency within traditional *jugum-caput* or *çift-hane* system. What Stahl finds in the documents supports the idea that the peasant economy was indeed based on the small peasant family-farm system.[72] Village communities, Stahl indicates,[73] were composed of the peasant families in possession of a certain amount of land called *delnita.* Stahl calls it "famille-ménage," and in all legal transactions the peasant family is described always with its patrimonial land. "Chaque ménage- paysan", he asserts, "finit bientôt par être considéré comme *une unité d'exploitation autonome* rentrant en tant que telle dans le patrimoine du boyar." "Le ménage paysan est donc considéré", he continues, "cette fois comme étant une *unité économique individualiste,* figurant en tant que telle dans les registres fiscaux de l'État." "C'était toujours cette possession d'une 'delnita' qui entraînait le droit d'user des biens communs". "Le paysan serf était vraiment maître de son patrimoine". "Le boyar mesure donc ses propres droits patrimoniaux par unités de ménages". These observations suggest the features of the Byzantine *stasis* or Ottoman *çift-ḫāne.*

4. Russian and East German Historiography

The most recent account of "Ottoman feudalism" has come from a Soviet Russian orientalist, C. F. Oreshkova.[74] According to Oreshkova,[75] in Ottoman society, "feudal relations shaped the system of land law", and it is therefore necessary to investigate the typology of these relations. Before anything else, she says, the Ottoman social system or "Ottoman feudalism" should be distinguished from nomadic

72 *Op. cit.*, 191, 200-203. Apparently Stahl is under the influence of the theory of "mir", Slavic rural community in which periodic partitioning of land was practiced. The theory, also applied to the Byzantine landholding system in the Balkans, is duly criticised by Paul Lemerle, "Esquisse....", 59-60; the basic independent character of family-farms does not allow a real communal ownership and disposition of land in the Byzantine *khorion* or Ottoman *karye* (köy). Communal rights on pastureland, forests, treshing lot etc. seems to be misinterpreted, see "The Cift-Hane" article in this volume.

73 *Op. cit.*, 200-203.

74 "Osmanskii Feodalizm...", in *Tipy obshchestvennykh otnosheni na Vostoke v srednie veka* (Types of Social Relations in the East in the Middle Ages) (Moscow: 1982), 111-132.

75 *Ibid.*, 112.

feudalism.[76] The problem is to determine which type of feudal society the Ottoman "social type" falls into in asmuch as it is incorrect "to see [the Ottoman type] as a basic stage in society's development". Very different feudal types existed in the societies included in the Ottoman Empire; and the Ottomans themselves, at the beginning of their history, underwent a feudalization process uniquely of their own. Following Mutafčieva, she asserts that typical Ottoman feudalism later emerged as a compound fused with an 'advanced feudalism' that had come into being in the pre-Ottoman Balkans.[77] Thereafter, the Ottomans tried to spread and establish this typical feudalism of theirs in parts of the Empire. According to the Russian writer,[78] it is necessary to accept this as "a variant kind of feudalism possessing generic and structural features uniquely of its own". The most important rule of this feudal system was that land was the property of the Sultan, i.e., *miri.* Another of its features was that an important segment of these lands, in the form of *wakf* and *mulk,* belonged to the upper layer of "the dominant feudal class". Oreshkova asserts[79] that the high and low ranks of the ruling class formed two groups which engaged in a sort of class struggle. But she agrees that Ottoman society as a whole was essentially composed of two main classes: the so-called '*āskerī* or "feudal" class, representing the Sultan's authority and the dependent *reaya* class, consisting of tax payers.

According to Oreshkova, since land ownership manifested itself in various forms, various feudal types existed side by side in the Ottoman empire. On the *miri* lands granted by the Sultan as landed property (*temlik)* or as pensions *(arpalık, ocaklık*) or *miri* lands farmed out for life-term (*malikane-iltizam*), the different status of land and peasant paved the way for different types of feudal relations. While Oreshkova points out that the organization of the *timar* differed from the European form of feudal production, along

76 *Ibid.*, 112-114.

77 *Ibid.*, 116, 119-121.

78 *Ibid.*, 123.

79 *Ibid.*, 126.

with Mutafčieva she touches an extremely important point which I shall pause ahead to discuss. "Timar holders", she says, "were not merely rent gatherers, they, to a degree, organized the exploitation of the land as well".

In general, Oreshkova proposes as a basic thesis that Ottoman feudalism was a unique regime which, like Japanese feudalism, was characterized by the dominant position of the state. An emphatically centralized state establishes an equilibrium by playing the role of referee among mutually antagonistic groups. According to Oreshkova,[80] centralized "despotic" state power was able to survive by means of this role. On the other hand, like Mutafčieva and some Turkish writers,[81] Oreshkova, too, is of the opinion that state ownership of the land was always a barrier to Ottoman feudalism's evolving into the type of classical, 'advanced' feudalism as we see in the West. In the eighteenth century, however, the regime of the provincial notables (*âyan*) was, to a degree, a significant development in this direction.

One of the writers who examined the formative period of Ottoman history within the framework of Marxist theory is the East German historian Ernst Werner.[82] Werner's synthesis of the research which has been made up until now on early Ottoman history does not present an interpretation much different from that of east European historiography as far as Ottoman socio-economic structure is concerned.[83] His work after summarizing

80 *Ibid.*, 125-129.

81 See pp. 18-24 above.

82 *Die Geburt einer Grossmacht: die Osmanen (1300-1481), Ein Beitrag zur Genesis des türkischen Feudalismus*, fourth enlarged edition: *Forschungen zur Mittelalterlich Geschichte*, Bd. 32: (Weimar: Hermann Böhlaus Nachfolger, 1985).

83 *Ibid.*, 346-358, 401-403; *idem*, "Überlegung zum Problem der Stagnation im türkischen Feudalismus: das 15. und 16. Jahrhundert", *Jahrbuch für Geschichte des Feudalismus*, V (Berlin, 1981), 125-147; *idem*, "Methoden und Möglichkeiten komparative Mediävistik", *Zeitsch. für Geschichtswissenschaft*, XXI (Berlin, 1973), 542-547.

nomadic feudalism on the basis of Soviet research,[84] attempts to explain the process of "feudalization" in the first century of the Ottoman state as a historical process, and to show how "Turkish nomads, peasants and workers" were integrated into "die feudale Klassenstruktur".[85] *Staatsfeudalismus* represented the combined interests of the dominant class. Continuity between Byzantine, Balkan and Ottoman socioeconomic structures is emphasized in the process. In general, "the militant feudalism" of the Ottomans corresponded with an economically stagnant society. However, "with the *pax turcica,* after the turbulant decades", he asserts, "a period of relative peace and security started for the Balkan *raya*". In his view, *Staatsfeudalismus* began to disintegrate after the seventeenth century, and "the integration of the urban sector in the imperial state structure", a characteristic of *Hoch-Feudalismus* begins to become apparent. [86]

Marx and Engels themselves had felt that the FMP was not adequate paradigm to interpret the social formations which we find in the great empires of Asia where the state had such formidable centralist power and absolute control over land and peasant labor.

B. Asiatic Mode of Production Theory

In the 1960's renewed academic attention in France and Great Britain was focused on Marx and Engel's Asiatic Mode of Production (AMP) theory.[87] As a result of this interest, a definition of Ottoman

84 Die *Geburt*, 24-29.

85 *Ibid.*, 357.

86 *Ibid.*,401 ff.

87 Discussion following the discovery and publication of Marx's essay on pre-capitalist social formations, *Grundriss der Kritik der politischen Oekonomie*, published for the first time in 1941 (distributed in 1953), first English trans. E. J. Hobsbawm, *Pre-Capitalist Modes of Production* (London: Lawrence and Wishart, 1964); and first French trans. *Fondements de la critique de l'economie politique*, (Paris: Anthropos, 1967); Turkish trans. M. Belli, *Kapitalizm Öncesi Ekonomi Şekilleri*, (Ankara: Sol, n.d.); for later discussions see. *Sur le Mode de Production Asiatique*, (Paris, 1969), and *Recherches Internationales*, 57-58 (January-April

social formation within the framework of AMP began to gain currency among academics in Turkey.[88] The AMP offered a certain

1967): numéro special: *Premières sociétés de classe et Mode de Production Asiatique*, contribution to the volume by S. Divitçioğlu, "Essai de modèles économiques à partir du M.P.A.", 277-293; R. Hilton, *The Transition from Feudalism to Capitalism*, (London: New Left Books, 1976); a structuralist criticism of AMP, B. Hindess and P. Hirsch, *Pre-Capitalist Modes of Production*, (London: Routledge and Kegan Paul, 1975), 178-220; for an analysis of the origin of the theory, P. Anderson, *Lineages of the Absolutist State*, (London: NLB, 1974), 462-549; Irfan Habib, "Problems of Marxist Historical Analysis", *Enquiry* (Delhi), n.s. III-2 (1969), 52-67; Jon Elster, *Making Sense of Marx*, (London: CUP), 241- 317; B. Chandra, "Karl Marx, His Theories of Asian Societies, and Colonial Rule", *Revie-lw*, V (summer 1981), 13-91; H. Wolpe (ed.). *The articulation of Modes of Production* (London, 1980); and a recent selection of articles, published by A. M. Bailey and J. R. Llobera, *The Asiatic Mode of Production: Science and Politics*, (London: Routledge & Kegan Paul, 1981).

88 For a short history of the discussions on the AMP as a model for the Ottoman socio-economic structure see, Selâhattin Hilâv, "Asya Tipi Üretim Tarzı ve Türkiye Sosyalist Hareketi", *Asya Tipi Üretim Tarzı*, ed. İ. Keskinoğlu, (Istanbul: Ant Y., 1970), 10-22; the first systematic study by the economist S. Divitçioğlu, *Asya Tipi Üretim Tarzı ve Osmanlı Toplumu*, (Istanbul: İktisat Fak. Y., 1967); the theory became popular in Turkey particularly because social scientists believed it to have brought an answer to the question of why Turkey had an underdeveloped socio-economic structure, and why its efforts to modernize have not been successful; among numerous studies repeating this theme, the following are worth mentioning: M. A. Şevki, *Osmanlı Toplumunun Sosyal Bilimle Açıklanması* (Istanbul: Elif Y., 1968); M. Sencer, *Osmanlı Toplum Yapısı* (İstanbul: MAY, 1969), 186-378; K. Boratav, *Tarımsal Yapılar ve Kapitalizm*, (Ankara: SBF, 1980); R. Aktan, *Türkiye İktisadı*, 3rd edition, (Ankara: SBF, 1978); Ç. Keyder, *Toplumsal Tarih Çalışmaları*, (Ankara: Dost, no 198); for a general sociological approach see İbrahim Yasa, *Türkiye'nin Toplumsal Yapısı ve Temel Sorunları*, 2nd ed., Ankara 1973; also see, E. Kongar, *Türk Toplum Bilimcileri*, (İstanbul: Remzi, 1982); J. Hinderink and M. B. Kıray, *Social Stratification as an Obstacle to Development, A Study of Four Turkish Villages*, (New York: Praeger, 1970); for an attempt to interpret the Ottoman history within the AMP theory, see, S. Yerasimos, "Le mode de production asiatique et la société ottomane." unpublished thesis, translated into Turkish by B. Kuzucu, *Az gelişmişlik Sürecinde Türkiye*, 3 vol-, (İstanbul: Gözlem, 1974).

perspective which influenced how the Ottoman social system was to be perceived. Societies belonging to the AMP, it is argued, are those in which isolated and self-sufficient peasant communities exhibiting a primitive division of labor are the foundation of the society. These communities do not engage in commodity production for the market. A military stratum originating from outside the community incorporates the peasantry into its imperial system through conquest. The village communities are obliged to surrender a part of their surplus to this dominant class. However, the process of appropriation is neither a consequence of social or economic integration of the society, nor does it lead to it. The state does not provide anything in return to the peasant communities. Thus, the connection between the state and peasant communities is entirely political in nature, reflecting the absolute hegemony of the state. The state constructs a political-legal superstructure which establishes a close control over land and the peasant labor. The resulting form of appropriation is therefore nothing more than a form of usurpation in the guise of tax or rent.

The conflict which arises in such a social structure is between rival groups within and without the "system", who wish to gain control of the surplus. These politically antagonistic parties do not represent the constellation of social elements which constitute the productive basis of the society. Rather, they are self-imposed despots who are integrated within the disarticulated society only through the process of appropriation. In other words, the dynamics of historical progression provided by class conflict is lacking in these societies. They are non-evolving, stagnant societies without history.

Sencer Divitçioğlu[89] is the forerunner among those social scientists in Turkey who use "the AMP as a working hypothesis in order to understand Ottoman society". He chooses to qualify his approach with recent historical research while remaining faithful to the theoretical underpinnings of AMP. Divitçioğlu observes that the sultan's grant of freehold rights to some of his men did not change

89 For his main publication on the subject see note 87.

the basic structure because land grants constituted an insignificant part of agricultural land, and the "prebend" categories, i.e. timariots, acquired access to the land only as state functionaries. The existence of landowners, he argues, independent of any connection to the state, could not have been possible under the Ottoman system. Although forms of access could vary, the land regime was unified under the principle of state control. Divitçioglu adhering to Marxist notions interprets the appropriation of surplus in the form of tax, and underlines the absolute subordination of the peasantry and the resulting stagnancy of the social formation as a consequence of the state's control over land. While this description draws parallels between the AMP and the Ottoman social structure, it is, Divitçioglu agrees, far from being fully capable of characterizing the Ottoman system.

In the same way that Marxist historians have revised their generalizations in the light of historical data available since the time of Marx, social scientists in Turkey have arrived at modifications of the AMP in light of the research historians. The outcome is more than a revision; it attempts to inject subtlety into a rather rigidly defined AMP elements leading to new questions and hypotheses for a better understanding of a social structure which had otherwise been characterized as "immobile". In essence this has been an effort to identify the distinctive nature of Ottoman society and the result has sometimes been to define Ottoman social formation outside both the AMP and FMP.

The salient features of this characterization are twofold. First, the ability of the Ottoman state to preserve its strict control on agricultural land had been a consequence not of the ruler's absolute power, but of a particular form of social interaction. In fact, the state was able to prevent the rise of a "class" of big landowners which always tended to exploit peasant labor as much as possible. As a result, serfdom did not develop in the Ottoman situation. Ottoman conquest took the form of seizing the land not of the peasant, but of the landlord. Thus, during the Ottoman expansion there was a tacit agreement between the Ottoman state and the peasantry against their "feudal" overlords.

Second, under the Ottoman regime, Divitçioglu observes,[90] a significantly large part of the surplus that was being accumulated in the hands of the dominant class was directed to public services in the form of *wakfs*. This functionalist interpretation of the Ottoman *miri* land regime is shared generally by historians and social scientists in Turkey.

According to Divitçioğlu,[91] Ottoman social formation actually shares the characteristics of both the AMP and FMP. The presence of an authentic form of urbanization under the Ottoman regime, a certain economic integration between urban and rural areas and the relatively advanced state of commerce and monetized economy all point toward characterizing the Ottoman social structure as a special case, or AMP cannot be applied to the Ottoman empire at all.

As far as Ottoman social formation and its internal dynamics are concerned, H. İslamoğlu-İnan and Ç. Keyder[92] propose to develop a paradigm on the basis of the theories of Asiatic Mode of Production and I. Wallerstein's capitalist world economy and peripheralization theories. Such a paradigm, they argue, can integrate the diverse elements of the structure into an intelligible whole. However, in such an integrative approach toward Ottoman history the dominancy of the AMP cannot be overlooked although certain characteristics of Ottoman society distinguish it from the kind of AMP originally suggested by Marx and Engels. They regard as inadequate my concept of "institutionalist functionalism", on the grounds that it is "characterized by an inability to integrate both in structure and in time its various areas of concentrations". Also, those before them trying to use the AMP to interpret Ottoman history remained "within a narrow perspective without recourse to such essential concepts as social formation or dominance". They stress

90 *Op. cit.*, 86-87.

91 *Op. cit.*, 89-95.

92 "Agenda for Ottoman History", *Review*, I-l (1977), 31-55.

that the basic concepts to be followed are totality of social formation and disarticulation of state control in its process of dissolution. It is essential, they argue, to recognize the state's dominant part in "the division of labor within the system", and the "political control over the economy". The state "integrates the system in the Asiatic Mode of Production, cutting through the economic, political and ideological levels". Drawing, however, on the results of recent empirical research and repeating Divitçioğlu İslamoğlu and Keyder observe that with "a highly monetized economy with a developed division of labor ... and a system of regional and inerregional markets" as well as close dependency between rural and urban production, the Ottoman social formation presents quite a different picture. In a separate paper, Keyder[93] puts special emphasis on the political control of the state over production. Being the dominant element in the Ottoman version of the AMP the weakening of the state control brought about a structural "disarticulation" or "evolution" in the whole social formation. This, he believes, means at the same time a gradual economic articulation with the capitalist world economy. Following the Marxist theory of class conflict for social evolution İslamoglu and Keyder find that these latent "contradictions" were factors for change once penetrated by the capitalist economies and led to the eventual dissolution of "the world empire" of the Ottomans.

The principal social dynamic "is not graspable in the production experience" (i. e., between peasant and the state), but in intra-class conflict. The actual factions in the Ottoman Society were the Janissaries, *ulema,* bureaucrats and other groups in the ruling class which struggled for a larger share of the peasants' surplus.

The dissolution of the system, or the state's failure "to reproduce the system which depended on the maintenance of small property in the countryside" is also discussed by İslamoğlu and Keyder. The struggle accompanied by basic structural changes such as the rise of the provincial notables (*a'yān*), and the emergence of commercial estates

93 "The Dissolution of the Asiatic Mode of Production", *Economy and Society,* V-2 (May 1976), 178-196.

(*çiftliks*) both of which were essentially considered as the outgrowths of spread of the tax-farming system and other phenomena related to the weakening of the central government. A true peripheralization process, they suggest, began with the commercialization of agriculture and the formation of commercial *çiftliks.* This was the end of the Ottoman social formation as "a world empire". And "becoming a periphery is identical with entering the world division of labor, and thus ceasing to be a self- contained unit of production". The process became complete in the second half of the nineteenth century. Within this perspective, modernization and reform simply meant "the transition from a state mechanism of the Asiatic type to a colonial state". In brief, as Divitçioğlu had previously argued, the Ottoman example deviates from classical AMP theory in a number of crucial structural particulars. Although İslamoğlu and Keyder duly stress the role of the state, they do not offer an explanation for it or its function to maintain a specific socioeconomic system.

Recently Perry Anderson offered[94] an analysis of the AMP theory with a summary of views on the Ottoman social structure. This analysis is of special interest for Ottoman studies because it explains why the Ottoman or "Asiatic" state was envisaged in western intellectual tradition as antithetical to the western state system and how the notion was in fact used, as a justification and selfdefinition of European political ideology.[95] He also shows how the Marxist theory of feudalism, when applied to oriental empires, is paradoxical. The theory which presupposes the existence of a military class or state established for the forceful appropriation of the surplus-product of a dependent population is so elusive that it can be applied to almost any historical society. "The superstructures of kinship", Anderson says,[96] "religion, law or state necessarily enter into the constitutive structure of the mode of production in pre-capitalist formations. They intervene directly in the 'internal' nexus of surplus extraction....

94 *Lineages of the Absolutist State*, (London: NLB, 1974).

95 *Ibid.*, 405-407.

96 *Ibid.*, 403.

These are what determine the type of extra-economic coercion that specifies them". "Today", he adds, "even those historians who admit the basic importance of the articulation of productive forces in a social formation have the consensus to deal with each society in its totality as the Marxist notion of social formation itself infers. Thus, the essential characteristic attributed to the Ottoman feudal system, i.e., the divorce of political and legal superstructures from the economic basis is methodologically misleading". The Ottoman case in particular, as illustrated through solid archival evidence, provides strong argument for the idea that only the state *and* economic basis taken together can explain total social reality. In a social formation such as the Ottoman empire the state's absolute control of landed property (and labor) was actually a decisive factor determining and reproducing a particular 'mode of production'.

In his analysis of the origins of the "Asiatic mode of production" idea, Anderson notes that the characteristic components of the "despotic" empires of Asia were formulated as state proprietorship of land, the absence of a hereditary nobility and historical immutability (stagnation). Montesquieu and Hegel added that oriental empires shared a servile social equality. All of these points were borrowed by Marx and Engels for a definition of the social formation of "Asiatic" empires.[97] Since 1960, however, there have been "modern attempts to build a developed theory of the 'Asiatic mode of production' ".

Anderson himself suggests a revised version of the theory for the Ottoman empire. For Anderson, the emergence in Islamic lands of Turkish states which had their own particular structural characteristics proved to be of "most significance for the development of Islamic social formation as a whole." Like the Seljukid and Indian Mughal regimes, that of the Ottomans also was characterized by a more autocratic, centralist regime than before. It was based on a more complete monopoly of land ownership and a better disciplined and equipped imperial army at *the expense of commercial interests.* "All these

97 *Ibid.*, 462-472.

Islamic states," he asserts,[98] "like the Ottoman empire itself, were essentially warrior and plunderer in caste: founded on conquest, their whole rationale and structure was military... A scribal bureaucracy did not develop much beyond the needs of tax collection. The state machine was largely a consortium of professional soldiers... It was the combination of military predation and contempt for agrarian production that seems to have given rise to the distinctive phenomenon of elite slave guards who again and again came to cap the state apparatus itself... They (tribal warriors) were not readily convertible into a rural nobility, living on hereditary estates, or a scribal bureaucracy, organized in a civil administration". Anderson's characterization of the Ottoman, and Mughal Indian social formations agrees in its essential lines with the Asiatic mode of production theory, with the difference that it puts less emphasis on the self- sufficient village community and "unchanging, stagnating" character of its socioeconomic structure.[99]

Under the Ottomans "the fundamental agrarian pattern of the Balkan countries," Anderson asserts, "remained based on petty production, amidst increasing overpopulation, divided holdings and village debts, the recession of Turkish rule". Briefly, Anderson finally subscribed to the theory of "landlordism" set against the Ottoman nomadic background and the "inimical relationship of the Ottoman state to cities and industries".[100]

1. Karl Wittfogel: Despotic Bureaucratic Power

Marx explains the establishment and survival of Asiatic empires solely in terms of direct force, conquest and terror. This is hardly an explanation. History testifies that in these extensive complex societies, no state power survived for long on the basis of force alone. The theory that a centralized power for large- scale hydraulic works and their

98 *Ibid.*, 505.

99 *Ibid.*,

100 *Ibid.*, 375, 393-394; on Ottomans and economy now see *An Economic and Social History of the Ottoman Empire.* H. İnalcik (ed.) Cambridge: CUP, 1994.

constant supervision by a highly specialized bureaucracy to maintain a distinct organization of forces of production under special ecological conditions was indeed an ingenious idea. The significance of the system's bureaucratic machine was fully developped by Karl Wittfogel.[101] But, even in this expanded form, the theory did not explain why total power states also existed in lands where there were no such large-scale irrigation works. In his critique of Wittfogel's thesis, Jullan H. Steward[102] points out that the integration of independent communities into a large polity required "state functions and enterprises other than the managerial controls of irrigation. "But, then, Steward, too, turned eventually to the conquest factor both in the initial acquisition of territory and in the specialization of functions as society continues to expand by conquest.

What appears to be always valid in Wittfogel's analysis is that certain conditions, not exclusively those required by irrigation, must be taken into account to explain the creation and long life of a state based on centralized total power. Such special conditions for the Ottoman empire consisted of the challenge to defend a specific social formation based on a belief system and its exclusive culture complex against the massive onslaught of a determined foe, Europe. On the other hand the omnipotent state was aware that its military power depended on a particular agrarian system for its power basis. Thus, Wittfogel's theory has to be expanded if it is to be applied to all "despotic" empires.

The idea of the omnipotent state and its all-controlling bureaucratic machine is basic to Wittfogel's theory. "State power" he said,[103] "more than any other factor, shapes the fate of both the members of the ruling class and the commoners. The state had to create a central controlling apparatus to serve those ends. Under the

101 *Oriental Despotism, A Comparative Study of Total Power*, fifth printing (New Haven and London: Yale Univ. Press, 1964).

102 "Initiation of Research Trend: Wittfogel's Irrigation Hypothesis", *Society and History, Essays in Honor of Karl August Wittfogel*, ed. G. L. Ulmen (The Hague: Mouton 1978), 11-12.

103 Op. *cit.*, 318.

state's regulative power economic differences among peasant households were minimal".[104] "The state." Wittfogel observes,[105] "actively supported village communities" by encouraging peasants to bring to it their complaints about local authorities' abuses of imperial laws. In other words, the state's prime concern was to protect the peasantry. In order to do so, it had to be able to deliver quick and unquestioned punishments against offenders on the most distant peripheries of the realm. This modified version of Wittfogel offers a social rationale for the "despotic" state which was accepted by the empire- builders and peasants themselves.

In fact, Wittfogel suggests that the hydraulic economy was typical only in arid and semi-arid landscapes. He admits[106] of different forms in their humid periphery.[107] The Ottoman empire was founded in such a landscape. While remaining faithful to his hydraulic society, Wittfogel hierarchizes the Asiatic empires according to their structural relation to the typical hydraulic core society. In his diffusionist theory[108] he explains how hydraulic statecraft, which originated in the valleys of the Nile, Euphrates and Indus diffused and gave rise to "marginal hydraulic societies" on the periphery.[109] Thus, "the great traditions of agromanagerial statecraft" diffused, and the despotic state reproduced itself under different conditions in societies separated from the hydraulic East.

For the diffusion of the tradition, Wittfogel adds,[110] "no primitive non- agricultural group has played as important a role as the pastoralist." The Arab conquests were responsible for the spread of "oriental despotic patterns of government" to North Africa and

104 *Ibid.* 329.

105 *Ibid.*, 330.

106 *Ibid.* 161-227.

107 *Ibid.* 161-227.

108 See G. Childe, "A Prehistorian's Interpretation of Diffusion", *Readings in Cultural Geography*, ed P. L. Wagner and M. W. Mikesell, (Chicago: UCP, 1962), 212.

109 Wittfogel, *op. cit.*, 69, 80, 295.

110 *Ibid.*, 204.

Spain. Turkish states in general belonged to the category of "marginal hydraulic societies". The Greek world, after being orientalized during the Hellenistic and Byzantine periods, was restored "to a loosely hydraulic society" through Turkish conquest.[111] Interpreting all these developments in terms of his hydraulic theory, Wittfogel suggests that nomadic conquests actually caused a change from a high to a low hydraulic density.[112] Consequently, "hydraulic enterprise may be of little importance" or "form a fraction of the politically dominated territory."

The third category of states, he suggests,[113] appears on the submargin of the hydraulic system. These states employ conspicuous elements of orientally despotic statecraft, "but their institutions are of a definitely non-hydraulic character".

While hydraulic empires were long-lived and possessed a solid institutional base, nomadic steppe empires had a more precarious existence. Founded on the margin of hydraulic civilization, the Ottoman empire nevertheless followed "the great traditions of agro-managerial statecraft". True, whether or not Osman's people were pastoral nomads, the state which developed on the frontiers of the bureaucratic Seljukid and Byzantine states was based on the true traditions of Iranian-Near Eastern absolutist statecraft. According to Wittfogel,[114] "the later development of Ottoman Turkey combines the features of the Byzantine and the Russian patterns. The Turkish empire resembled the Byzantine with whose territory it was largely congruent in that it also originally controlled classical areas of hydraulic economy; and it resembled Tsarist Russia in that it was also deeply influenced by the industrial society of modern Europe.

It differed from Byzantium in that the loss of its hydraulic provinces virtually coincided with the decline of its political prominence; and it differed from Russia in that the growing economic and cultural influence of the industrial West was accom-

111 *Ibid.*, 208.

112 *Ibid., 226.*

113 *Ibid., 226.*

114 *Ibid.*, 181, 215-225.

panied, and partly preceded, by a successful encroachment upon Turkey's sovereignty".

Let us open a parenthesis here and point out that the Ottoman provinces of Egypt and Mesopotamia where irrigation agriculture continued without interruption were never truly absorbed into the classical Ottoman administrative system of *timars* and *çift-hane.* They were "autonomous" provinces, constituting a margin on the Ottoman core lands. This state of affairs can be taken as evidence that the classical Ottoman system cannot *directly* be a derivative of a hydraulic society. Wittfogel's diffusion theory appears to be correct only in that the Ottomans did adopt the tradition of a powerful centralized bureaucracy but they did so in response to a challenge unrelated to flood control.

A complex centralized bureaucracy maintaining complete control over land and peasant labor through careful surveying and registration was indeed the basis of the classical Ottoman political system. Historically, the Ottomans inherited the system through the Sasanian, Caliphal, Seljukid-Iranian and Ilkhanid-Iranian traditions.[115] The text books the Ottoman bureaucrats studied and applied, and the *munshī-kātib,* state secretaries, who joined the Ottoman chancery mostly from Iran, were the actual vehicles of transmission for the tradition.

In his insightful analysis of the bureaucratic machine, Wittfogel also touched on the problem of the peculiar landholding system employed by the centralized empires. He stressed the fact that the despotic character of the Asiatic empires actually stemmed from the state's need for complete "control over land and people".[116] He makes a point of state ownership of agricultural lands for its concern to maintain "small farming" both in hydraulic societies and in societies that adopted hydraulic statecraft.[117] Most of the land is, in

115 See, M. Fuad Köprülü, *Alcune osservazioni intorno all' influenza delle istituzioni bizantini sulle istituzioni ottomane,* (Rome, 1953).

116 *Op. cit.*, 220-221, 230, 263, 271, 273.

117 *Ibid.*, 230.

one way or another, regulated by the government. Beside the government-managed land there was another category of land which, though still under government regulation, was in the possession of small farmers. They "work for or pay tax and rent to the government."[118] In China, Muslim India and the Ottoman empire "a normally functioning despotic regime determines the fate of its serving men and the lands alloted to them." This was the case with "the Turkish Sultan Sueliman, who characteristically demonstrated that a well-functioning despotism could abolish office land as easily as it would create it."[119] Thus, peasant-possessed land as well as sinecure land are kept, under the strict control of the state.

Although criticized on scholarly as well as political grounds Wittfogel's contribution to the analysis and description of centralized bureaucratic empires of the Ottoman type is undeniable. Wittfogel failed to recognize the role of the family-farm system of agrarian production in bringing about an omnipotent state formation in regions outside his hydraulic society.

Observations in View of the Marxist Paradigms

A. Tribute, Conquest and Protection

Under the FMP, land and labor are directly controlled by a class of landowners whereas in the AMP, they are subject to state control. But in both theories, this control is politico-legal, relying on force, and not the result of socio-economic articulation. This coercive mechanism is organized as the "feudal" state.[120] Therefore, our examination of the theory must start with the examination of the nature and function of the imperial power in these "autocratic", "despotic" empires.

---

118 *Ibid.*, 271, 295.

119 *Ibid.*, 274.

120 For an update discussion of FMP and AMP as far as the Ottoman-Turkish formation was concerned, see K. Boratav, *Tarımsal Yapıtlar ve Kapitalizm* (Ankara: SBF, 1980), 11-17.

The form of direct "extraction", or "usurpation", of revenue by the conquering power seems clearly to apply to the tribute stage of relations. But even here, it is possible to speak of a social function, protection, which was guaranteed by the conqueror.[121] For example, in placing Wallachia and Moldavia under tribute, the Ottoman protectorate guaranteed peace and protection; these countries were effectively protected from raiders coming from the north or the east (Cossaks or Crimean Tatar raiders). Also, as seen earlier,[122] supplies shipped to the Istanbul market from these countries played a significant role in the development of the Wallachian and Moldavian economies. In this way, the Ottoman tribute system offered a more complex network of relations than a dependency based purely on compulsion and predatory exploitation.

The direct rule over conquered land, however, was inherently different from a tributary relationship. The right of booty and spoils was legitimized in Islamic law only in time of war, and submission brought about the immediate protection of the conquered by the Islamic state.[123]

---

121 F. Oppenheimer, *Der Staat*, (Frankfurt, 1907); for status, social function and reward, see, M. M. Tumin, *Social Stratification, The Forms and Functions of Inequality*, (Englewood Cliffs: Prentice-Hall, 1967), 19-46; R. Bendix and S. M. Lipset, *Class, Status and Power*, (Glencoe, I11.: The Free Press, 1953); L. Krader, *Formation of the State*, (Englewood Cliffs: Prentice-Hall, 1968), VIII, 187, defines the basic role of the State as "controlling and directing the life of the people under it by centralized power in the hands of a few," also see, Chapter 3: Ankole: "Formation by Conquest," 43-51, and Chapter 6: "The Tatar State: Turks and Mongols," 82-103; on the theory of total social control of the State, see, R. Thurnwald, *Die Menschliche Gesellschaft*, vol. 4, (Berlin- Leipzig, 1935), and, E. Meyer, *Geschichte des Altertums*, (1921), vol. 1, parts 1-2.

122 Supra, "Romanian Historiography".

123 For the two stages of the Ottoman conquest, see, H. İnalcık, "Ottoman Methods of Conquest", *The Ottoman Empire: Conquest, Organization and Economy*, (London: Variorum Reprints, 1978), no. I; for the early pursuit of these two opposing but eventually complementary policies in the Turkmen principalities in western Anatolia, see H. İnalcık "The Rise of the Turcoman Maritime Principalities in Anatolia, Byzantium, and the Crusades", *Byzantinische Forschungen*, IX (Amsterdam, 1985), 191-203, 216-217.

There are historians who could see that the Balkan peasantry in general turned against their feudal masters, and tacitly favored the Ottoman centralist regime, which in a sense restored the eastern Roman tradition. When we discuss this aspect of the Ottoman conquest we must carefully consider the role of the *istimālet* (conciliatory) policy of the Ottoman central government and distinguish it from the conduct of the frontier *ghazis.* The upper echelons of the Byzantine and Balkan feudal aristocracy had alienated themselves from the peasantry not only in economic and social terms, but also ideologically by being "latinized", allying themselves with the Latin West and following their life style, and even their faith. The great economic, social-cultural crisis which was shaking the Byzantine and Balkan societies in the fourteenth century has only recently been the subject of serious study.[124] The Ottomans themselves were not unaffected by or unaware of this political and cultural dichotomy.[125] The point I am trying to make is that the Ottoman conquest of the Balkans cannot be explained as an abrupt invasion of conquerors or a juxtaposition of an alien dominant society over another. Rather it was the outcome

124 I. Ševčenko, *Études sur la polémique entre Théodore Métochite et Nicéphore Choumnos*, (Brussels: Byzantion, 1962); *idem*, "Intellectual Repercussions of the Council of Florence", *Church History*, 24 (1955), 291-232; A. Laiou, "The Byzantine Aristocracy in the Palaeologi Period", *Viator*, 4 (1973), 131-151; D. Geanakoplos, *Byzantine East and Latin West, Two Worlds of Christendom in Middle Ages and Renaissance*, (Oxford, 1966); A. E. Vacalopoulos, *Origins of the Greek Nation, 1204-1461*, (New Brunswick: Rutgers U. P., 1970); A. Pertusi, *Venezia e li Oriente fra tardo Medioevo e Rinascimento*, (Florence, 1966); S. Runciman, *The Last Byzantine Renaissance*, (Cambridge, 1970).

125 F. Taeschner, "G. Gemistos Plethon, ein Vermittler zwischen Morgenland und Abendland zu Beginn der Renaissance," *Byzantinische und Neugriechische Jahrbücher*, VIII (1931), 100-113; F- Babinger, *Johannes Darius (1414-94), Schwalter Venedigs im Morgenland und sein griechischer Umkreis*, (1961); G. Amakis, "Gregory Palamas among the Turks and Documents of his Captivity as Historical Sources", *Speculum*, 25 (1951), 104-118; in early Ottoman popular chronicles, *Die altosmanischen anonymen Chroniken*, ed. F. Giese, (Breslau, 1922), 29-34, criticism of the Ottoman elite's imitation of Italian manners is voiced; a study on cultural interaction between Ottoman Turks and Levantine Italians might yield surprising results.

of a long process of compromise and integration of two societies in which the centralist Ottoman regime proved to be the final solution to the questions stirring these fundamentally peasant societies. It is an anachronistic distortion by modern nationalist or marxist historians to visualize the pre-Ottoman Balkan landlords or "Latinized" elite as the advanced feudals apt to lead these societies to a western type feudalism and thence to capitalism. What actually the bulk of the population then wanted was the restoration of "free" peasant exploitations under the protection of a Basileus, Tsar or even a Sultan. In this, while Stefan Dušan failed, the Ottomans succeeded.

According to Islamic legists, the state's right of ownership over agricultural lands arose from the prerogative of conquest. In their correspondence with foreign sovereigns, the Ottoman Sultans spoke of "lands conquered by the sword", or "right of the sword". Thus, at this point, the Ottoman sources themselves rationalize rights of control over land and subjects by referring to the fact of the conquest.[126] Once the land and peasants had been taken under a certain status, this signified an objective legal order, binding on the state as well. In Islam this obligation was assumed before God, that is, it was a duty of religious sanction. Like all Islamic sovereigns, so too the Ottoman Sultans spoke of their subjects as "the trust of God" *(vadī 'atu' Allāh).* Whatever the ideological expression, this situation was not merely a tribute relationship. It was a matter of direct protection of the peasants, with a particular system of land possession and labor organization. And this entire system was guaranteed by objective laws and acquired continuity. Thus, the Islamic-Ottoman state came to fulfill certain functions for the ruled, primarily the peasantry. It should be remembered that from

126 On the great Ottoman legist Ebussuud's interpretation of land ownership see, H. İnalcık, "Land Problems in Turkish History", *The Muslim World*, vol. 45, (Hartford, 1955), 221-22, reprint: *The Ottoman Empire: Conquest, Organization and Economy*, (London: Variorum Reprints, 1978), no. IV; also H. İnalcık, "Islamization of Ottoman Laws on Land and Land tax", *Festangabe an Josef Matuz, Osmanistik - Turkologie - Diplomatik*, Ch. Fragner and K. Schwarz, eds., Berlin 1992, 101- 116.

the beginning, Islamic legal theory sought to justify and legalize the matters in accordance with dogma on the one hand, and social reality on the other. To ensure smooth functioning of the social system the ruler was recognized to formulate further laws called *kanuns.* In the classical period, the Ottomans followed a code of practical laws which were absolutely independent from the rigid Islamic rulings as far as landholding and peasant conditions were concerned.

If we consider that life and property in the Middle Ages were precarious, it is obvious that protection was of vital importance. Individual production was possible only under the effective protection of the state, and in its absence, the local feudal lord was the best available choice.

Village communities, isolated and without defence in the wilderness were particularly vulnerable. The peasants, living in constant fear of violence, wanted before anything else, an effective protection. Suffice it to mention the horrible conditions in the French countryside at the end of the Hundred Years War and the Great Flight in Anatolia during the Djelālī depredations in the period 1596-1610. The fear of loosing the land to the local notable or usurer was not less distressing. Nothing speaks more eloquently of the need of a protective power than the innumerable petitions of peasants to the Ottoman Padishah for the final refuge for protection or redress of abuses.[127] The interdependence of the peasant and the imperial power was obvious and expressed emphatically in political manuels. For the empire, protection of the peasant meant, in a more concrete way, *the maintenance of an agrarian system based on "free" peasant families which was believed to be the guarantee for their subsistence.* It was believed that the wealth and power of the empire, too, came from such an order.

In their imperial titles, Ottoman sultans refer to their dominions as "well protected lands" (*mamālik-i maḥrūsa).* Acts of violence and

127 A volume of complaints from Ottoman archives was recently published by H. G. Majer, *Das osmanische "Registerbuch der Beschwerden"*, vol. I, (Wien: Oesterreich. Akademie, 1985).

robbery were the greatest concern of the imperial bureaucracy, and were punished accordingly under a particularly severe penal code. In oriental political theory, this kind of state protection is idealized as the ruler's 'justice' ('*adālet*).[128] At any event, it does not seem logical to think that the great masses of peasants in the Christian Balkan countries could have been held for centuries under submission merely by sword.

As noted above, state protection and control were accepted as the precondition for the continuation of a certain organization of production which was seen traditionally as the most efficient and profitable agrarian system (see the *Çift-Ḫāne* System in the next article in this volume). Extracting state revenue at a maximum level, which depended on holding the productive power of the peasantry at a maximum level, was always the greatest concern of the central bureaucracy, whether in Persia, in the Islamic caliphate, or in the Ottoman state. Thus, a convergence of interests, or an equilibrium arose between the conqueror and the conquered, or between the dominant class and the dependent class.[129] In other words, the factor of protection, which was ensured by the state or military-dominant class, emerged as a determining factor in the 'articulation of the forces of production'. Many Marxist writers simply ignore the distinction between a condition of pure tribute and a system of production in which the centralist state takes land and labor under its direct control and protection.[130] As we shall see in the *çift-*

128 See, H. İnalcık, "Adâletnâmeler", *Belgeler*, II (Ankara, 1967), 49-63.

129 Eastern "Mirror-for-Princes" literature or treatises on politics which take the idea of equilibrium between the ruling class ('class of sword and pen') and *reaya*, i.e., dependent people engaged in economic production as the basis of polity; summarizing these ideas Kınalızâde, *Akhlāḳ-i 'Alāī*, II, (Istanbul; 1860), says that an ideal polity is based on four classes *(tā'ife)*, that of trade, that of handicrafts, that of agriculture, and that of the military (*sipahilik*). The latter one is necessary because "it protects the polity from the enemy from outside and internal outlaws." He considers it (r. 7-8) as part of the wealth producing classes in the same footing as the others.

130 Occasionally even in its "primitive" phase some Marxist historians admit the involvement of "the feudals in the process of production".

hane system, it would have been impossible for the *distinct social formation* referred to as the 'Asian empire' to have emerged without this type of state supervision of land and labor.[131]

B. Dissolution Process of the Centralist Empire

Under certain conditions, when a centralized empire is unable to carry out its basic functions, such as ensuring security, protecting "the powerless" and collecting taxes, local authorities gain influence and strengthen their control over the land and peasantry and eventually gaining the role of the central government. This process began primarily as a financial, fiscal crisis caused by the long disastrous wars. Local great men (the *dynatoi* of the Byzantines, the tax farmer-governors of classical Islam and Ottoman *āyan)* emerged mostly from among the urban, military leadership in the provinces. These men became over time tax farmers with hereditary tenure. In the large areas they controlled they were empowered to sell rights over local revenue sources, that is over land and peasants, to small tax farmers. In this way, a true hierarchy similar to that in western feudalism emerged. It was under such circumstances as these that the *āyan* system emerged in the Ottoman provinces.[132] Under the tax-farming (the *mukataa-iltizam)* system, which provided the material foundation of their power and influence, the *āyan* also came to acquire administrative and military powers. That is to say, their control over land and the

131 A purely structuralist theory does not bring an explanation for the autocratic empire formation because it dismisses the historical process in favor of a deterministic scheme of evolution and change. See, H. İnalcık, "L'Empire Ottoman", in *Variorum Reprints*, 1985, and "Mehmed II" *İslâm Ansiklopedisi*, vol. V.

132 H. İnalcık, "Centralization and Decentralization in Ottoman administration". *Studies in Eighteenth Century Islamic History*, eds. T. Naff and R. Owen, (London, 1977), 27-52; Y. Özkaya, *Osmanlı İmparatorluğunda Ayanlık*, (Ankara: DTCF, 1977); Y. Nagata, *Materials on the Bosnian Notables*, (Tokyo: Institute for the Study of Languages and Cultures of Asia and Africa, 1979); in the Byzantine empire *dynatoi* consisted of provincial dignitaries; Ottoman *āyan* originated mostly from among the local military chiefs or *ulema.*

peasantry was progressively strengthened. However, at no time was the *āyan* ever able to reduce, in principle, the land to true freehold private property and the peasants to the status of serfs, as in western feudalism. The state always stayed as the sole legitimizing authority, and even the most powerful *āyan* sought to obtain the symbols of legitimation from the Sultan. On this point, I believe, for the sake of the theory, the Balkan Marxist historians fall into exaggeration. Even in those regions strongly penetrated by western capitalist economy, for example western Anatolia or Macedonia, the *āyan* do not appear to have dominated a manor or plantation-type farm. Rather, as before, the *çift-hane,* and/or sharecropping methods, remained the dominant mode of production.[133]

True, in the Ottoman land system, there were always freehold and endowment lands which to some extent escaped the control of the central bureaucracy, and assumed the character of private property, and this process, gaining momentum under certain conditions can be considered as introducing a structural change. Evidently, it was for this reason that sixteenth and seventeenth century Ottoman "advice literature" (Mustafa ʿĀlī, Aynī Alī, *Kitāb-i Musteṭāb,* Koçi Bey) viewing from the central bureaucracy's standpoint strongly criticized such a trend in landholding; they believed that the real reason for the decline of the empire was the passage of state lands as properties into the hands of dignitaries and palace favorites. The period of the *āyan* and the subject of the big *çiftliks* have only recently been somewhat better illuminated by research.

The fundamental factor in the big çiftlik formation which expressed a change in the Ottoman socio-economic order, is related to the general loosening of the state-controlled *(miri)* system in favor of the individual. Studying the formation of the so-called big farms during the seventeenth century two points must be kept

133 H. İnalcık, "The Emergence of Big Farms, *Çiftliks:* State, Landlords and Tenants", *Contributions à l'histoire économique et sociale de l'Empire Ottoman,* (Louvain: Peeters, 1984), 105-126; Y. Nagata, *Some Documents on the Big Farms* (çiftliks) *of the Notables in Western Anatolia,* (Tokyo, 1976).

in mind.[134] First, the process was not, in general, appropriation of land as freehold property by the "powerful" men in the provinces, and the peasants' exclusion from it. What happened was simply the establishment in one way or another of the powerful men's control over the agrarian units, *raiyyet çiftliks* or *çift hanes*. *Reaya* continued always to be the direct producers; in this period general economic conditions in the Ottoman empire in most areas were not yet favorable to the formation of large scale farm exploitations. Second, where we find big landed properties, more or less organized for market, these appeared mostly to consist of the reclaimed or deserted lands which were no more in the possession of peasant families who abandoned their lands because of insecurity, excessive tax burden, usury and judicial malpractices. It can be said that, in general peasant desertion of land appears to have been a common process in the dissolution of the agrarian system in the Byzantine and Ottoman empires where the "powerful men" took advantage of the situation to establish their own control over land.

In the big *çiftliks* it was simply the right of collection of rent or state taxes farmed out to rich and in fluential men. Peasants stayed on the lands and no change was introduced in the process of production. In the eighteenth century real changes occured on the lands reserved for the cultivation of cash crops such as cotton and tobacco. Compared to the First category such lands were to be found on certain coastal areas open to international trade and consisted mostly of deserted or newly reclaimed lands.[135]

Annales School, Empirical Research

Omer Lûltfi Barkan, a student of Marc Bloch and the founder of the Turkish school of agrarian history, emphatically affirms the state's

134 It is important to distinguish between *ekābir çiftliği*, *çiftliks* of the important men and *raiyyet çiftliği*, those of reaya, peasants.

135 Bruce McGowan, *Economic Life in Ottoman Europe: Taxation, Trade and the Struggle for Land, 1600-1800*, (Cambridge: CUP, 1981), 121-173; also see notes 125 and 126.

pervasive role in the whole Ottoman social system. Stressing its monopolistic policies, he says: "The Ottoman system was basically one of imperial self-sufficiency. In order to systematically exploit the vast resources of wealth of the empire, and to preserve its political and economic integrity and unity, the Ottomans sought to establish a tightly closed economic order ... They attempted to develop meansby which the different economic zones of the empire would complement one another" and "the robust consititution and political power of the empire in its first centuries enabled it to pursue an economic policy that was highly favorable to it". Economic integration and autarchy, and above all a centralist autocracy which made possible to pursue such a policy formed the dominant characteristics of the empire. Barkan particularly stressed the omnipotent (*ḳādir-i kül)* nature of Ottoman state power which, he says, possessed and organized everything, men and things, for its own purpose.

In Europe, in addition to the control of land by an aristocratic or feudal class, servage and labor services and seigneurial rights of justice over serfs constitute the key elements but all have a fundamentally diverse meaning in a centralized empire. In studies completely based on archival materials Barkan discussed these topics in the context of the Ottoman empire. In his study on the *ortaḳdji-ḳuls*,[136] sharecropping slaves who as war captives were settled on the *miri* (state-owned) lands in the vicinity of Istanbul by Mehmed II (1451-1481) he concluded that they carried the characteristic features of western serfs. In contrast, the typical Ottoman peasants defined as *reaya* who constituted the overwhelming majority of the Ottoman peasantry were "free" men with a status totally different from the "sharecropping slaves." Barkan also indicated that within three or four generations, the state had to extend to all its serfs the status of *reaya.* The change was due to the difficulty and great cost of supervising this group in the midst of the *reaya* masses as well as to the inefficiency in production. It is extremely important for us to

136 "Toprak İşçiliğinin Organizasyon Şekilleri", *Istanbul Üniversitesi, İktisat Fakültesi Mecmuası*, I and II.

note that by this fact once more the state had to admit that *the most efficient organization of agrarian production was the* reaya *system based on the free family-farm unit* or *çift-hane* system.

On the other hand, as we tried to show in a monograph on rice cultivation,[137] the omnipotent state, when it found it necessary for its own purposes, did not hesitate to impose conditions which reduced the *reaya* to a status quite close to that of a serf.

The *reaya* was "free" in the sense that nobody had rights over his person or could arbitrarily impose upon him services considered normal for a slave. Thus, labor services were carefully restricted and were strictly defined in the laws and regulations. Ottoman lawmakers seemed to realize that forced services, arbitrarily imposed and multiplied, might result in actual serfdom or slavery. However, the state reserved for itself the right to require forced services and recognized certain feudal labor services necessary to maintain its *sipahi,* cavalrymen, in the villages. The whole question of whether or not there was serfdom in the Ottoman empire or whether or not the Ottoman *reaya* could be considered free should be discussed within this basic policy. As for the attempts of the local members of the military class to impose "illegal" labor services upon *reaya* which resulted in reducing peasants to the status of a quasi serf, see our study of the *çift-hane* system in this volume.[138]

The *Annales* school's method of analysis[139] with the long and total perspective in the time and space of economies and societies, in particular Fernand Braudel's perception of the Ottoman empire as an integrated part of the Mediterranean world revolutionized Ottoman studies, bringing new dimensions to questions concerning Ottoman socio-economic structure. Braudel's great talent was to show how the Ottoman east experienced and followed the western

137 "Rice Cultivation", *Turcica* XIV, 59-141.

138 Also see *An Economic and Social History of the Ottoman Empire,* ed. H. İnalcık, Cambridge 1994, 143-154.

139 H. İnalcık, "The Impact of the *Annales* school on Ottoman Studies", *Review,* I, 3-4, 69-96.

Mediterranean in its monetary, demographic and other structural changes. In particular, following Earl Hamilton's bullionist theory on price revolution in Spain, Braudel extended it to the east to include the Ottoman zone. While Braudel's main source of evidence for the eastern Mediterranean was the Dubrovnik archives, Barkan, adding to it the evidence supplied by the Ottoman archives, confirmed and brought precision to Braudel's findings. Modifying the bullionist theory, Barkan included demographic and economic factors in his analysis, and offered a theory for "the structural crisis" of the empire during the second half of the sixteenth century.[140]

The West's increased stock of cheap silver, Barkan argues, enabled Europe to drain basic commodities such as wheat, hides, wool, copper and the like from the Ottoman zone in ever-growing quantities which upset the economic equilibrium established in the 'closed economy' of the empire. He suggests that the Ottoman economy could not adjust itself to the growing European demand for primary goods, wheat in particular, which entailed a tremendous rise in prices and shortages in the empire. In other words, the empire's agrarian economy was not geared to an expanding capitalist market.

By establishing price lists from original sources, Barkan was able to show that in approximatly one century between 1490-1586, the prices of basic foodstuffs increased 182.49 percent, but 427.79 percent in the next twenty years (the 1490 prices are assigned the price index 100). However, towards 1586 the actual value rate of gold to silver had increased from 11.52 to 13.10. Thus, inflation in terms of the silver/gold ratio was much less, 162 and 265 respectively during these two periods. Actually the increase in prices, Barkan asserts, was due to various factors: apart from the international inflation of silver, a dramatic population increase (between 1520 and 1580, 56% in Anatolia and 71% in the Balkans), soaring state expendi-

140 "The Price Revolution of the Sixteenth Century: A Turning Point in the Economic History of the Near East", trans. J. McCarthy, *International Journal of Middle East Studies*, 6-1 (January 1975), 4-5, the original in Turkish: "XVI. Asrın İkinci Yarısında Türkiye'de Fiyat Hareketleri", *Belleten* 34 (1970), 557-607.

tures because of long expensive wars and internal disorders in the period 1587-1618 as well as changes in the patterns of the external trade of the empire. The Ottoman reaction to the West's massive purchases was to restrict and prohibit the export of basic commodities which only led to large-scale contraband activities. In brief, the West's "economic penetration produced a grave inflationary current in the Ottoman empire." "Under the new conditions", Barkan argues, "European trade developed from an integrative partner of the Ottoman trade into a 'dominant' exploitative one."

Also, the "disastrous changes" in Ottoman handicrafts, he asserts, were the direct result of "European absorption of the reserve stocks of primary materials." Thus, Europe's capitalist market economy with mercantilistic methods such as buying cheap foodstuffs and primary goods from the Levant and expanding the Levant market for its finished goods, was the primary cause for the stagnation and degeneration of the native handicraft industries. At any rate, Europe's dominance and exploitation had already begun in Barkan's sense in the late sixteenth century before the Industrial Revolution.

Barkan says, a class of nouveaux riches, enriched by tax farming, or other speculative means and exploitation "oriented toward the countryside, became a factor in the destruction of the agrarian structure which characterized the last centuries of the Empire. Those who had profited from the country's economic disorders and from inflation became more and more interested in the countryside as a place for profitable investment. Using classic methods of usury and hoarding, they increased their agricultural exploitation, playing dual roles as usurers and country gentlemen." Barkan refers to "the founding of vast agricultural estates" in this period.

But such generalizations have not been substantiated. Although disruptions took place in Anatolia during the great turmoil of the *djelālī* depredations and the Iranian and Austrian wars, it is believed that it was too early to speak of the emergence of "vast agricultural estates" and "the destruction of the agrarian structure" in this period. On the other hand, it appears that the real cause of the

Ottoman monetary disorders stemmed mainly from the influx of western silver *counterfeit* or debased coins. Barkan does not discuss phenomena such as the dearth of *akçe* and its constant flight to the east, the increase of counterfeit and clipped *akçe* in the market and ultimately state devaluations of this monetary unit upon which all imperial price and salary systems had rested.

Following the traditional interpretation, and asserting that the main reason for the devaluation of the *akçe* was simply to increase the monetary stock of the treasury Barkan was not able to explain these seemingly contradictory phenomena.[141]

Parallel monetary upheavals and state bankruptcy taking place in the kingdom of Naples in the same period can be referred to in order to explain the Ottoman case. Devaluation was actually a necessary step to correct the monetary disorders. The Ottoman government realized that European counterfeit coins invaded the Ottoman market because of their high rate to gold and low silver contents compared to *akçe.* While *groush* officially circulated at the rate of 80 *akçe,* its silver content was only worth 65. As a result, good money, *akçe* left the market or whenever it reached the market it was clipped or counterfeited. In 1589 by a monetary refom, the Ottoman government devalued *groush,* fom 80 *akçe* to 70 to keep the *akçe* circulating in the market. Of course, the background to the disturbance was the growing disparity in the silver/gold ratio between east and west and frantic exchange of silver and gold between two zones during this period.[142]

141 See H. İnalcık, "Impact", mentioned in note 137.
142 *Ibid.*

III

THE *ÇİFT-ḪĀNE* SYSTEM AND PEASANT TAXATION

The basic fiscal and agrarian system of the Ottoman empire is revealed to us in what is called *çift-resmi,* the farm-tax, or peasant-tax system. In tax and population censuses, this particular tax precedes all other taxes. In addition to the originally Islamic taxes such as *djizya,* and tithes, the Ottomans continued most of the non-Islamic or *'urfi* taxes and impositions under the name of *rusūm* or the *tekālīf-i 'urfiyye* and *'awāriz-i dīwāniyye* system to which the *çift-resmi,* was related.

Based upon pre-Ottoman customary dues or state taxes, *rusūm* and *tekâlif* constituted the basis of the Ottoman taxation primarily reserved for the military in the provinces. Outside of those *tekālīf* which were approved and sanctioned by the government there was a category of *tekālīf* taxes called *shāḳḳa,* exactionary, which were condoned by the state as local customs. But when they were abused and became subject to complaint, they were denounced and abolished by the central government as "oppressive injustices" *(meḫā'if).* However, as was true in all medieval societies, custom was generally respected as the most dependable and just rule by both the government and the subjects. Pragmatically they were considered as rules long-tested and established in the society. Custom, *'ādet-i ḳadime* or *ologelmiş,* was the third important authority referred to after *defter* (official register) and *ḳānūn* (state law) in the case of disputes over a matter by the administration. The importance of the Islamic legal principle of consensus *(idjmā')* in Muslim society might have been a further support for this attitude. At any rate, extensive reference by the Ottomans to the living custom became a basis of their elaborate system of state laws *(ḳānūn)* and of integration of Byzantine and Balkan taxation practices into the body of Ottoman law.

Rusūm or *tekālīf* were regular permanent taxes, while *'awāriz-i dīwāniyye* were services and contributions which were, in principle, temporarily imposed for emergency situations. They were always imposed by and reserved for the government, thence the term "accidental government levies" *('awāriz-i dīwāniyye).* For our discussion of peasant tax, it should be noted that both *tekālīf-i 'urfiyye* and *'awāriz-i dīwāniyye* included a number of labor services to be fulfilled either for the local military or the government.

Family-Farm Unit and Taxation

As for the *raiyyet-resmi* or *çift-resmi,* our peasant or farm-tax, let us begin with the term itself. *Çift,* from Persian *djuft,* meant a pair of oxen and, by connotation, a piece of land which could be cultivated by a pair of oxen and which constituted a unit of peasant family production. *Ra'iyyet çiftlik* or simply *çiftlik,* or *çift,* meant a farm with a pair of oxen belonging to a peasant family *(ḫāne).* The same was meant in the Roman or Byzantine empires under the terms of *jugum* or *zeugarion* respectively. Actually, the words *çift, djuft, jugum* and *zeugarion* come from the same root. Now, composed of a peasant family *(ḫāne),* a pair of oxen as animal power *(çift)* to cultivate, and a piece of land large enough to sustain an average peasant family, this unit was the basic organization of agrarian production and as such, it was the standard for fiscal survey and taxation. Taking this unit as a fiscal basis, a survey was easily made without an elaborate and costly cadaster of arable land; and taxation is conveniently determined on this standard unit. In other words, *ra'iyyet çiftlik* was both a type of agrarian organization and fiscal device.

The system should be studied at two levels – socio-economic and political-financial. Here, let us focus first on the fiscal aspect of it with its political implications, taking into consideration, in particular, the struggle between the provincial elite and the central bureaucracy for the control of this basic unit of peasant labor and land. With the family-farm unit as the basis of agricultural production and agrarian taxation, the central bureaucracies in the Byzantine and Ottoman empires had a vital concern in maintaining it as the foundation of the entire fiscal-political system against the attempts of the powerful men, *ḳudretli kimesneler* in Turkish, or *dynatoi* in Greek, who strove to turn the land into big estates, either preserving basic family farm units, or when possible or profitable, reorganizing them into manor-like agricultural units or enclosures *(ekābir çiftligi* or *proasteion).*

Thus, when we speak of the socio-political structure and dynamics in Ottoman society we have to make a distinction between the conflicts of the different groups within the ruling elite itself on the one hand, and between these groups and the peasantry on the other whereas the changes in the family farm unit *(çift-ḫāne)* as the particular organization of agrarian production is an area of investigation of socio-economic history.[1] Obviously, we cannot overlook close relationships between these two sets of processes. The changes in the military- fiscal framework, however, might not necessarily entail changes in the basic socio-economic organization, that is, the type of agrarian production based on the family-farm unit. But it is also true that the imperial-fiscal framework was responsible, to a great extent, for maintaining and shaping this socio-economic basis. The imperial bureaucratic control was maximized when the central authority was strong enough, and when the bureaucratic group which formed the key agency in the whole state machinery was working well to perpetuate the system.

Viewed from this standpoint, it can be suggested that in medieval times the struggle of a ruling elite against a foreign power representing another ruling elite was, in the last analysis, a process of the same character – a struggle between two "imperial" groups

1 I found in an official survey book the term in the form of *ḫāne-bā-çift*, or *the peasant family with çift.*

striving to achieve or maintain control over the mass of peasant farm units with the promise to restore the basic prerequisites of the system. In fact, in their conquest of the Balkans, the Ottomans consciously and systematically appealed to the peasantry with the promise to eliminate the innovations, labor services in particular, introduced by a forceful provincial body of magnates which tended to change the age-old agrarian system based on family- farm units. It can safely be said that what the Ottoman empire actually did was to substitute an imperial regime in which the central bureaucracy had lost all control over peasantry and land. Once in control, the Ottomans, always conciliatory as long as their central imperial authority was guaranteed, reduced the local Christian lords, now as Ottoman *tīmār* holders, to their former position vis-à-vis the imperial government and the peasantry. In brief, the basic fact in Ottoman conquest was the restoration of central authority and bureaucratic control vis-à-vis a provincial elite which was in a way to undermine an age-old socio-political system. Of course, this may be true only when such a development is considered sociologically, not in terms of ethnic or religious terms. But we should remember that the Ottoman imperial regime did not mind whether the old *pronija*-holders were converted to Islam or not.

Çift-Ḫāne, Family-Farm Unit

The basic instrument of the imperial bureaucracy was the survey and registration of the peasant family-units. It was the most important task for the Ottoman government, immediately after the conquest of a region, to take a survey registering the *çift-ḫānes.*[2] Corresponding to the *colonus* in the Roman empire and the *stasis* in Byzantium, the Ottoman *çift-ḫāne* as a fiscal term meaning a peasant family with two oxen and sufficient amount of land, was the unit to be preserved at all times.

2 For Ottoman survey see H. İnalcık, *Hicri 835 Tarihli Sûret-i Defter-i Sancak-i Arvanid*, Ankara: Turkish Historical Society, 1954, *Giriş*.

As a rule, the *ḫāne,* peasant family as the labor unit of the agricultural organization, is recorded in the detailed survey register (*defter-i mufaṣṣal*) together with *çift,* that is the land and oxen, which always made up two other basic element of the unit.

In the *defter-i mufaṣṣal* the name of the family head, a married man, had the letter *ç or nīm* under it to indicate that he possessed a *çift* or half a *çift* respectively. The unit and its possessor, once recorded in the survey register, as the basis of tax assessment, could not theoretically be changed until a new survey.

First, the Ottoman law is clear about the indivisibility of peasant farm- unit. It reads: "The *re'āyā çiftlik* can never be portioned out." If a *çiftlik* is found divided among several possessors it was to be restored to its original form, and if the head of the household in possession of the *çiftlik* died leaving several sons, they were to possess it collectively. Furthermore, the central government instructed the surveyor-assessor to integrate the plots of land so as to create new units of *çiftlik.* The great majority of the arable lands in Anatolia and the Balkans were organized as *çift-ḫāne*s or family-units of production and taxation.[3] All these features of the Ottoman *çiftlik* are to be found in the Byzantine *zeugarion* or *stasis.*

The great Ottoman legist Ebū's-Su'ūd, interpreting the principle of the unity and indivisibility of the *çift* set forth a fiscal argument saying that, if divided, it was almost impossible for the government or *tīmār*-holder to collect *çift-resmi* or farm-tax. At any rate, this was a strong bureaucratic argument. But at the same time, it touched on the gist of the problem, referring to the combined nature of land and family as the basic fiscal unit.

Here we cannot go into details of how the central government took the necessary measures to keep the *çiftlik* undivided as far as inheritance rights were concerned.[4] Since the Islamic law stipulated the distribution of the inheritance among all the children, male and female, and the spouse, it was considered necessary that a category

3 H. İnalcık, "Osmanlılarda Raiyyet Rüsûmu", *Belleten*, XXIII (1959), 576-610.

4 Now see H. İnalcık, ed. *An Economic and Social History of the Ottoman Empire*, Cambridge Cambridge: University Press, 1994, 103-178.

of agricultural lands had to be excluded from this rule since the first century of Islam.

Since most of the Ottoman lands fell within the category of land originally conquered over the non-muslims (the so-called *ḫarādjī* or *fay'* lands of Islamic Law), most of the agricultural lands in the Ottoman empire were excluded and subjected to a special regime of state ownership, known as *mīrī arāzī*. This was carried out through the state's fundamental right to make, apart from the religious law, state laws or *ḳānūns*. In the Byzantine times this type of land definitely existed though the extent of it cannot be verified due to the fragmentary character of the evidence. However, the Ottoman surveys can be referred to in assuming that even in the last period of the Byzantine history, this category of agricultural lands must have been quite extensive since the Ottoman surveys show that the Ottoman state apparently did not have to make large-scale "nationalization". Except for the *wakf*s and the lands granted by the emperor's special diplomas and put under the private ownership of the members of the ruling elite all the rest of arable lands reserved for grain cultivation in rural areas were considered as state-owned lands.

As for the family, essential element of the family-farm unit it was not allowed to abandon the farm-land, and measures were taken to keep the family together at all times as a labor unit on the land. If the husband died and the children were minors, the law allowed the widow *(bīve)* to take possession of the land on the condition that by hiring labor, or cooperation of her male relatives she could manage cultivation and continue production and payment of the taxes. If the children were grown up and able to do work, the eldest is recognized as the sole legal possessor of the *çiftlik* and responsible for the taxes. It was left to the family to arrange each one's share in the payment of the taxes.

If the head of the family ceased to cultivate for three consecutive years without a legally acceptable excuse – illness, flood, etc. – he lost the title to the *çiftlik* and it was given by auctioning to the highest bidder from among the village community and then from outsiders.

Preemption also was recognized for the daughter and close relatives in certain areas. The possession of the land gives only some restricted rights on the *çiftlik* such as direct inheritance by his son or sons or widow and continuous usufruct but excluding the rights of selling, giving away as charity or surety, or exchange with another property, or making changes in the customary use of the land.

In brief, the whole Ottoman administrative, financial and military structure rested on the *çift-ḫāne* system. The system consisted of an organization of agricultural production on the basis of peasant households, *ḫāne*s, each of them having a pair of oxen and being given possession of a *raiyyet çiftlik,* i. e., a plot of land sufficient in size to sustain one peasant household and pay "the rent to the landholder who could be either directly the state or its agent. The size of the land varied with the fertility of the soil from 50 *dönüms* to 150 or from about 5 to 15 hectars. It is interesting to note that the size of the Roman and Byzantine family farm also varied between these limits. Professor Laiou suggested that the average size of a farm in Macedonia was 163 *modioi* or about 14 hectars (the *modios* is taken to be 888.7 m^2).

I might add that the army veterans of Rome received on their retirement 10 or 12 *iugera* of land, 50 *modii* of wheat seed and one yoke of oxen, the three elements forming the normal family-farm. A *çiftlik* is defined in Mehmed the Conqueror's law code as a piece of land to be sown with four *muds* of seed. In the in fourth-century Italy, it was recommended to sow 4 *modii* of seed in one *iugerum.* Now, this unit was not to be divided. The definition of land by the amount of seed must be related rather to the sharecropping system. In the Ottoman practice sometimes a *çift* was defined as a pair of oxen, thus *çift-lik* meant a piece of land large enough to be cultivated by a pair of oxen.

One is surprised to see in thousands of documents how zealously the Ottoman central bureaucracy was concerned with keeping *re'āyā çiftliks* intact and converting all arable land to this type of agrarian production.

Just as the guild system was considered the keystone of urban industries and urban society, so *çift-ḫane* was regarded as the foundation of agricultural production and rural society. The Ottoman bureaucrats, believing that the imperial system could survive only by maintaining these two fundamental institutions, were scrupulously supporting guild system in the towns and *re'āyā çiftliks* in the rural areas. This was a kind of constitution of the traditional imperial system until the western-inspired liberal policies of the Tanzimat reformers in the nineteenth century tended to change it at least in its inheritance rules.[5]

Needless to say, the Ottoman rural society was not solely composed of the *çiftliks* and *half-çiftliks* which were the ideal units for this agrarian-fiscal system. There were families or single men who possessed land less than half- *çiftlik* or no land at all. Originally there were wanderers or so-called unattached or "free" peasants who were not registered in state survey books and consequently not considered part of any agricultural unit. Being mostly peasant youth leaving family and land in search of livelihood elsewhere, these wandering men were called *hāric-ez-defter*, unregistered ones, in the Ottoman terminology, *eleutheroi* or "free-men" in the Byzantine-Roman system. All of these groups were put fiscally under the conventional system of *çift*-tax.

Çift-tax as the expression of the combination of family labor with land is the key to understanding the social stratification in Ottoman rural society. In a study published in 1959 I attempted to explain the system in detail.[6] The *çift*-tax constitutes a fiscal system which includes *çift*-tax, half *(nīm) çift*-tax, *bennak* or married peasant tax and *kara* and *mücerred* poor or unmarried peasant tax. *Tütün- resmi,* or hearth tax, *dönüm* tax and some other minor taxes also fell within the same system. Broadly speaking, in this tax system both the amount of land and the number of working hands

5 However, the Ottoman land law of 1858 still tried to maintain the *ra'iyyet çiftlik* unit on *mīrī* lands.

6 "Osmanlılar'da Raiyyet Rüsûmu", mentioned in note 1, above.

determined the tax status and labor services. The registration of the peasants at a given time in the imperial survey book established his status and obligations until the next survey. The book or *defter* was the final and decisive reference in all kinds of disputes over status and tax obligations. A peasant family in possession of a *çift* was to pay the full *çift*-tax which was originally equivalent to one gold piece, the same amount that was established by the Roman Emperor Diocletian for *coloni* and continued in the Byzantine and Ottoman empires.

Below a certain amount of land, that is below the half-*çift*, it was the labor force that was considered to determine the tax. If the peasant possessed less than a half-*çift*, then tax rates were determined by his marital status, that is, the potential labor force which he represented.

The full tax was originally 22 *akçe* per one *çift-ḫāne,* its fractions were 12, 9, and 6 akçe per half-*çift*, for married poor (*bennak*) and unmarried poor *(kara)* respectively. A married man was supposed to control a larger amount of labor irrespective of the amount of land in his possession. However, the moment he entered into possession of a *çift* or half-*çift* he was to pay higher rates incumbent on a *çift* or half-*çift.* That *bennak* tax, or married man's tax, was interpreted as a family tax is illustrated by the fact that when a married peasant abandoned his *çift* or half-*çift* land his status changed and he paid only 9 akça *bennak* tax. Finally, the minimum 6 *akçe* tax paid by a *caba* or *kara,* a landless umarried peasant, is interpreted as the equivalent of a man's labor capable of earning an income. Since the family was considered a single work team only those unmarried sons of a peasant who were not in the service of their fathers and who made their own living separately were subject to *kara* tax. At any rate, here we find that *çift*-tax was personalized and the peasant's labor became an object of tax assessment.

Çift-resmi was also called *ra'iyyet* or *ḳulluk akçesi* which discloses its nature or origin more precisely. *Ra'iyyet* or *ḳulluk* means the status of being a slave, dependent or subject and this cash obligation was the equivalent of what the peasant owed to the landlord for labor services. The fifteenth century Ottoman law codes and survey books leave no doubt about that interpretation. A 22 *akçe* tax or its fractions for each particular status are shown as cash equivalents of certain labor services or *ḳulluks* owed to the lord, namely 3 *akçe* for 3 days personal service, 7 *akçe* for a wagon load of hay, 7 *akçe* for a half wagon load of straw, and 2 *akçe* for service with a wagon. As the law code of the Conqueror states, "if money is to be taken for these seven services then twenty two *akçe* will be taken." Here for personal labor service only 3 *akçe* is reckoned. On the other hand, a landless unmarried peasant had to pay 6 *akçe* of tax, since, as the same law code explains, landless peasants usually earn money by working as agricultural workers or carrying goods for people with their animal or cart, or were occupied in crafts. With the exception of this personal labor for the lord or three days work or three *akçe*, the four other services were services that only peasants with land and capital equipment could perform. Here, once more, we find the combination of personal labor with family agricultural activities. It is interesting to note that in the Roman empire each peasant family was to pay one gold piece for *iugatio-capitatio* and the poorer peasants paid it in fractions of a *nomisma* divided into 24.[7]

In the Byzantine empire the dependent peasants, *paroikoi* were classified in the tax registers in the same way as in the Ottoman Empire.[8] A *zeugarate,* one in possession of a pair of oxen or a definite amount of land, corresponds to our *çift.* One *nomisma* was paid as a land-and-hearth tax. A *boidate,* one possessing one ox or half of the land of a *zeugarate,* corresponds to our *nīm-çift.* And, *aktemones,* peasants without land, or more exactly, a plot of land less than a half-*çift*, correspond to the Ottoman *bennak.* The difference has not been determined between *aktemones* and *pezoi,* but surely this class of peasants corresponded to the Ottoman poor peasants.

7 A. H. M. Jones, "Capitatio and Iugatio", *The Journal of Roman Studies*, XLII (1957), 88-91; A.Déléage, *La capitation du Bas-Empire*, Mâcon 1945.

8 See A. Laiou-Thomadakis, *Peasant Society in the Late Byzantine Empire*, Princeton 1977.

In the last analysis this head-land tax can be interpreted as what Marc Bloc termed labor rent owed by the peasant family to his lord.

Evidently, unable to use labor services, the state had to turn them into a lump cash tax and thus provided an important cash revenue for the treasury. By the same act the state abolished most of the personal services which could easily be abused by the local lord or *sipahi.* In Byzantium an attempt to convert labor services into a cash tax is reported under Andronikus II (1282-1328). Incidently, the state while abolishing feudal labor services kept for itself the right to impose upon reaya services and contributions – the so-called *'awāriz-i dīvāniyye* – in the Ottoman Empire. The conversion of labor services into a cash tax was a revolutionary change introduced by the state in favor of peasantry. The state claimed this kind of control and restrictions on the basis of its capacity of having *raḳaba* or *dominium eminens* over all arable land and having the supreme lordship over the subjects. It is a fact that attempts of absolute control by local lords over the land and labor of the peasants were always challenged by imperial authority in Byzantium as well as in the Ottoman state. The protection of *reaya* or *paroikoi* was declared as the "imperial justice" or the supreme goal of the empire.

The *sipāhī* implemented the state regulations on the transference and use of land by the *re'āyā.* Since the *dīnārs* were indivisible and unalterable units as recorded in the survey books, the *çift-hane* or peasant family units too were held indivisible and unalterable in order to protect the fixed *tīmār* income. But on the other hand, the rigidity of the system and the state's maintenance of the *çift-ḫāne* were perhaps reasons why the organization of agricultural production in the Ottoman Empire remained unevolvable and economy stagnant.

Heavy exploitation by the provincial lord or *tīmār*-holder who tried to increase labor services and rent resulted in the peasants' widespread discontent and protest. To abandon the land and thereby ruin the source of revenue of the lord was the most efficient weapon the medieval peasant could resort to for protest.[9] From an economic point of view that was a logical thing to do for the peasantry because once the lord's demand exceeded the surplus that was left for the peasant's subsistence, there was no reason to continue cultivation. Despite efforts to tie down the peasant to the estate land, the flight of *paroikoi* to the neighboring lord's estate or even to the lands under foreign control was not an infrequent occurence in late Byzantine rural history.[10] In a time of labor scarcity this was the most dreaded thing that could happen to the lord as well as to the state. It is also a commonplace that the Ottomans with their so-called *istimālet* policy of enticement, greatly profited from peasant protests in their conquests, and, indeed, making the preservation of the family-farm system with its customarily established rules a paramount state policy they could relatively easily eliminate petty dynasts and provincial lords in the Balkans.[11]

At any rate, *çift-tax* and its components made up a complete tax system comprising the whole agrarian structure. It is clear that the *çift-tax* or the annual fixed cash tax paid by a registered, dependent peasant actually represented a tax paid for the *productive labor force of the peasant* in possession of a certain amount of land. We have already seen that in early Ottoman laws the *çift-tax* was simply and exclusively interpreted as certain labor services computed for cash. It meant the labor or its cash equivalent which was owed to the ruler or to the local military man representing the ruler. These labor services or *tekālīf*, impositions, had been established by custom and were necessary for the maintenance of the military–labor to cultivate the reserve land for the sustenance of the soldiers' or lords' family, to mow the hay for his horse, to supply fire wood and straw. Without these basic labor services, the cavalrymen could not survive and perform their services in royal campaigns or in

9 See "Mazra'a", (H. İnalcık), *Encyclopaedia of Islam*, 2d ed. vol. VII.

10 P. Lemerle, "Esquisse pour une histoire agraire de Byzance", *Revue Historique*, CCXIX (1957); Laiou, *op. cit.*

11 Sec H. İnalcık, "Ottoman Methods of Conquest", *Studia Islamica*, II (1954).

securing the protection of the peasantry and agriculture against the marauders. Since these services were usually abused and resented by the peasantry, the Ottoman bureaucrats tried to change them into a lumped cash tax wherever economic conditions allowed to do so.

In sum the peasant labor was considered a taxable object and its rate varied according to whether it was the labor of a whole peasant household in possession of a *çift,* or it was only half of this unit, or a peasant household with little or no land, and finally, an adult unmarried man with no land. The system required that a peasant in possession of a *çift* would be a married man capable of supplying the necessary labor for it, and perform all these services, or instead pay the *çift- tax* in full in the amount of 22 *akçe* which originally corresponded to one gold piece in the early fourteenth century.

The fact that productive labor was considered the basis of tax assessment in the system becomes clear when land was no longer a consideration in rating the *çift-tax.* An unmarried adult male peasant without land in his possession still had to pay the tax though at the lowest rate of 6 *akçe.* Those who did not have any independent productive power, that is the very old people *(pīr-i fānī),* children, slaves, monks, and "priests who live only on alms", were all exempt from this tax. Women who were not actually the head of a farm unit did not pay. However, implicitely, married women and children were always considered components of the labor force of the peasant family, a reality today in the Turkish countryside; but a single woman was not subjected to this tax. That labor force was a tax object can be seen with manumitted slave agriculturists. An *ortaḳcı ḳul,* sharecropper slave, when manumitted, had to pay between 45 and 60 *akçe* even if not engaged in agriculture. This was the equivalent of one gold piece in the fifteenth century and the subsistence or earnings of an adult male was estimated between 7 and 10 gold pieces at that time. It appears that the government fixed the tax rate of fifty *akçe* for the labor of an adult male in many categories in the rural population. The so-called *ellicis,* that is, those who pay fifty *akçe,* or *florici,* or those paying one gold piece as personal tax included many groups of the *re'āyā* which were considered outside the regular body of peasant population.

As mentioned earlier the *çift-resmi* is occasionally termed in the state regulations as *kulluk akçesi,* or money for services which a dependent peasant had to fulfill for the state or *tīmār*-holder. When the state assigned certain services to a group on a permanent basis such as guardianship at a mountain pass or work in the mines or salt-works and the like, the rate of the *çift-resmi* was substantially reduced because of this labor service. The regulations are explicit on the reason for reduction or exemption.

Historians still argue whether this kind of taxation, for example *ḫarādj-i muvaẓẓafa* in Islam or *jugatio-capitatio* in the Roman world is a head tax or a land tax.[12] But when we take into account the family-farm unit in which labor and land is combined and the cases when labor of person is considered separately as an object of taxation because of its income producing potential, the enigma, I believe, is resolved.

I believe, the analysis of the peasant tax leads us to a key principle of tax assessment in the whole ancient and medieval world. The peasant was not considered only a producer of soil products and thus subject to pay tithes on them, but also as representing a potential labor force capable of meeting services or creating other kinds of economic value. Since as such this was a personal tax, it was also applicable to productive people living in the towns. All of the members of the ruling class were exempted from it because they were not producers of goods. Rather, they were considered as spending their time and energy in the task of protecting the producer. The personal tax assessed on the labor force of an adult married male in his full capacity of production was set at the rate of one gold piece from Diocletian's time or perhaps earlier in the Mediterranean world and western Europe. This stable standard of taxation did not change in the subsequent periods. We find it under the Islamic caliphate

12 See H. T. Modarresi, *Kharāj in Islamic Law*, London 1983; F. Lot, *L'impôt foncier et la capitation personelle sous le Bas-Empire et à l'époque franque*, Paris 1928.

as *djizya* or *ḫarādj*. In the countryside it was the peasant household representing the production unit that was taxed. In the Byzantine empire the tax was one *nomisma* called *zeugaratikion*, and under the Ottomans 22 or 25 *akçe* as *çift- resmi* or *ispence*.

It is interesting to note that in this tax system the basic unit of one gold ducat was divided into 24, and various categories of peasant population classified according to their economic conditions – having two oxen with land, or married without land or single – were charged at various rates on the basis of a duodecimal system. The question of why the Ottomans retained 22 *akçe* instead of 24 was answered, I believe, by the fact that one *mithkal* of gold was worth 22 *akçe* in the 1330's according to a record in the *Resalä-yi Falakiyya*, an Iranian-Ilkhanid financial treatise written around 1334. As Nicolas Svoronos showed in his publication of the Byzantine cadaster of Thebes, the agrarian tax followed the same duodecimal system of 24, 12, 9, 6.[13] Obviously, the whole system was a convenient bureaucratic device in assessment of various rates of personal or combined tax according to the means of the tax payer, since for tax assessment the establishment of elaborate cadaster of land or personal income lists were practically impossible. It may be remembered that the duodecimal tax system was also taken by the bureaucracies in ancient and medieval empires as the basis of the weights and measures.

As a footnote, I would like to touch upon the long controversy on the nature of *iugatio-capitatio* and *zeugaratikion* in the pre-Ottoman empires.

Ferdinand Lot in his studies of the land-head tax, *iugatio-capitatio,* in the late Roman empire, and Marc Bloch in his analysis of the socio-economic nature of medieval *mansus* showed that the family-farm unit continued to exist after the decline of the Roman empire in western Europe as the basic cell of the rural society. Always referring to the enigmatic nature of this peculiar head-land tax, "iugatio-capitatio", Ostrogorsky[14] linked it to Diocletian's tax reform and defined

13 "Recherche sur le cadastre byzantin et la fiscalité au XI et XII siècles: le cadastre de Thebes", *Bulletin de Correspondance Hellenique*, 1959.

14 *Pour l'histoire de la féodalité byzuntine*, Brussels 1954.

the "iugum", which corresponds to our çift, as "a piece of land that can feed a *caput,* and the caput stands for the human labor expended on a *iugum.*" The tax actually imposed upon the peasant family was always related to "the occupation of a definite unit of land."

The problem of *capitatio* and *iugatio* in the late Roman empire has provoked much controversy, and many theories have been offered for solutions. Recently, in his paper on *capitatio and iugatio,* Arnold Jones agrees that there is "a system of assessing land tax and other levies on *iuga,* fiscal unit of land, and *capita,* poll tax, which are combined in some way, and this is still a problem to be investigated. The laws, census records and lists of estates give only fragmentary evidence and it is not possible to make a full description of the system." But one point, Jones asserts, is clear. In a number of laws "iuga or iugatio and capita or capitatio are coupled together as the units of assessment for various taxes and levies." "A tax might be levied on both units combined (as was usually the case) or on one only." On the nature of *iuga* he agrees that "there is no question: they were units of land", whereas *capitatio* covered human beings or *coloni* and animals at the same time. In the list of estates in western Anatolia we find *zugokefalai* or *zugokefali* in which Jones points out that farms and *coloni* are combined as an "assessment unit".

Now I believe a complete description of the Ottoman *çift-hane* system, which is possible to make with the utilization of the detailed Ottoman survey registers, clarifies to a certain extent, the nature of *iugatio-capitatio* in the late Roman and Byzantine system. A person's productive force must be considered as the basis of tax assessment which varied of course according to whether he controlled simultaneously the labor of his wife and children as a married man, or whether or not he possessed a piece of land with the necessary animal power. The family-farm unit was the economic and fiscal unit in the whole system- Despite the changes in the political super-structure, the peasant family-farm always remained as the backbone of the rural economy and fiscal organization throughout the medieval East to be inherited finally and vigilantly maintained by the Ottoman empire.

IV

LES RÉGIONS DE KRUJE ET DE LA DIBRA AUTOUR DE 1467 et 1519

d'après les documents ottomans

Selon les méthodes ottomanes de conquête, la domination ottomane en Albanie a été établie en passant par diverses phases.[1] Au lendemain de la victoire ottomane dans la bataille de la Savra en 1385, les seigneurs féodaux qui dominaient différentes régions du pays, reconnurent comme suzerain l'État ottoman et furent obligés de s'acquitter des conditions suivantes de vassalité : tribut annuelle, obligation d'ost et envoi de leurs enfants comme otages à la cour des Ottomans. La deuxième phase commença lorsque les Ottomans mires directement sous leur domination des parties différentes du pays. Durant cette phase était nommé un *sancakbeyi* et des *kadi,* des commissions enregistrèrent sur régistres officiel (*defter*) les habitants et les ressources, et enfin ces ressources étaient partagées comme *hàs* et comme *timar.*[2] À la tête de l'administration ottomane du pays se trouvait un *sancakbeyi,* qui y représentait le pouvoir du Padischah et était, dans le même temps, le commandant des *sipahi* timariotes du pays. Les notes sur les régistres officiels des régions de Premedi et de Korçe (Görice) dans le sud indiquent de toute évidence que dans ces pays s'étaient installés des timariotes ottomans depuis les temps de Bayezid Ier.[3] Il est très probable qu'en ces temps-là était comprise sous la domination ottomane la région de Gjirokastër (Ergiri,

1 Sur les méthodes ottomanes de conquête consulter : H. İnalcık, "Ottoman Methods of Conquest", *Studia Islamica* II (1954), pp. 122-129.

2 *Ibid.*, et sur le cadastre H. İnalcık, *Sûret-i Defter-i Sancak-i Arvanid*, Ankara 1954, pp. XIII- XXIII.

3 *Ibid.*

Gynokastre). Naturellement, cet état de choses était l'aboutissement de la deuxième invasion ottomane en Albanie durant l'année 1394. Les opérations de Bayezid ont représenté une réaction contre Venise, qui avait entrepris à s'installer en Albanie, dans la Morée et ailleurs, dans ces temps- là. C'est pourquoi Bayezid préféra prendre les devants et installer sa propre domination directe dans les pays qui formaient l'objet des visées de Venise.

L'installation du pouvoir ottoman a été réalisée sous différentes formes en passant d'une zone à l'autre. Les Ottomans, dans les régions où ils ne pouvaient pas instaurer le système du timar et l'administration du *sancak* dans la pleine acception du mot, laissaient les feudataires aborigènes comme timariotes ottomans dans leurs domaines antérieurs, et c'est sous cette mention qu'ils les enregistraient sur les registres des timars. Dans de tels cas, les fonctionnaires ottomans enregistraient et octroyaient les revenus au seigneur féodal du pays à titre de timar. Pour ce faire il fallait le relâchement d'un *berat* de la part du Padischah. Ce *berat* constituait le document le plus important, indiquant que dans ces pays avait été installée la domination ottomane. Ainsi, en étudiant le temps de l'installation de la domination ottomane en Albanie du nord, on doit tenir compte de tous ces aspects. Dans ces circonstances, il n'est pas possible de donner exactement les dates d'installation des Ottomans dans ces zones. Après la victoire des Ottomans au voisinage de la Savra en 1385, on comprend qu'aussi les feudataires de l'Albanie septentrionale ont admis la suzeraineté ottomane. La défaite à Plošnik en Bosnie (27 août 1388), qui se termina par la perte des forces ottomanes, avait été incité, comme l'attestent les sources narratives ottomanes, par le seigneur de Shkodër (İskenderiye). On sait qu'à cette époque à Shkodër dominaient les Balsha, qui durant cette période étaient hostiles aux bans de la Bosnie (expédition de Georges Ier Balsha contre la Bosnie en 1379).[4] D'après les sources

4 V. A. Gegaj, *L'Albanie et l'invasion turque au* XVe *siècle*, Paris 1937, p. 18. D'après un document publié par N. Iorga, *Notes et extraits*, IIe série, Paris 1899, pp. 97-98, déjà en 1403 Raguse cherchait l'alliance avec les Balsha contre la Bosnie et tentait de s'assurer des troupiers turcs à la solde.

narratives ottomanes, le *tekvur* du château-fort de Shkodër, c'est-à-dire son seigneur, s'était soumis au Padischah, auquel il versait la tribut.[5] Il avait présenté au Padischah la situation de la Bosnie et avait sollicité son concours. D'après nos sources, le sultan Murad Ier lui donne vingt-mille *akıncı* sous le commandement de Lala Şahin et les fait partir pour la guerre. Nos sources affirment qu'un quart de cette troupe d'*akıncı* fut anéanti par l'attaque improviste de l'armée de la Bosnie. Cette défaite est attribuée à la trahison du seigneur de Shkodër. Ces sources prétendent qu'il s'était entendu en secret avec les Serbes et les Bosniens. Les points les plus importants donnés par ces sources narratives, sous l'angle de notre objet, sont les suivants : vers 1388, le gouverneur de Shkodër, Georges Ier Balsha, était sous la protection ottomane. Il voulait tirer avantage de la puissance de son souverain, dans la lutte contre le prince de la Bosnie, son rival dans l'Albanie septentrionale. Quant à Lala Şahin, le commandant ottoman dont il est porté mention, on peut affirmer avec certitude qu'il ne s'agit point de Lala Şahin, le *beylerbeyi* de la Roumélie aux temps de Murad Ier. Ce Lala Şahin était mort en ces temps-là.[6] Du reste, il y a peu de probabilités que ce Lala Şahin ait été envoyé avec une force d'*akıncı.* Mais il y a un deuxième Lala or Kavala Şahin, dont parlent les sources vénitiennes : il a eu une activité importante avec ses *akıncı* sur les frontières de l'Albanie. Quand il se trouvait aux frontières, il était appelé par le nom de Kefalya (Kephalia ou *subaşı)* Şahin. Le titre de *Lala,* qui lui a été donné, peut résulter de la métathèse du mot *Kefalia>Kavala>Lala,* ou bien les historiens postérieurs ont confondu le Kavala Şahin avec le Lala Şahin. En fait, Aşık Paşa-zâde le mentionne sous le nom de *Kavala Şahin.* Ce qui plus est, ce Şahin est devenu *beylerbeyi* en 1446, et précepteur

5 Cette version est empruntée à Rūhī et figure sous une forme plus ample chez Neşrī (Cf.notamment l'édition par Fr. Taschner, *Gihānnümā*, Leipzig 1951, pp. 64-66).

6 Cf. Aşık Paşa-zâde, éd. 'Āli, Istanbul 1332 H., pp. 61-62. Neşrī considère les deux Lala Şahin identiques et essaie de concorder les événements. Il n'est point de doute que le *beylerbeyi* de la Roumélie soit mort avant la bataille de la Savra.

(lala) du prince héritier Mehmed (Mehmed II).[7] D'un document daté du 6 mars 1409 il résulte que les Ragusains se plaignaient que leurs charges d'étoffes envoyées en Albanie étaient ouvertes par les Vénitiens et soumises à des droits de douane élevés. À cette occasion, ceux-ci citaient d'exemple que cela n'avait pas eu lieu ni aux temps des seigneurs de la Zenta, ni aux temps des Turcs, ni antérieurement encore.[8] D'après N. Jorga (Iorga), qui a publié le document, après la bataille de la Savra, Georges II Balsha avait abandonné Shkodër au Turc Şahin. Il est certain que le Kavala (Kephalia) Şahin a été un *subaşı* ottoman des marches, qui déployait son activité en Albanie du nord durant les années 1385-1389.

Après la mort de Murad Ier dans la bataille de Kossovo en 1389, l'insurrection en Anatolie obligèrent le Sultan à se retirer de Roumélie. De cet état de choses s'avantagea Venise, qui consolida son influence sur les seigneurs albanais aborigènes. Après que Bayezid Ier eût amélioré la situation en Anatolie à l'avantage des Ottomans, il passera encore en Roumélie en 1393 et s'emparera de la Bulgarie. A une année de là, il invitera à Karaferye (Verrai) tous les princes des Balkans. Par cet acte, il pensait consolider ses droits souverains sur les princes, qui, durant son absence, avaient penché vers la Hongrie et Venise.[9] Cette politique se manifesta par l'envoi d'une armée d'invasion en Albanie en 1394, en vue de faire refouler notamment l'influence de Venise et d'exercer de la pression sur les seigneurs féodaux du pays. Nous avons vu que l'installation directe de la domination ottomane dans l'Albanie méridionale était rattachée à cette expédition. Il semble que ces opérations militaires constituaient un commencement de l'installation directe du régime ottoman aussi dans l'Albanie septentrionale. Même, les Ottomans n'avaient installé jusqu'à cette date leur domination totale que sur

7 Aşık Paşa-zâde, 129, 142, 190. Ce Kavala Şahin est le fameux Şihabeddin Şahin Paşa (cf. İnalcık, *Fatih Devri Üzerinde Tetkikler ve Vesikalar*, Ankara 1954, Index).

8 N. Iorga, *ibid.*

9 Cf. "Bāyezīd I", *Encyc, of Islam,* IIe éd., vol. I, p. 1151.

les seules routes qui menaient en Albanie. Le Paşayigit Beg avait pris en 1391 Shkup (Skoplje, Üsküp) et avait transformé ce pays en un point solide de marche et un centre de départ des expéditions militaires, en y portant et y installant des Yürük de Saruhan. Plus au sud, Monastir et Ohrid (Ohri) avaient été aussi transformés en bases solides d'opérations contre l'Albanie. Les forces ottomanes, parties de ces marches, purent tenir l'Albanie sous un contrôle strict.

Kruje aussi (Akçahisar, Kruye), sans nul doute aux temps de Bayezid Ier (plus probablement entre les années 1394-1396), a passé sous l'administration directe ottomane. Dans le registre ottoman de l'an 1432[10] y est noté que Yakut Paşa et Hoca Firuz ont relâché à Kruje des documents de remise des impôts. On sait que Hoca Firuz Paşa était, dans les dernières années du règne de Bayezid Ier, *beylerbeyi* de la Roumélie. Avant ce dernier, ce poste était occupé par Yakut Paşa. Les sources occidentales admettent que Kruje a été conquise en 1396.[11] Après la défaite d'Ankara (1402), l'influence ottomane en Albanie s'affaiblit et les Vénitiens font augmenter leur pression sur les seigneurs du pays, notamment sur les Balsha. Ils s'emparent du château-fort de Shkodër et des autres forteresses de cette région. En ces temps-là, Balsha III était en guerre contre les Vénitiens. Entre les années 1410-1415, Kruje fut prise par un féodal albanais (Nichita Thopia).[12] On voit que Mehmed Ier, après avoir garanti l'unité ottomane, avait consolidé comme partout, aussi en Albanie, son influence et sa domination. Les sources occidentales confirment que derechef, en 1415, le château-fort passa entre les mains des Ottomans. Des notes des registres ottomans il n'est pas possible de suivre en détail ces changements. Néanmoins, la note que nous venons de mentionner sur le registre de l'an 1432, ne laisse nul doute qu'aux temps de Mehmed Ier, les Ottomans dominaient à Kruje. Cette note fait état que l'exemption de la population du château des impôts avait été approuvée aussi par Mehmed Ier.

10 *Sûret-i defter-i Sancak-i Arvanid*, p. 103.

11 Gegaj, p. 19.

12 *Ibid.*, p. 389.

D'après le registre de 1432 Kruje résulte être un centre de *subaşılıḳ*. Il n'est point de doute que Kruje, même avant cette date, était un *subaşılıḳ*, car les indications des revenues de Timar appartenant au *subaşı*, vont jusqu'à l'époque de Mehmed Ier. Après le *sancakbeyi*, le *subaşı* est le commandant des sipahis timariotes d'une zone et, dans le même temps, aussi l'administrateur de cette zone. Chaque sancak est divisé en plusieurs *subaşılıks*. Dans les XIVe-XVe siècles les *subaşıs* avaient plus d'influence que dans les périodes postérieures. D'après le régistre de l'an 1432, à Kruje on fait les *subaşı* en ordre chronologique, les titulaires suivants: en 1432 Hızır Bey, en novembre 1438 encore Hızır Bey, en avril 1440 Umur Bey. Vers 1438 İskender Bey, fils de Jean, avec le kadi de Kruje ont délivré des certificats *(biti, mektub)* sur des transferts de *timar*, opération qui indique que İskender Bey (Scanderbeg le Kastriote) avait été nommé *subaşı* de Akçahisar (Kruje), avant que ne soit nommé à ce poste pour la deuxième fois Hızır Bey. Les *subaşıs* avaient la compétence de délivrer des certificats de ce genre. Par ce *biti*, Iskender Bey témoigne de l'attitude correcte d'Urani (Urana, Uran), lequel, lors d'une attaque ennemie, entra à Akçahisar et prit part à sa défense. Cet acte permit à Skanderbeg de lui assurer comme adjonction de fief le village de Marmur (Marmuras). On doit signaler qu'il est possible que cet *Urana* ne soit autre que le Comte Uran, qui a servi fidèlement Skanderbeg aux temps de son insurrection (Skanderbeg avait confié la défense de Kruje à Uran, au temps où celle-ci avait été assiégée par Murad II en 1450, tandis que Skanderbeg avait préféré se battre en dehors de ses murs).[13] Puisqu'il est porté mention d'Urana dans notre régistre, et qu'il est le père du scribe appelé Zaganos, il faut conjecturer qu'il devait être en âge assez avancé. On sait que le Comte Uran est mort en 1458.[14] D'une note dans le même document on apprend qu'en mai 1438,[15] neuf villages du *vilâyet* de Dhimitër Jonima (Dimitri Gönima, Gionima), dans le Mati supérieur, et

13 *Ibid.*, p. 73.

14 *Ibid.*, p. 119.

15 *Sûret-i defter*, p. 120.

qui appartenaient à Skanderbeg, avaient été octroyés à André Karlo. Selon toute vraisemblance, cela est à rattacher à la révocation de Skanderbeg du poste de *subaşı.* Ces neuf villages, toujours selon le registre en question, étaient situés dans les terres de Jean (Yuvan-ili), c'est-à-dire qu'ils appartenaient aux domaines de Jean Kastriote, le père de Skanderbeg. Jean, quoique ayant réussi, devant la pression de Mehmed Ier, à garder pour un certain temps encore ses positions sous le protectorat vénitien, dans les premières années du règne de Murad II, fut absolument obligé d'entrer sous la vassalité ottomane. La note en question, datée de 1438, ne laisse subsister aucun doute que c'est autour de cette date que ces terres avaient été registrées dans la *defter.* Quoique l'État ottoman considérât ces terres des domaines d'État attribuables en *timar,* pour Skanderbeg il s'agissait des domaines seigneuriaux de son père. Jean Kastriote est mort en 1443. Comme nous le dit Chalcocondyles,[16] après la retraite des Ottomans dans les Balkans en 1443 devant J. Hunyadi, les anciens seigneurs se dépêchèrent de tous les côtés à rentrer en possession des domaines de leurs pères. Skanderbeg abandonne l'armée du Sultan, vient et s'empare de Kruje, et, en sa qualité de seigneur de Kastriote, prend possession des domaines de son père, qu'on avait octroyé à d'autres.

En été 1444, comme tous les autres du reste, Skanderbeg, aussi était convaincu que les Ottomans allaient être chassés complètement des Balkans. Cependant, la défaite subie par les Croisés à la bataille de Varna, fit s'évanouir ces espoirs.

Après avoir traité brièvement du lien qui passe entre l'insurrection de Skanderbeg avec Kruje, nous pouvons retourner aux notes qui figurent sur les registres ottoman toujours pour ce qui concerne Kruje. Dans le registre[17] de l'an 1432, nous trouvons la note suivante : "Akçahisar (Kruje) même est un château de pierre, gardé par les suivants : selon les documents délivrés par le regretté sultan (Mehmed Ier) et le sultan de notre temps (Murad II), les habitants sont exemptés de la dîme des produits et de l'*ispence,* de la dîme pour les

16 Ed. Darko, II, p. 96.

17 p. 103.

vignobles et les courtils et d'autres redevances mais ils versent au comptant la capitation. Ils sont en possession aussi d'attestations (*temessükleri*) délivrées par Yakut Paşa et Hoca Fîruz Paşa: à titre de compensation pour Akçahisar a été cédé Kollojke (Kllojke) avec toutes ses dépendances. Aux temps du sultan Kollojke est devenu *hâs* du *subaşı* avec 125 familles, 19 veuves."

De la note ci-dessus on apprend que 125 maisons chrétiennes avaient été chargées du service de garder le château. Ces maisons ne versent que la seule capitation *(cizye),* ayant été exemptées des autres contributions. En d'autres termes, ils ne versent pas la dîme sur les céréales, les vignobles et les courtils. De même ils ne versent pas la contribution de l'*ispence.*[18] On doit faire remarquer que l'administration ottomane avait confié la garde du château aux habitants chrétiens eux-mêmes. C'est une politique que les Ottomans ont appliqué aussi dans d'autres pays. L'exemption des impôts garantissait aussi le rattachement de ces populations à la domination ottomane. D'autre part, on sait qu'une telle exemption fut accordée à Kruje aussi par Andronic Paléologue II, empereur de Byzance. Des exemptions de ce genre avaient été reconnues aussi aux châteaux d'Istuluş (Stelush), Petril (Petrele), Madriç, Kocacık (Sfetigrad). D'après un registre des temps de Suleyman Ier le Législateur (Archives du Conseil des Ministres, Istanbul, No 367), de ces exemptions des chrétiens s'avantagent 58 miasons et 10 célibataires *(mücerred),* tandis que 4 individus sont indiqués spécialement comme ouvriers pour la réparation du château. Tous ceux- ci, comme antérieurement du reste, étaient exemptés de toutes les autres contributions (impôts) en dehors de la capitation *(cizye).* À cette époque on voit qu'à côté de la citadelle ont été installés 65 maisons de musulmans. Ils avaient la tâche de servir le *sancakbeyi,* effectuer des services militaires et aider les fonctionnaires du Padischah qui arrivaient. Contre ces services, ils ne versaient au possesseur du timar que la dîme, sans nulle autre contribution. Il est très vraisemblable que cette population musulmane privilégiée

18 Sur ces impôts voire *Sûret-i defter*, pp. XXXI-XXXIII.

ait été installée dans ce lieu par le gouvernement ottoman. Mais le château est resté toujours entre les mains des chrétiens. Sur la base de notes remontant à la deuxième moitié du XVIe siècle, les 47 maisons chrétiennes dans la forteresse faisaient les services suivants: ils entretenaient et réparaient le pont du château, long de 20 *zira* (13 m 50), le palier et la maison en bois à la tête du pont, les deux grandes maisons et les accès des veilleurs de nuit. De même ils réparaient les maisons de propriété publique dans le château, c'est-à-dire les maisons de l'État, les fonderies de canons, les trois entrepôts, les affûts des canons et d'autres réparations. Pour ces services ils étaient exemptés de toutes les taxes, à l'exception de la capitation *(cizye).* Mais plus tard, peut-être vers la fin du XVIe siècle, ces exemptions furent annulées et la population chrétienne fut soumise aux règles appliquées pour les gardiens des défilés *(derbendciler).* D'après celles-ci, ils furent grevés de l'impôt de 1900 *akçe.* Pour cette raison ils s'adressèrent au Divan royal à Istanbul, demandant d'être exemptés de la capitation et de toutes les autres redevances, sauf des 1900 *akçe* qu'ils verseraient chaque année au *sipahi* de Kruje. Etant donné que les restaurations dans le château furent considérées des plus nécessaires, ce fut par un ferman du Padischah que furent acceptées leurs demandes. Mais cette exemption fut limitée à seulement 47 maisons. Une autre note de ce registre laisse entrevoir qu'aussi les musulmans de la citadelle de Kruje continuaient à jouir de l'exemption contre quelques services importants. Ces musulmans n'habitaient pas à l'intérieur de la citadelle de Kruje, mais en dehors de celle-ci, dans la cité *(varoş),* et quand il était besoin de quelque service gouvernemental, ils accompagnaient le *sancak beyi,* aidaient les *emin* envoyés par les sultans ainsi que les percepteurs de la capitation. En cas de besoin, ils étaient censés de garder et défendre le château. Contre ces services, ils avaient été exemptés de tous les impôts, sauf de la dîme de production sur les moissons.

Compte tenu de ces exemptions d'impôts, il serait exagéré de considérer Kruje une ville privilégiée ou bien une ville affranchie.

*

Après que Skanderbeg se fût emparé de Kruje en 1443, il s'empara des embranchements des routes principales portant dans l'Albanie septentrionale, de Sfetigrad (Kocacık) et Dibra. De même tombèrent entre ses mains aussi les châteaux de ces régions, mais d'une importance de deuxième main, comme Petrele et Stelush. Murad II s'empara, durant la campagne de 1448, de la forteresse de Kocacık et mit en son pouvoir le chemin qui portait en Albanie. Le siège mis à Kruje par Murad II en 1450 n'eut pas de succès, étant donné que le château fut défendu à son intérieur par Uran et à son extérieur par les attaques de surprise de Skanderbeg. C'est la première victoire militaire de Skanderbeg. Enfin, Skanderbeg s'assura, contre le puissant État ottoman, la protection d'Alphonse V (accord du 26 mars 1451), et l'installation à Kruje d'un contingent envoyés par Alphonse.

Du registre daté de mars 1467 (*şaban* 871)[19] on comprend que Skanderbeg, malgré tout son effort, perdit le contrôle sur la route qui portait en Albanie du nord, et qu'au voisinage de Kruje les Ottomans sont devenus directement les maîtres. Ainsi, Skanderbeg a sous son contrôle seulement un territoire à l'ouest de Kruje.

Nous reproduirons maintenant, sous une forme résumée, les indications que nous porte ce document important, qui fait ressortir la situation de la région entre la Dibra et Kruje aux temps que Skanderbeg vivait encore. Tout d'abord nous ferons ressortir les zones avec tous les villages d'après l'ordre suivi dans le cadastre, et ensuite d'après les zones nous indiquerons les possesseurs de *timar*. Au cours de notre dépouillement, nous tâcherons d'exposer de la façon la plus complète le matériel du cadastre.

Le Defter de 1467

À la tête du *defter* se trouvent les *hâs* du mir-livâ (*sancakbeyi*). Il n'est point de doute qu'il s'agit du *sancakbeyi* d'Ohër (Ohrid). Le

19 Le registre provenant des archives de *Başvekâlet*, Maliyeden Müdevver N° 508. Il s'agit d'un *defter-i mufassal* comprenant en détail les habitants, les revenus et les timar. Le secrétaire a enregistré sur le *defter* avec soin et clarté tous les noms qui sont reproduit ici dans leur forme Ottoman.

sancak d'Ohrid comprenait les *nâhiyet* suivants : Prespa, Dirça, Mokri, Gura, Basse-Dibra, Dulgoberda, Jupa, Çermeniça, Ryeka, Mati, İvraka, Akçahisar, Dimitri Gönima, Kurbin (Beneda, Karli). Les *hâs* du *mir-livâ,* selon les *nâhiyet (vilâyet)* étaient les suivants :

1. Dans le *vilâyet* de la Haute-Dibra (Dibri) : Rahonik.
2. Dans le *vilâyet* de Dulgoberda (actuellement Golloborde) : Ivladi-Miric, Manastriça, Yablaniça, Tumyani, Bulkiza.
3. Dans le *vilâyet* de Çermeniça : Lika, Curani.
4. Dans le *vilâyet* de Mati : Kilos, Bilekamen, Forharya, Liz, Ciyay (Citay ?), Midha, Martinaş, Gik, Buk, Kıstil, Laç, Selita, Kilişt, Miçale.
5. Dans le *vilâyet* de Dimitri Gönima : Viştol, Solomon, Kayryl, Birzan, Gaybi, Bukati, Koryasot, Fiko, Mataris, Iskandani, Napizi, Duş, Dulak, İskopidhi, Luzdi, Kolaşi, Koştanya, Lendije.
6. Dans le *vilâyet* de Kurbin : Zevalbinişta, Lac, Birşat, Kaçular, Mali- Bardh, Selita, Galata, Likapay, İsmak, Kurbin, Madhiş.
7. Dans le *vilâyet* d'Akçahisar : Mişgrad, Mavruşak, Novay, Cizin, Gönimi.
8. Dans le *vilâyet* de Beneda : Piyac, Muniz.

Les revenus du *hâşş* dans tous ces villages qui appartenaient au *mir-livâ* atteignaient le montant de 46 567 *akçe* (approximativement 1000 ducats d'or).

Dibra était un *zeâmet,* et à l'époque de ces événements se trouvait entre les mains d'Ahmed Bey fils de Yurema (un albanais ?). Les villages *hâs* d'Ahmed Bey dans la Haute-Dibra et la Basse-Dibra sont les suivants :

1. Dans la Haute-Dibra : Banişta, Kuma Kırçişta, Lijani, Şipanci, Selişte, Dena-Çavişte, Çinci, Potasti, Timovik, Bohmagu (?), Kloboçişta, Damtiyar (?), Pakli, Terapçi, Makilar, Ulasik.
2. Dans la Basse-Dibra : Peskopiya (il y avait un monastère exempté sur ordre du sultan), Tirana, İstarovis, Biloye, Çiryani, Brezdan, Kubilani, Kalçişta, Kuma-Brasti, Vinca, Şimbat, Tirpişte.

Les revenus des villages que comprenait le *zeâmet* de la Dibra dans 233 familles montent à 29 793 *akçe.* Le père d'Ahmed Bey, Yurema, était sans nul doute le seigneur ancien de cette zone. On sait que dans la même zone avait défendu ses droits Moïse Dibra, qui, ralliant Skanderbeg, s'était battu à ses côtés. Moïse (Moysa) fut chassé de là, sûrement après 1448.

Le deuxième *zeâmet* de notre cadastre est celui de Ryeka (Reke), et son *subaşı* est Karagöz Bey.

Dans notre *defter,* après le *zeâmet* du sancakbeyi et celui de la Dibra, viennent les timar. Plus loin nous reproduisons les noms des villages distribués en timar, d'après l'ordre sur le registre.

I. *Haute-Dibra* (Dibri) : Kovaçiça, Dolna, Kıçişta, Hobuk, Kurnay, Tırbaç, Pelaşci, Dolna Buroyani, Herbil, Rinbari, Sohoriçani, Topolyani, Ohşatina (s'y trouve le monastère de Thotok, il possède du sultan l'ordre d'exemption), Raşati, Blatu, Çarnani, Suşani, Blaçe, Kars, Buçivo, Humiji (?), Kraykovişta, Grajdani, Gradiç et Çiyok, Solokik, le château de Kocacık (48 chrétiens du château sont exemptés de la capitation et tous les autres impôts contre le service comme gardiens du château, il a notamment aussi trois chrétiens comme menuisiers, en tout 51 individus exemptés), Ustolnica, Jitinyani, Pariş, İstrajavişta, Braştani, Provalanik, Balani, Guranci, Novak Dulgas, Fuçişta, Ulahlar, îslavyani, Selic, Ayokâni (?), Ayoluc (?) (ces neuf derniers villages ont été abandonnés, c'est-à dire que leur population s'en est allée), Mamitar, Rumil, Banişa, Pisyak, Potasti.

II. IL *Basse-Dibra* (Dibri) : Beliça Zagrad, Bukova, Şimbarbola, Sohodol, Maklişta, Darda, Ivranyovo, Nimiravi, İskrapniça, Ariza, Tarik, Kiraş, Lur, Radibodişta, Kirupi, Kitirova, Dolna Brasti, Haute-Kidhine, Basse- Kidhine, Haute-Setina, Basse-Setine, Şaşar, Gur, Grande-Rayç, Petite- Rayç, Periga (Priga) (?), Kolojanci, Raşîopol, Luzinye, Velişte, Toroyak, İzdolani, Bulac, Kilişaviç, İslatina, Lugan, Îçvatos, Milani, Diyuştita, Palamişta, Kudhon, Siçani, Zimorna, Şilubod, Drimjani, Dopyak, Vitişta, İslavyani, Kurna Burovyani,

Kuştilanez, Istaniçani, Garid Poşti, Gırkâni, Mohor, Şivasil, Bizova, Nizazi, Limyan, Ketherova, Peskopya, Kal.

III. *Dulgoberda* (Golloborde) : Radovişta, Golemo-Ostrani, Dıranova, Mali- Ostrani, Zirklani (?), Sopot, İsmolnica, Birzdan, Okştun, Kinovic, Dranok, Peskopostina, Lukova, İlasiça, Ciranci, Viçişta, Koriça, Kolovişta, Divolyani, Hotişani, Miraş, Tuçapi, Godivya, Lişniçani, Çirkoviçani, Ilişova, le château de Modric, Drestila, Kilani, Zabzon, Burova, Istablova, Kukrova, Bas-Prepatnik, Çirnobok, Trebişta, Selbişta, Kırvaviça, Izviri, Pasinik, Sirpitova, Kurna Virinca, Dolna Virinca, Lopolis, Malakas.

IV. *Ryeka* (Reke) : Dolna-Menliçani, Goma-Menliçani, Dolna-Kostovrast, Kurna-Kostovrast, İskodrina, Movirça Yançi, Prisovinça, Radostoşi, Novak, Radosac, Bituşa, Trabişta, Orahova, Bulitin, Vidoşa, Tihopoli, Jimovic, Virbyani, Bogdevo, Sinçi, Vukovya, Timiça, Virbyen, Bileçiça, Keçniça, Liyeskova, Yetçepori, Kurakomiça, Brodiç, İstrazmir, İştroviça, Jojoli, Nistrova, Ribniça, Ribniçiça, Ostoya, Gari, Yagorica, İgladhino, Tirasimci, Silci, Dirimmini, Galicnik, Pesyagorica (ces neuf derniers villages ont été abandonnés, c'est-à-dire n'ont pas d'habitants), Suşiça, Traşinca (abandonné), Bituşa, Bitimiça.

V. *Vilâyet de Çermeniça* (Çermenike) : Babyani, Kinajavic, Mirak, Liborajde, Duruzi, Gradic, Dardan, Lubnik, Niçeta, Kostinyani, Buzigar, Vulçani, Korikuk, Şinimiri, Filoka, Litimya, Koşarişta, Zibişta, Şemil, Brayungini, Nulari, Viçani, Hotolişta, İzgoşt, Konyarmaniz, Dragostunya, Orahova, Pudil, Fanaris, İzranişta, Şingerg, Padhul, Kasale, Şenimiri, Şingin, Fuvaçiç.

VI. *Vilâyet de Mati :* Kinine, Selita, Çipor, Gur, Kurragij, Bisar, Baliş (abandonné), Kıranik, Dardas, Flokit, İftoni, Paskolati, Giyame, Brisk, Maluteza, Biyan, Maçukal, Sindthimi, Boyan, Diryan, İştiyaktiz, Şilya, Şindiliştir (?), Vakar, Kalovelec, İnbaş, İştuyit, Pelişkaş, Buriyil, Midha, Yadhira, Pilaş, Şenkol, Çiruya, Kukonin, Patira, Birşi,

Kijova, Duzdar, Miştira, Gur, Istuluş (les habitants de la forteresse ont été exemptés des taxes à condition de garder la forteresse), Kilos, Liz.

VII. *Vilâyet d'Ivraka* : Diriçi, Malthi, Irkale.

VIII. *Vilâyet Dimitri Gönima* : Zuymyia, Şukadhe, Şilaz, Pidhani.

IX. *Vilâyet d'Akçuhisar* (Kruje) : Dom, İskonil, Kukâni, İşkilaz, Vilyeze, Jiye, Birth, Rudheş, Priska, Şin, İştiyakiz, Şindeli, Boyla, Buvazi, Pirezi, Asani, Makrik, Bilasik, Ozgurdiş, Vriyon, Şingerg, Barkıneş, Kurseng, Burnik, Bogmeş, Kithnami, Kalmeti, Pinyari, Patize, İkriskoza, Domi, Dolna Kaşar, Bobotiş, Bubik, Boytul, Kolakaş, Mazerak (à l'exception des cinq premiers villages, les autres ont été abandonnés, c'est-à-dire la population s'est enfuie).

X. *Nahiyet Beneda* : Bastari, Kulure, Beniş, Buşuniş, Bulaşeş, Şingin, Favriş, Selita, Lunza, Şinpal, Kutisi, İmdoş, Brusa.

Du nombre des villages de Kruje, la plus grande partie de la population a abandonné son foyer. Dans cette région, des 35 villages, 30 ont été abandonnés. On comprend qu'ils ont émigré dans les enclaves vénitiennes ou bien en Italie. Or, le vilâyet du Kruje, d'après le registre de 1432, formait une vaste région avec des villages assez riches sous l'administration d'un *subaşı (zaîm).* Des seuls 27 villages avec 369 maisons, le *hâs* du *subaşı* avait un revenu de 32 668 *akçe.* Dans les villages abandonnés, mentionnés plus haut, il y avait comme maisons : 3 à Şingerg (Shingjergj), 12 à Asani (Asan), 5 à Kurdsan (Kurtseng), 37 à Kolakşi (Kolakaş), 8 à Dom (Domi), 9 à Mazerak, 18 à Ozgurtaş (Ozgurdiş), 9 à Bogomis, 29 à Viryon (Viriyon), 11 à Barkin (Barkaneş), 17 au Bas-Kuşari (Bas- Kaşar), 9 au Haut-Kuşari (Haut-Kaşar).

Le *vilâyet* de Ryeka est la zone où se trouve un grand nombre de villages abandonnés (13 villages). Cette zone qui s'étend entre la Dibra et la forteresse de Kocacık était devenue un champ de bataille. La population des villages entre la Dibra et Kruje était fortement réduite. La plupart de ceux-ci n'ont qu'une à dix maisons. Les villages comptant 20-30 maisons constituent une exception. Les villages qui comptent plus de 20 maisons sont les suivants : Kovaçica dans la

Haute-Dibra 24 maisons, Borova dans la Basse-Dibra 27 maisons, Luzinye 46 maisons, Şemil de Çermeniça 42 maisons, Lubnik 30 maisons, Mirak 30 maisons, Brayungini 24 maisons, Jirnovic de Ryeka 22 maisons, Radovişta de Dulgoderda 21 maisons, Giyk d'İvraka 21 maisons. Les autres villages comptent au-dessous de 20 maisons.

Le Defter de 1519

Or, dans le enregistrement[20] fait dans la même zone en 1519, l'attention est attirée par le fait que les villages en général comptent une population bien plus grande et des revenus considérables. Par exemple, dans le village de Kurdsan, qui en 1467 était vide, en 1519 il y avait une maison musulmane et 23 maisons chrétiennes, à Bulaşaş 2 maisons musulmanes et 32 chrétiennes, à Selite 79 maisons chrétiennes, à Uzgurtaş (Uzguriş) 30, à Şinmiri 35, à Dom 1 maison musulmane et 36 chrétiennes, au grand Şingin 80, à Şingerg 158 et à Şipal 70. Les villages comptent en général 20 maisons. Se basant sur ce tableau, on peut affirmer sans nulle hésitation que les batailles entre Skanderbeg et les Ottomans ont représenté une véritable catastrophe et une période de dévastations pour l'Albanie septentrionale.

Examinons maintenant ci-dessous les possesseurs des *timar* d'après l'ordre d'enregistrement dans le *defter :*

I. *Dans la Haute-Dibra* : le Kadi Bahadir, dépendant affranchi de Hızır Bey; Yakub, fait de nouveau musulman; Haci de Germiyan, le Turc Ahmed, Hamza, le Janissaire Ali, Ismail le ferreur; Yakub, dépendant affranchi d'Isâ Bey, fils d'Evrenuz, İstanişta et Greg. Come on le voit, deux des timariotes sont chrétiens. Il n'est point de doute qu'ils appartiennent à la couche militaire des anciens possesseurs aborigènes, qui se sont unis aux Ottomans.[21] Il convient de noter ici Yakub,

---

20 Archives de la Başvekâlet, Istanbul, Registre N° 81. C'est un *defler icmal*, qui a des lacunes dans les premières pages. Dans une note marginale il porte la date de 925 de l'Hégire.

21 Sur cette question voire H. İnalcık, "Timariotes chrétiens en Albanie au XVe siècle", *Mitteil. des Österreichischen Staatsarchiv*, Bd. IV, 1952 ; H. İnalcık, *Fatih Devri Üzerinde Tetkikler ve Vesikalar*, pp. 137-84.

nouvellement converti à l'islam, qui prit prisonnier Moïse Dibra, le fameux compagnon de Skanderbeg. Il doit s'agir d'un des aborigènes albanais, qui a rallié les Ottomans et qui a abjuré. Du nombre des timariotes figurent trois individus venus de l'étranger, comme soldats du Sultan ou de quelque bey. L'un de ceux-ci était janissaire. Le Turc Ahmed et Haci de Germiyan doivent avoir été, sans nul doute, des volontaires turcs provenant d'Anatolie dans les zones de marche. Isâ bey, fils d'Evrenuz, dont le nom vient d'être mentionné ci-dessus, est le fameux bey de marche qui, dans les années 1445-1449 était *sancakbeyi* des territoires albanais (Arvanid-ili). Celui-ci, en 1455 et 1459 entreprit deux offensives réussies contre Skanderbeg. Il semble qu'après ces offensives, ses hommes soient entrés en possession de fiefs. Quant à Hızır bey, dont il est porté mention ici, il semble n'être autre que le même Hızır bey, nommé à deux reprises *subaşı* de Kruje, comme rival de Skanderbeg. Les beys pouvaient concéder à leurs gens des certificats pour obtenir des timars.

Le *defler* porte mention de la forteresse de Kocacik, comprise dans la juridiction de la zone de la Grande-Dibra. Après que Skanderbeg se fut emparé de Kocacik (Hocacik d'après les anciens textes), c'est-à-dire de la forteresse de Sfetigrad, le pouvoir ottoman en Albanie entra dans une phase extrêmement précaire. Après cette victoire de Skanderbeg, le sultan Murad II vint personnellement en Albanie à la tête d'une forte armée, mit le siège à la forteresse et s'en empara (1448). Cette forteresse avec ses environs, d'une importance stratégique notable, fut nouvellement renforcée par les Ottomans. Naturellement, les *yürük* doivent y avoir été installés très tôt pour la garantir. Etant donné qu'ils étaient appelés les *yürük* de Kocacik, on peut supposer que c'est de ceux-ci que découle aussi le nom donné à la forteresse.[22] Dans notre *defter,* il y a comme population dans cette forteresse appelée "Kocacık Hisarı" (Château de Kodjadjık) 48 chrétiens. Cette note marginale

22 T. Gökbilgin, *Rumeli'de Yürükler, Tatarlar ve Evlâd-i Fâtihân*, İstanbul 1957, pp. 90-97.

dans le *defter* indique qu'ils avaient été exemptés des taxes contre le service à défendre la forteresse : "Au château de Kocacık même. Ils ont entre leurs mains l'ordre (*hükm*) de notre

Padischah, - que sa victoire soit sanctifiée - ordre auquel se soumet le monde entier. Aux termes de celui-ci ils sont exemptés de la capitation et des autres '*avâriz,* contre le service qu'ils prêtent comme défenseurs du château. "Dans le château séjournent comme châtelains timariotes 9 individus. Des trois *timar* établis sur les terres autour du château, l'un appartient à Süleyman qui sonne du clairon, l'autre à *l'imam* du château Musa Fakih, et le troisième au *dizdar* du château, Muhiddin.

Dans le vilâyet de la Haute-Dibra il y a aussi des *voynuk.* Ils sont en tout 24, et avec eux se trouvent 8 *eşkinci.* Les *voynuk* se trouvent dans les villages suivants : Hırbil (aujourd'hui Herbeli), Mamita, Divolyani (aujourd'hui Dovolyan), Banişta, Topolyani (aujourd'hui Topoyani) et Rahonik. Ces villages se situent sur les versants ouest du mont Deşat se trouvant presque au nord de la Dibra. Un de ces villages, qui porte actuellement le nom de *Vojnika,* sur la route Kruje-Dibra, doit représenter sans nul doute l'un des villages de ces *voynuk.* Au- dessus du nom de Divolyani se trouve la note suivante : "Cet une territoire qui au temps de Skanderbeg était resté vide comme pays de *voynuk.* Il était antérieurement du domaine de Yani Bobovik. Sur la base du document de Haci Bey ce pays est devenu une propriété de *voynuk* au nom de Georges fils de Todor et frère de Çirin (?) et de Nicolas, compte tenu qu'il s'agit de chrétiens utiles, à condition qu'ils rejoignent l'armée tour à tour. Écrit le 5 *Şaban* de l'an 877 à Constantinople. " De cette note marginale du 5 janvier 1463 on voit que le territoire en possession d'un *voynuk* appelé Yani Bobovik est resté vide. D'après le document délivré par le gouverneur ottoman Haci bey, ce pays a été donné à Istanbul aux trois *voynuk* chrétiens, considérés des hommes utiles. Ils doivent participer tour à tour à la guerre et jouir de la possession des territoires du *voynukluk,* selon les dispositions sur les *voynuk.* L'attention y est attirée par le fait que les territoires appartenant aux *voynuk* sont encore laissés en jouissance aux *voynuk.* Et encore de cette note on apprend que cette zone naguère était comprise dans les domaines de Skanderbeg.

Cette note concernant les *voynuk* de la Basse-Dibra fait état de l'origine de ces *voynuk* : "Quand ce pays fit sa reddition sans guerre l'ordre a été donné pour tous que les *bashtine,* dont ils étaient propriétaires depuis longtemps, restent en leur jouissance comme naguère. C'est pour cette raison qu'elles leur furent relâchées." Cette note est à indiquer qu'on est en présence de troupiers aborigènes, qui possédaient des *bashtine* aussi avant l'occupation ottomane.[23]

On sait que les *voynuk* étaient une organisation militaire restée de l'Empire de Stéphane Dušan, qu'ils étaient des paysan-soldats qui s'occupaient des travaux du sol sous les pronoïaires. Ceux-là avaient pour tâche, à l'époque, de garder et de défendre les châteaux. Durant la période que nous examinons ils ont été chargés de garder les gorges ou bien d'entrer comme combattants actifs dans l'armée du sultan.[24] Les notes que nous avons présentés sont à indiquer que les *voynuk* gardaient encore la même forme d'organisation qu'ils avaient dans l'empire serbe. Par exemple, à la tête des *voynuk* du village de Mamita est mentionné un *lagator* appelé Progon. Ses assistants sont Nicolas Potrak et Radoslav. Du nombre des *voynuk* il y a aussi ceux qui possèdent des noms complètement albanais (Gjon, Gjin). On apprend ainsi que les Ottomans, à la tête des principales routes provenant d'Ohrid ou de Shkup (Skoplje, Üsküb), ont désigné au service de la défense d'une part les *yürük* et d'autre part les *voynuk* aborigènes. Ces *voynuk* apparaissent aussi dans d'autres *vilâyet,* c'est-à-dire dans l'Albanie entière.

De même, aussi dans le vilâyet de la Haute-Dibra se trouvaient 12 fauconniers (*doganci*) chargés d'assurer à la cour 12 faucons annuellement.[25]

23 *Bashtine:* une terre suffisante à garantir la vie à une famille, possédée en commun par des *voynuk.* Des informations plus détaillées sur les *bashtine* sont données dans *Fatih Devri Üzerinde,* pp. 171-174.

24 Sur les voynuk de celle période v., *Fatih Devri Üzerinde,* pp. 171-179.

25 Sur l'organisation des fauconniers voir s/v *Doganci,* dans *l'Encyc, of Islam,* IIe édition.

II. Dans le *vilâyet* de la Basse-Dibra il y a 17 timariotes, dont les noms sont les suivants : Çeri-başı Ali, Tur bey fils d'Umur, Vardarlu Ali, Karagöz, Karagöz dépendant affranchi de Hızır Bey fils de Barak Bey, Ismail, Mihayil, Olivir et Progon, trois frères chrétiens, Süleyman fils d'Ahmed, Mustafa fils de Yusuf, İsmail de la Dibra, le Janissaire Ali, Ibrahim de la Dibra, Süleyman fils de Bahşayiş, Nebi fils de Hızır, Hamza, Devlethan de Kırçava, Georges, Nicolas et un autre Georges en commun. Deux timars sont en jouissance de chrétiens, dont l'un est possédé par trois frères, l'autre par quatre individus. Aussi ici on voit que les timariotes, comme dans la Haute-Dibra, sont composés par des dépendants *(kul)* des beys, par des chrétiens aborigènes, par des aborigènes convertis en musulman (Ibrahim de la Dibra, Ismail et Devlethan de Kırçava), ou bien par des nouveaux-venus des pays étrangers. Dans la Basse-Dibra il n'y a pas un *zaîm* à la tête des spahis, mais un *çeri-başı,* qui est le commandant des spahis timariotes sous le *subaşı (zaîm).* Dans ce *vilâyet* il y a 14 *voynuk* et 4 *eşkinci (eşküncü).* L'exemption des impôts de la population du château de Kocacık (l'exemption de la capitation est très importante) ainsi que l'abandon des *bashtine* dans les mains des *voynuk* représentent des mesures prises en vue de rapprocher et rattacher aux Ottomans la population de ces lieux. Ces mesures prises par les Ottomans en vue de ralentir la résistance opposée à la conquête de l'Albanie ont été appliquées aussi dans d'autres régions.

III. *Le vilâyet du Dulgoberda (Dulgobrdo, Golloborde).* Les timariotes de ce pays sont les suivants: Karaca Aşçı, İskender, Sa'di Hoca, Karagöz des soldats de la forteresse de Kocacık, Şirmerd, Hızır Madik, Abdullah, Sinan le dizdar de la forteresse de Modriç (au sud du château de Kocacık), Ali Ozgur (Sguras), Haci Mehmed, Yusuf dépendant affranchi du Kadiasker, Kılavuz (Kulaguz) İlyas.

Dans ce *vilâyet* aussi il y a 23 *voynuk* et 7 *eşkinci.* Il y a aussi 3 fauconniers chargés de la tâche d'envoyer 2 faucons et 1 faucon royal *(şahin).*

IV. *Le vilâyet de Ryeka (Reke).* Cette zone est un *vilâyet* administrée par un *zaîm (subaşı).* Le *subaşı* de Ryeka obtenait 18 287 *akçe* de revenus de 227 familles. On n'y a qu'un seul timar octroyé comme adjonction à Süle et Turasan de Kırçava (Krçevo). Dans le *vilâyet* de Ryeka il y avait beaucoup de *voynuk*: 31 *voynuk* et 10 *eşkinci.*

V. *Le vilâyet de Çermeniça (Çermenike).* Dans cette zone, où a sa source le fleuve Shkumbin, les timariotes sont les suivants: Ulûfeci ilyas, Hacı Ya'kub, Karagöz *gulâm* de Hızır Bey, Yusuf et Gön (d'après la note marginale, ces deux ont pris prisonnier "le traître nommé Muzak", et tous les deux prennent part chaque année à la guerre); İlyas ve Karagöz convertis nouvellement à l'Islam. Ali fils de Hacı Barak, İbrahim, Avâre Hızır, İlyas fils de Paşayiğit, Bahadır Kethüda du châtelain du château d'İlbasan, Samed, Solak İsmail, Temirhan, Ayas *gulâm* de Balaban Aga, Hüseyin *gulâm* de Balaban aga.

Dans le *nâhiyet* de Tamadhya, compris dans la Çermeniça, se trouve enregistré un timar sous le nom de Yusuf, nouvellement converti à l'Islam.

VI. *Le vilâyet de Mati.* Les timariotes, dans le bassin du fleuve Mati, entre Kruje et la Dibra, sont les suivants : Le Voyvode Karagöz des dépendants de Davud Bey, Barak de Monastir, Balaban *gulâm* de Karaca Bey, Yusuf, Dragoslav, Tomaş, Petro Vılık et Mavro en commun *(müşterek),* (deux de ceux-ci sont dans la l'armée chaque année), Aleksi Diye, le Turc Isa, le Papas Peter, Hızır Ginak, Ali neveu de Balaban Aga, Kali Gierg, Gönima, Gierg, Todor ensemble (deux de ceux-ci rejoignent l'armée chaque année), Kolosirod (?) et Peter Ginak, Hızır l'Albanais.

Ce qui attire l'attention dans le *vilâyet* de Mati est le fait que, par rapport aux autres *vilâyets,* les timariotes sont chrétiens pour la plupart. Ainsi, des 14 timar, 6 sont entre les mains des chrétiens.

Étant donné que les timariotes chrétiens jouissaient de leurs timar en commun *(müşterek)*, comme nombre ils forment la majorité. Ils les possèdent en commun dans la mesure de 2 ou 4 personnes, et ce n'est que deux de ceux-ci qui rejoignent l'armée chaque année. On sait que ces timar sont donnés en commun aux cousins ou bien aux individus qui sont proches. L'un des timariotes est un prêtre. De même il résulte parfaitement que des deux derniers timariotes, l'un est Turc et l'autre Albanais. Dans ce cas aussi on constate qu'on a octroyé des timar à la mouvance des beys.

Balaban Aga, qui a accordé des timar à ses propres soldats dans la Basse- Dibra et dans la Çermeniça, ainsi qu'à son neveu à Mati, doit être ce même Balaban Aga, sancakbeyi d'Ohrid, connu pour ses batailles sanglantes contre Skanderbeg. On peut supposer que Balaban Aga soit le fils de quelque seigneur albanais de ces régions. De plusieurs exemples on sait que de tels seigneurs ont pris l'initiative à octroyer tout d'abord des timar dans leurs zones anciennes à leurs garçons et à leurs cousins.

Dans Mati figurent 15 *voynuk* et 5 *eşkinci.* Encore dans ce *vilâyet,* le Padischah avait accordé aux habitants du château d'İstuluş (Istuluzzi) un firman, par lequel ils étaient exemptés des impôts, à condition de tenir en état de sécurité la forteresse.

VII. *Le vilâyet d'İvraka.* Dans le *vilâyet* d'İvraka, presqu'à l'Est de Mati, dans la vallée de la rivière d'İvraka, il y a trois timar, dont les posseseurs sont Tanuş Pirlat, Uzatay (?), İzvendenko (?) Pirlat. Il convient de faire noter que tous ces chrétiens ont été laissés à leurs places. Il s'agit d'anciens soldats chrétiens laissés dans leurs propres pays montagnueux et difficiles à franchir. Il ressort aussi que deux de ceux-ci sont du même cousinage.

VIII. *Le vilâyet de Dimitri Gönima.* Ce *vilâyet,* attribué à Dimitri Gönima, un des fameux seigneurs albanais, se trouve dans la vallée supérieure du fleuve Mati. Dans notre *defter* il est question d'un timar dans le *vilâyet* de Dimitri Gönima, c'est-à-dire du timar d'Abdullah, un dépendant affranchi de Hızır Bey, fils de Barak Bey.

IX. *Le vilâyet d'Akçahisar* (Kruje). Les noms des timariotes de cette zone sont les suivants: en commun les frères Nicolas et Georges; trois frères Pierre Suma, André Kımbeza et Demètre en commun; İlyas, converti nouvellement à l'Islam, Oğurlu. Et un autre timar attribué au nom du nouveau musulman Dogan.

Ils doivent appartenir aux familles aborigènes restées fidèles aux Ottomans, après la retraite de Skanderbeg, qui doivent avoir gardé leurs timar, ou bien avoir obtenu plus tard des timar.

Tableau récapitulatif sur les connaissances données plus haut à propos des formations militaires

Vilâyet	**Subaşı**	**Timariotes**			**Voynuk**		**Fauconniers**	**Forteresses**
		Musulmans						
		Spahis	**Gardiens de château**	**Chrétiens**	**Voynuk**	**Eşkinci**		
Haute-Dibra	1	8	9	2	24	8	12	Le château de
Basse-Dibra		15		2	14	4		Kocacık
Dulgoberda	–	13	–	–	23	7	3	
Ryeka	1	1	–	–	31	10	–	
Çermeniça	–	16	1	–	–	–	–	
Mali	–	8	–	6	15	5	–	Le chateau
Ivraka				3				d'İstuluş
Dimitri Gönima	–	1	–	–	–	–	–	
Akçahisar	–	3	–	2	–	–	–	
(Kruje) Beneda (nâhiyet)	–	2	–	2	–	–		
Total	2	67	10	17	107	34	15	2

V

OTTOMAN ARCHIVAL MATERIALS ON *MILLETS*

Ḳadi Court Records

The *ḳadi* court records, *sicillāt,* constitute an extensive collection,[1] scattered across the former area of the empire, and perhaps the most important source for the social life and actual legal conditions of the non-Muslims under Ottoman rule. This happened not only because the non-Muslims, the *ahl al- dhimma,* were under the jurisdiction of *ḳadis* in so many areas of the law, but also because the *dhimmīs* often preferred to seek a *ḳadi's* decision or certificate. The use of Muslim courts provided greater assurance, or the means to escape the more rigid stipulations of their own religious law in such matters as marriage, divorce, and parenthood rights, which were supposed to be under the exclusive jurisdiction of the Christian or Jewish authorities. In the eighteenth century the Greek Patriarchate had to take serious measures to prevent the latter practice, as a result of which the infiltration of Islamic and customary law was being seen in such areas as marriage and dowry practices.[2] At any rate the *ḳadi sicillāt* abound with court decisions, as well as contracts,

1 For a bibliography of the *sicillāt* in Turkey, see Osman Ersoy, "Şer'iyye Sicillerinin Toplu Kataloğuna Doğru", *Ankara Üniversitesi, Dil ve Tarih-Coğrafya Fakültesi Mecmuası,* 21 (1963), pp. 35-65 and Mücteba İlgürel, "Şer'iyye Sicillerinin Toplu Kataloğuna Doğru," *Istanbul Üniversitesi Edebiyat Fakültesi, Tarih Dergisi,* 28-29 (1975), pp. 123-166.

2 N. J. Pantazapoulos, *Church and Law in the Balkan Peninsula During Ottoman Rule,* Salonica, 1967, pp. 91-112.

transactions, certificates and other kinds of documents, drawn up not only between Muslims and non-Muslims but also between non-Muslim parties.

Since the *sicilāt* were deposited in the *ḳadi* courts of the cities and towns throughout the empire, their rediscovery has given existence from the 1930s on to many local archives in the lands once under Ottoman rule – Yugoslavia, Bulgaria, Albania, Greece, Syria, Turkey, Israel, Jordan, and Egypt. One of the most extensive, and for obvious reasons the most important collections, is that in Istanbul, under the office of the *mufti.* About ten thousant well-preserved volumes of the *ḳadı* records of Istanbul, Galata, Eyüp, and adjacent districts, collected under Abdülhamid II, have been barely touched for study. The Bursa collection, comprising the oldest *kadi* registers dating back to the 1460s, is the best known to the students of Ottoman history, and has been exploited since the 1930s.[3] Also, a number of publications have been made from the collections in such centers as Monastir, Sarajevo, Vidin, Sofia, Salonica, Cyprus, Damascus, Jerusalem, and Cairo.[4] Documents from the *sicillāt* of Vidin and Sofia concerning the Church and ecclesiastical matters have been collected and studied by Joseph Kabrda.[5]

Monastery Archives

Ottoman documents preserved in monastery archives bear a special interest not only for the history of particular monasteries and the administration of monastic properties under Ottoman rule, but also for Ottoman history in general, since some monasteries preserved

3 See H. İnalcık, "Bursa şer'iye sicillerinde Fatih Sultan Mehmed'in fermanları," *Belleten*, 11 (1944), p. 693. *Sicillāt* were extensively exploited for local history in the publications made by *Halkevleri* in Turkey.

4 For the publications made in these places see J. Reychman and A. Zajaczkowski, *Handbook of Ottoman-Turkish Diplomatics*, revised ed. A. S. Ehrenkreutz and T. Halasi-Kun, The Hague and Paris 1968, index.

5 In his book, *Le système fiscal de l'Église orthodoxe dans l'Empire Ottoman*, Brno, 1969, and his articles, cited in the book's bibliography, p. 163.

documents from the earliest Ottoman times, even the fourteenth century. Monastic documents have been published by Paul Wittek and Paul Lemerle, Elizabeth Zachariadou-Oikonomides (Greece), D. Ihčiev (Bulgaria), P. Džansazov and J. Jastrebov (Yugoslavia), Eutimo Castellani (Jerusalem), Klaus Schwarz (Sinai) and Zdenka Veselá-Prenosilová (Sinai).[6] It should be added that the Ottoman survey registers of the fifteenth and sixteenth centuries preserved in the central archives in Istanbul contain complete lists of the monasteries in Ottoman territories and often copies of their *fermans* and statutes.

Collections in the Central Archives (Başvekâlet Arşivi, Istanbul)

The collection of *Mühimme* registers in the Ottoman archives, containing copies of the decrees decided upon in the Imperial Council, and covering the period from 1553 to 1905, is definitely one of the most important sources for affairs concerning the non-Muslims and their organizations in the Ottoman Empire. Among the collections of documents on this subject selected from this source, those published by Ahmed Refik Altınay and Uriel Heyd are particularly worthy of mention.[7] Ahmed Refik, in his selection, included principally documents concerning the non-Muslim communities in Istanbul and their organization. Uriel Heyd selected those on the Jews in Palestine. A brief examination of these publications will suffice to show that the *Mühimme* collection documents deal with all aspects of the relations of non-Muslims individually or collectively with the Ottoman government. They also show the government's concern for matters affecting its *dhimmī* subjects, especially in relation to taxation, security and peace among them. A great number of the decrees are concerned with the enforcement of the restrictions that Islamic law

6 See for a bibliography, Klaus Schwarz, *Osmanische Staatsurkunden des Sinai-Klosters in türkischer Sprache*, Freiburg-im-Breisgau, İ970, pp. 197-205.

7 Ahmed Refik (Altınay), *Istanbul Hayatı*, 3 vols., Istanbul, 1930-1935; U. Heyd, *Ottoman Documents on Palestine*, Oxford, 1960; also see Bernard Lewis, *Notes and Documents from the Turkish Archives*, Jerusalem, 1952.

imposed upon non-Muslims as, for example: the bans upon selling wine in public, upon dressing as Muslims, riding horses, possessing slaves, having houses too close to Muslim places of worship, upon any contraction of churches or synagogues beyond the maintenance of those Mehmet the Conqueror had permitted to remain in use. A need to reinforce restrictions of this sort was apparently felt in times of war against Christian powers and in times of public distress, when the sultan made a show to the Muslim public of the fact that he was scrupulously applying the prescriptions of the *Sharī'a.*

On the other hand, since the *dhimmīs* were involved in every aspect of public life in the Ottoman Empire, the papers and registers dealing with public affairs, especially with public finances, are important, such as the *māliye aḥkām*, the *muḳaṭa'a* registers, the *'avāriz-i dīvāniyye* registers, and the registers of the petitions and complaints, *şikāyāt* and *aḥkām.* Of special interests is a register called *Avrupa [tüccārı]* containing decrees and diplomas issued to non- Muslim merchants of the empire who were engaged in trade with European countries and who were given special privileges and tax exemptions to enable them to compete on an even footing with those enjoying capitulatory privileges.[8] It is important to emphasize that these documents show that the Ottoman government dealt with non-Muslims directly as its *dhimmī* subjects.

The *taḥrīr,* or *tapu, defterleri,* the population and tax survey books of the Ottoman state,[9] are of basic importance for statistical data on the non-Muslims in the areas of demography, economic conditions, and taxation. Frequently the contents of important *fermans*, or of diplomas granting exemptions or appointments, as well as laws and regulations, *ḳānūnnāme*s, are entered in these registers along with the persons or groups to whom they apply. These are the best known

8 For all these *defters* see Midhat Sertoğlu, *Muhteva Bakımından Başvekâlet Arşivi*, Ankara, 1955; and B. Lewis (cited n. 7), pp. 2-4.

9 See Ö. L. Barkan, "Türkiye'de imparatorluk devirlerinin büyük nüfus ve arazi tahrirleri ve hakana mahsus istatistik defterleri," *İstanbul Üniversitesi Iktisat Fakültesi Mecmuası*, 2 (1941), pp. 20-59, pp. 214-47; B. Lewis (cited n. 7), pp. 4-5.

registers in the Ottoman archives and a number of publications have already been made based on them with full reproductions or summaries.[10] Mention should be made here of the surveys of imperial *evḳāf,* comprising valuable statistical data on the non-Muslims who paid their taxes to *evḳāf.* The best example is the sultanic *evḳāf* of the *Fatih* mosque (Tapu registers n. 240, dated 952 cumadelûlâ 1/1545 July, and no. 210),[11] which is a mine of information on the Greek, Armenian, Jewish, and European (*Efrenciyan*) communities of Istanbul. From this register we learn, for example, not only the population of each district and the taxes paid, but also individual and group places of origin. These records attest to a large immigration of Armenians and Greeks from Anatolian towns into Istanbul before 1545. As for the nineteenth century, starting from 1831 several detailed population surveys have been the subject of research and publication by E. Z. Karal, K. Karpat, and J. McCarthy.[12]

As for the principal registers concerning only the non-Muslim communities in the Ottoman Empire, they are:

1. the *cizye* registers, registers of the Islamic poll tax, which go back to the fifteenth century. The important *cizye* register of the year 1489 has been studied and published by N. Todorov and Ö. L. Barkan.[13]
2. the *peskopos muḳāṭa'ası* registers, on which we will focus our attention below.

---

10 For a bibliography see Reychman and Zajaczkowski (cited n. 4), pp. 24-103.

11 See H. İnalcık, "Istanbul," *EI*², vol. 3, pp. 244-45.

12 See H. İnalcık, "Impact of the *Annales* School on Ottoman Studies and New Findings," *Review*, 1(1978), p. 76; K. Karpat., "Ottoman Population Records and Census of 1881-1893," *IJMES*, 9 (1978), pp. 237-74; mention should also be made of the important data in the *Sâlnames or* Yearbooks of the Ottoman Provinces, for a bibliography of these see H. R. Ertuğ, "Osmanlı devrinde salnameler," *Hayat Tarih Mecmuası*, 9 (1973).

13 N. Todorov, "La situation démographique de la péninsule balkanique au cours des XVᵉ et XVIᵉ siècles," *Annuaire de l'Université de Sofia, Faculté de Philosophie et d'Histoire*, 53 (1959); Ö. L. Barkan, "894 (1488/1489) yılı cizye muhasebesine âit muhasebe bilançoları," *Belgeler*, 1 (1964), pp. 1-117.

3. the *cemā'āt-i gayr-i Muslime* registers, altogether eighteen registers containing copies of papers on all matters of affairs concerning the non- Muslim communities from the year 1837 on.
4. the *kilise defterleri,* which start in 1837, and contain permissions for construction and repair of churches, schools and other buildings, as well as cemeteries, run by the non-Muslim communities or foreigners.

From 1916 on imperial orders, *irādes*, were classified in dossiers according to individual subject. Among the *irāde dosyaları,* dossier no. 62 is devoted to the non-Muslim communities and includes such important documents as petitions from the Greek Patriarchate for the appointment of a new patriarch, the reaffirmation of the regulations governing the Armenian Patriarchate, and the resignation of the Haham-başı, Hayim Nahum.

In the nineteenth century important events involving the non-Muslim communities prompted special investigations by the government and resulted in such special *defters* as that on the *Rum fesādı,* the Greek insurrection, a survey of all Greek merchants in Istanbul *hāns,* one on Serbian affairs, and other registers on the Bulgarian uprising in Vidin, the question of the Bulgarian Exarchate, the disorders in Lebanon, and the question of Crete.[14]

Briefly speaking, all of these documents show that the Ottoman government treated the non-Muslims simply as its *dhimmī* subjects, and that their religious leaders were given full independence of action only in matters concerning the church hierarchy and property. It was only in 1764 that for the first time the sultan gave the Greek and Armenian patriarchs direct authorization to punish troublemakers in their community without having to bring the case to the attention of the Porte; at the same time *ḳadi* courts were ordered to refuse cases involving dubious marriages.[15]

14 See M. Sertoglu (cited n. 8).

15 See A. Refik, *Istanbul Hayati, 1000-1100,* Istanbul, 1931, p. 206; for marriages see orders in Kabrda (cited n. 5), no. xxvi, xxviii, xxxiv and Pantazapoulos (cited n. 2), pp. 98-103.

A Study of the Peskopos Muḳāṭa'ası Registers[16]

In this series the introduction to register no. 2540-2 reads: "This is a register of the diplomas and decrees (*berevāt ve ahkām)* concerning the Office of the Public Revenues from the Appointments of Bishops (*Ḳalem-i Muḳaṭa'a-i Peskopos),* during the time of his Excellency 'Abdullah Nā'ilī Efendi, *Defterdār-i Şiḳḳ-i Evvel,* and 'Alī Efendi, secretary to the grand vezir's *kethudā* and chief secretary of the said office. First of Muharrem 1167/Oct. 29, 1753)."

The introduction makes clear the following points:

1. There is a special office at the department of imperial finances responsible for the collection of the revenues connected with appointments of the religious heads of the Christian communities in the empire.
2. The head of this office is a *hoca,* head-secretary, under the finance minister, but at the same time he is a secretary to the grand vezir's deputy, thus under the direct control of the grand vezir's office.

The register contains diplomas and decrees on appointments, changes and other matters concerning the title and jurisdiction of the metropolitans *(medrepolid)* and bishops *(peskopos)* in the empire. In other words the registers kept at this office are essential for the study of church organization throughout the empire and its relations with the Ottoman government. The records concern the Orthodox Greek Patriarchate of Istanbul and the Patriarchates of Jerusalem, Alexandria, and Antioch, Ohrid (Ohri) and Peč (İpek) as well as the Armenian Patriarchate of Istanbul. It also includes decrees concerning monasteries. The first register in this series contains documents from the period 1051-1061/1641-1651, but it also has notes on circumstances dating back to the sixteenth century as well as marginal records of the years 1061-1082/1651-1671. The office was then under the *Defterdar* of the *şiḳḳ-i s̱ānī.* There are four registers in this series, covering the period between 1051-1253/1641-1837. The office of *Peskopos Halifeliği Muḳata'ası*

16 Başvekâlet Archives, Istanbul, Kâmil Kepeci Tasnîfi nos. 2539-2542

was abolished in 1837; after that, diplomas and decrees concerning the non-Muslim communities were copied in the registers of the *Cemāʿat-i Gayr-i Muslima* in the *Dīvān-i Hümāyūn* under the direct control of the grand vezir or prime minister.[17]

The following list of the Metropolitan and Episcopal sees under the Patriarchate of the Orthodox Greeks (*Rūmiyān*) with the amount of *pīş-keş* is based upon the *Peskopos Muḳataʿası* register no. 2539 covering the period 1641- 1651.

	Piş-keş
Patriarchate of Istanbul, over the Christians in Istanbul and its dependencies. 105 *okka* meat per day for the Imperial gardeners *(bostancı)*	20,000 *kuruş*
Metropolitanate of the Christians in the *nāḥiyes* (counties) of Terkoz and Hâslar (area between Bosphorus, Marmara Sea and Black Sea) and the city of Galata	4 gold pieces
Bishopric of the town of Çatalca with the villages of Hamillu and Haridin and Büyük-Çekmece and its dependencies	800 akça
Metropolitanate of the Christians of Bigados and its dependencies	1440 akça
Metropolitanate of the Christians of the district (*vilāyet*) of Ereglü (Heraclea) and its dependencies	20 gold pieces
Metropolitanate of the *nahiye* (county) of Istanimaka and its dependencies	20 gold pieces
Metropolitanate of the district *(vilāyet)* of Siroz (Serrés) and its dependencies	65 gold pieces
Metropolitanate of the district of Zihne and its dependencies	9 gold pieces
Bishopric of the Christians of the village of Potemkale and its dependencies in the *ḳazā* of Argirikasrı	2000 akça

17 See M. Sertoğlu (cited n. 3), pp. 27-29.

Gumenot-i Manastır-i Prokri or Panaya along with the Christians of Kızıl-Kaya	5 gold pieces
Metropolitanate of the Christians of Salonica with the Bishopric of Liti and Andelissa in Sidre-Kapsi (Siderokavsja)	150 gold pieces
Metropolitanate of Arhi, and its dependencies in the *ḳazā* of Sidre- Kapsi	30 gold pieces
Metropolitanate of Kara-Ferye (Pherrai) and its dependencies	25 gold pieces
Kethudalık of the Christians of the *ḳazā* of Sidre-Kapsi	10 gold pieces
Kethudalık of the salt-works in the area of Salonica	730 akça
Metropolitanate of the Christians of the district of Varna and its dependencies	10 gold pieces
Metropolitanate of the Christians of the district of Kortos (Corinth) and its dependencies	130 gold pieces (100 for metropolitan and 30 for bishop)
Metropolitanate of the Christians of the church of Koron with Kalamata	15 gold pieces
Metropolitanate of the Christians of Narda with the church of Inebahtı and its dependencies	30 gold pieces
Fixed sum paid annually by the monks in the Aynaroz (Athos) monasteries	200,000 akça
For *żarar-ı kaṣṣā bān* and *kirbas-bahā* for the *bostancıs* as ordered in the year 1063/1652	200,000 akça
Metropolitanate containing the bishopric of the district of Moton (Modon)	8 gold pieces
Bishopric of the Christians of Yeni-Kale in the province of Morea with the districts of Moton, Koron and Arkadya, comprising fifty villages	7gold pieces

Metropolitanate of the Christians of the island of Sakız (Chios) and its dependencies	35 gold pieces
Tercümanlık (office of dragoman) at Sakız	500 akça
Metropolitanate of the Christians of the islands of Rhodes and Limnos and their dependencies	24 gold pieces
Bishopric of the Christians of the islands in the Marmara Sea	20 gold pieces
Bishopric of the Latin Christians (*efrenciyye)* in the *ḳazā of* Bar and its dependencies	1800 akça
Metropolitanate of the Christians in the villages of Ganos and Khora and its dependencies in the *ḳazā*s of Gallipoli and Magalkara	8 gold pieces
Metropolitanate in the district of Bursa and its dependencies	15 gold pieces
Metropolitanate of the Christians in Mudanya, Sigi (Sige), Pulad, Gusi and Subashı in the *ḳazā* of Kite	25 gold pieces
Bishopric of the Christians in the villages of Kurşunlu (Megas Agros), Mir-Ali and Yeni-köy	6 gold pieces
Kethudalık or Mir-Ali and its dependencies	30 gold pieces
Metropolitanate of the Christians in the district (*vilāyet*) of Amasya with the *ḳazās* of Sinop, Samsun, Bafra, Aydinat and their dependencies	40 gold pieces
Metropolitanate of the province (*livā-sancak*) of Canik with the church of Panaya	10 gold pieces
Metropolitanate of the Christians of Trabzon, Torul (Ardasa) with the districts (*nāḥiye*) of Gümüş (Argyropolis), Bayburt (Paipert) and their dependencies	50 gold pieces
Metropolitanate of the Christians of the district of Rize (Rizaion)	20 gold pieces
Metropolitanate of Konya and its dependencies	9 gold pieces

Metropolitanate of the Christians of the district of Niğde and its dependencies	12 gold pieces
Metropolitanate of the Christians of the district of Antalya	20 gold pieces
Metropolitanate of the Christians of the district of Aydıncık (near Cyzicus)	20 gold pieces
Metropolitanate of the Christians of the district of Kefe (Caffa) and its dependencies	50 gold pieces
Metropolitanate of the Christians of the district of Mangup	20 gold pieces
Metropolitanate of the Christians of Tat-Ili (in the Crimea) and its dependencies	15 gold pieces
Metropolitanate of the Christians of the district of Kay-seriye and its dependencies	12 gold pieces
Metropolitanate of the Christians of the district of Ankara and its dependencies	10 gold pieces
Metropolitanate of the Christians of the district of Filibe (Philippopoli) with the *ḳażās of* Hasköy and Tatar-Pazarı and their dependencies	50 gold pieces
Metropolitanate of the Christians of the district of Sofya (Sofia), and its dependencies	112 gold pieces
Metropolitanate of the Christians of the district of Ayaslug (Ephesus) and its dependencies	20 gold pieces
Metropolitanate of the Christians of the district of Izmir (Smyrna)	10 gold pieces

Under the Patriarch of the Christians of the island of Cyprus	**Piş-keş**
Patriarchate of the Christians of the province of Cyprus and its dependencies	73,500 akça

Dragoman at the Court of Cyprus	1,600 akça
Bishopric of the Christians of the *ḳazā* of Baf and its dependencies	5,400 akça
Bishopric of the Christians of the *ḳazā* of Kirine and its dependencies	1,400 akça
Bishopric of the Christians of the *ḳazā* of Gilani and its dependencies	2,400 akça
Bishopric of the Christians of the *ḳazā* of Limasson and its dependencies	2,400 akça
Bishopric of the Christians of the *ḳazā* of Lefkoşa and its dependencies	3,600 akça
Bishopric of the Christians of the *ḳazā* of Hirishora and its dependencies	2,800 akça

Under the Patriarch of Ohri (Ohrid)

Patriarchate of the Christians of the province of Ohri	1,000 gold pieces
its dependencies and the fixed lump sum to be delivered to the imperial treasury annually	60,000 akça
Bishopric of the Latin Christians (*Efrenciyān*) on the island of Andrea and its dependencies	8 gold pieces

Under the Patriarch of İpek (Peč)

Patriarch of the Serbian Christians of the province of İpek with the provinces of Budin (Buda), Temešvar, Bosnia,* Gyula, Egre, Kanija, İskenderiyye, Prizrin and their dependencies as found on July 1, 1615. Besides the *piş-keş* he agreed to pay each year to the imperial treasury a lump sum in the amount of 100,000 akça, as fixed down.	100,000 akça

* In a register of *muḳāṭa'a* dated 1479 (Başvekâlet Archives, Maliyeden Müdevver no. 176) the metropolitan of Bosnia (*Medrepolid-i vilāyet-i Bosna*) was to pay fifty gold pieces each year. The high rate of pīş-keş can be interpreted as an indication of the importance of the Greek Orthodox church in Bosnia at that time; cf. John Fine, *The Bosnian Church, A New Interpretation*, New York and London 1975, pp. 375-78.

Metropolitanate of the Christians of the districts of Iştip (Štip), Maleşeva, Kratova, Islavişte and their dependencies; later on with an addition of 6200 akça	45 gold pieces
Metropolitanate of the Christians of the province of İpek later on with addition that was fixed down as 3000 akça Since the aforesaid metropolitanate lies at İpek, the Patriarch himself holds it, and paying the *pīş-keş* he possesses it independently; this was decided on March 27, 1584.	22 gold pieces
Bishopric of the Christians of the church belonging to the Latin clergy (*ruhbānān-i Latin)* in the province of Bosnia, Kilis, Hersek and their dependencies. Bishop is nominated by the Patriarch of İpek	40 gold pieces
Metropolitanate of the Christians of the city of Budin (Buda) and its dependencies. Its holder is nominated by the Patriarch of İpek	10 gold pieces
Metropolitanate of the Christians of the districts of Sigetvar with Peçuy. Its holder is nominated by the Patriarch of İpek.	10 gold pieces

The following is a list of all the Metropolitan and Episcopal sees in their hierarchical order as found in the *berāt* renewed for Kyrillos, patriarch of the Greek Orthodox Church, on the occasion of Osman III's accession to the throne in 1753 (Register no. 2540/2, p. 39). For the titles Metropolitanate (M), Archbishopric (AB), Bishopric (B); we followed the list in T. Papadopoullos, *Studies and Documents Relating to the History of the Greek Church and People under Turkish Domination,* Brussels, 1952, pp. 82-122.

1. Istanbul and its dependencies (M)
2. Kayseriye (Kayseri) (M)
3. Lititisa (AB)
4. Kuş-Adası (Ephesus) (M)
5. Ereğli (Hrakleia) (M)
6. Radoscuk (Rodosto) (B)

7. Gelibolu (Kallioupoli, Gallipoli) (B)
8. Mirtofona (Miriofiton, Mürefte) (B)
9. Çatalca (Metrai) (AB)
10. Çorlu (Tsuralon) (AB)
11. Ankara (Ancyra) (M)
12. Kapıdağı (Cyzicus) (M)
13. Iznikmid (İzmit) (Nicomedia) (M)
14. tznik (Nicaea) (M)
15. Kadıköyü (Chalcedon) (M)
16. Selanik (Salonica) (M)
17. Çitroz (Kitros) (B)
18. Kapaniya (Kampania) (B)
19. Balatomina (Platamuno) (B)
20. Serfice (Setfion) (B)
21. Toyran (Tolvan) (B)
22. Petros (Petras) (B)
23. Ardamiri (Ardamerion) (B)
24. Aynaroz (Mount Athos)
25. Silstre (Dristra) (B)
26. Tırnovi (M)
27. Çirmen (Tsernevon) (B)
28. Lofca (Lovec) (B)
29. Şumnu (formerly Preslav) (B)
30. Edirne (M)
31. Ahtabolu (Agathopoli) (B)
32. Amasya (Amasea) (M)
33. Bursa (M)
34. Niksar (Neokaisaria) (M)
35. Konya (Iconion) (M)
36. Kara-Ferye (Pherrai) (M)
37. Antalya (formerly Pisidia) (M)
38. Talantova (Talantion) (formerly Athens) (M)
39. Girit (Crete) (M)
40. Trabzon (Trebizond) (M)
41. Yenişehir (Larissa) (M)
42. Tırhala (Trikkala) (B)
43. Narda (B)

44. İnebahtı (Lepanto, Naupakhton) (M)
45. Filibe (Philippopoli) (M)
46. Rodos (Rhodes) (M)
47. Siroz (Serez, Serrai) (M)
48. Dirama (Philippi) (M)
49. Zihne (Zichna)
50. Midillü (Mytilene) (M)
51. Yanya (Ioannina) (M)
52. Dimetoka (Didymoteichon) (M)
53. Alaşehir (Philadelphia) (M)
54. Menlik (Melenikon) (M)
55. Badracık (Neo-Patras) (M)
56. İstifa (Tsivon) (M)
57. Inoz (Enez, Ainos) (M)
58. Melo (Melos island) (AB)
59. Nakşa (Naxos)
60. Misivri (Mesambria) (M)
61. Vidin (M)
62. Ağriboz (Euboea) (M)
63. Sofya (M)
64. Vize (Byzon) (M)
65. Ahyolu (Anchialus) (M)
66. Varna (M)
67. Ibrail (Braila) (M)
68. Gömülcine (Komotene) (M)
69. Silivri (Silivria) (M)
70. Süzebolu (Sozopoli) (M)
71. İskete (Xanthi) (M)
72. Golos (Volo) (M)
73. Kefe (Caffa) (M)
74. Gözleve (Kozlov, Jevpatorya)
75. Sakız (Chios) (AB)
76. Limni (Lemnos) (M)
77. Imroz (Imbros) (M)
78. Hâslar (Villages between Istanbul and Bosphorus formerly Derkos or Terkos) (M)
79. Kördos (Kortos, Corinthos) (M)

80. Benefşe (Monemvasia) (M)
81. Ravendos (Reontos) (B)
82. Balya-Badra (Palaia Patra) (M)
83. Moston (Mothonis?) (B)
84. Mezistre (Misithra, Mistra) (M)
85. Arkadya (Christianoupolis) (M)
86. Anabolu (Nauplion) (M)
87. Marmara (Marmora island)
88. Ilıca
89. Santorin (Santorin island) (AB)
90. Mesta
91. Alosonya (Elassonia) (AB)
92. Sisam (Samos) (AB)
93. Istanköy (Karpathos) (AB)
94. Fenar (Phanarion) (AB)
95. Gümüşhane (Argyropolis)
96. Mezid Adası
97. Kesendire (Kassandra) (AB)
98. Değirmen Adası
99. Sifnos (Sifnos) (AB)
100. Andre (Andros) (AB)
101. Egin (Aigina) (AB)
102. Bogonyani (Pogonianis) (AB)
103. Kirine
104. Ayamavra (Levkas) (AB)
105. Ala-Kilisa (Phersalon?) (AB)
106. Kefalya (Kephallenia) (AB)
107. Istendin (Tinos) (AB)
108. Kördos (Corinthos) (B)
109. Eflak (Wallachia) (M)
110. Bogdan (Moldavia) (M)
111. Venice (M); in 1782 the patriarchate notified the Ottoman Porte that since 1557 the Orthodox Greeks resident in Venice had been electing a metropolitan for themselves with the approval of the patriarch.[18]

18 See the document published by A. Refik (cited n. 15), pp. 227-29.

The list of the metropolitan sees under Ottoman rule as established by T. Papadopoullos on the basis of seven *Notitiae Episcopatum* and the Synodal *Acta* can be checked against the above lists drawn up on the basis of Ottoman documents. The amount of the *pīş-keş* to be paid by each metropolitan or bishop can be an indication of the importance of the see and the size of the Orthodox population in the area under its jurisdiction. Among the *Notitiae* the one drawn up by the Patriarch Serapheim in 1759 is chronologically the closest to our document. The next *Notitiae* known is dated 1855, while the *Peskopos Muḳāṭa'a* registers contain lists of the same character for the whole period after 1641. The hierarchical structure of the Greek church during the Ottoman period, T. Papadopoullos said, exhibited essentially the same structure as it had in Byzantine times. Under the immediate jurisdiction of the Ecumenical Patriarch we find metropolitans at the head of diocesses, which constitute the essential subdivisions of the hierarchy. Under the immediate jurisdiction of a metropolitan is placed a bishop, *peskopos.* Those metropolitans under the direct jurisdiction of the Ecumenical Patriarchate who have no bishops under their own dominion, are considered higher in rank than a bishop but lower than an independent metropolitan. Otherwise, the metropolitans are all of equal importance, distinguished only according to an established order of precedence. As our document makes clear, the respective boundaries of metropolitan dioceses and espiscopal sees are determined by Ottoman administrative divisions. T. Papadopoullos stressed the fact that a metropolitan diocese or an episcopal see owes its historical continuity to the continuing existence of the Orthodox population in that particular area. They flourish, decline and disappear as the Orthodox population increases, decreases and disappears. Thus the actual geographic distribution of the Orthodox population is reflected in the *Notitiae Episcopatum.* The Ottoman *cizye* registers on the other hand furnish us with complete lists of the Orthodox population subject to the poll tax in Istanbul and the provinces; these lists can be used as reliable sources for actual population estimates.[19]

19 See note 13.

Peşkeş or Pīş-keş

Peşkeş or originally *pīş-keş* meaning gift, present in general usage, was actually "an offering made by an inferior as a mark of respect and dependence" (Redhouse). In the Ottoman Empire, *pīş-keş* was given at the moment of a governor's acceptance of his diploma of appointment. The rate for each rank was fixed by regulation in the sixteenth century. For example, the governor of Rumeli gave to the *mīr-'alem* at the Porte, ten thousand *akça.* Originally, the exchange of presents was a symbolic act, used to establish a bond of dependency between lord and retainer in the Turco-Mongol world. The exchange of presents was, from the beginning of Ottoman history, a persistent custom practiced by the Ottomans (as an early example see Sultan Orhan's *temlīknāme* in *Arşiv Klavuzu,* Istanbul, 1938, document no. 1). Officials of lesser grades paid a fixed amount of money called *resm-i berāt* accompanied by some costly presents from the sultan, such as a caftan, a horse with gilded saddle, or a sword. These presents symbolizing the authority delegated by the ruler in Islamic states were generally called *al-'alāmāt-i mulūkiyya,* (see *al-* 'Umarī, *Al-ta'rif,* Cairo 1312/1894, pp. 209-211). It should be noted that *pīş-keş* cannot be interpreted as bribery from the Ottoman viewpoint. The money paid by high clergy at the moment of receiving their *berāt* from the Porte was also called *berāt pīşkeşi, pīş-keş* paid for *berāt.*[20]

According to a tradition perpetuated in the circles of the patriarchate, Gennadios, at the time of his appointment as the first patriarch under the Ottomans, was granted one thousand gold pieces for his maintenance.[21] The contemporary historian Kritovoulos confirms that "the sultan loaded him with noble and costly gifts."[22] It is known from documentary evidence that before the Conqueror's time metropolitans and bishops were assigned

20 See Kabrda (cited n. 5), p. 59.

21 Pantazapoulos (cited n. 2), p. 25.

22 *History of Mehmed the Conqueror,* trans. C. T. Riggs. Princeton, 1954, p. 94.

regular income from the Ottoman treasury in the form of *timar*.[23] Hence, these metropolitans, as well as Gennadios, must have given customary *pīş-keş* to the sultan. What was, perhaps, striking for the contemporaries was the extravagant increase of the amount of *pīş-keş,* first to 2,000 gold pieces, and then to 2,500 by the rival metropolitans to obtain the patriarchate.[24] As a result of the competition for the patriarchal throne in the Greek church[25] and the growing tendency of the Ottomans to farm out public offices to the highest bidders, *pīş-keş* was over time substantially increased and considered a source of revenue for the state.

23 See *Sûret-i defter-i sancak-i Arvanid*, ed. H. İnalcık, Ankara, 1954, nos. 100, 122, 148, 162, 186, 200, 270, 299.

24 See M. Crusius, *Turcograecia libri octo.* Basel, 1584 cited by S. Runciman, *The Great Church in Captivity*, Cambridge, 1968, pp. 193-94; Pantazapoulos (cited n. 2), p. 25.

25 See for the situation in later times T. Papadopoullos. *Studies and Documents Relating to the History of the Greek Church and People under Turkish Domination*, Brussels, 1952, pp. 132-35; O. Kersten, *Das Patriarchal von Konstantinopel im ausgehenden 16. Jahrhundert*, Wien, 1970, pp. 82-83.

VI

SEPHARDIC JEWS IN THE OTTOMAN EMPIRE*

The scholarly papers read by the distinguished specialists in this historic meeting commemorate the quincentennary of the immigration of the Sephardic Jews in the Ottoman empire and celebrate Turkish-Jewish cooperation and friendship for indeed hundreds years. They have discussed all aspects of Jewish life in the Ottoman empire. In view of the richness and great variety of the sources available, the incomparable Ottoman archival collections, the Rabbinic literature, the archives of the Alliance Israélite Universelle, and also diaries, travelers reports and epigraphy, this conference actually but signals a starting point of a vast program of research on the Jews in the Ottoman empire. Through those papers drawn from the sources, we now have a clearer idea of the size and significance of the unexplored source material dealing with the six centuries of Jewish life under the Ottomans. Speaking only of the Ottoman archival materials, records clearly indicate that Jews served in public life as courtiers, physicians and advisers to sultans. They also performed as tax-farmers, financial agents and government experts. Moreover, in international and interregional trade and in the urban trades and industries, Jews were involved in all aspects of life in the Ottoman empire, playing a role of importance far beyond the size of the community. One finds Jewish activities in every kind of Ottoman archival documentation: in the *Mühimmes*, or proceedings of the imperial council, in the registers and papers of the finance department,

* Paper read at the *Conference on Sephardic Jews*, Istanbul, June 4, 1992.

in the *cadi* court records which deal with legal and commercial transactions and administration. Only a fraction of these vast collections has so far seen the light of day. Here the pioneering work of Bernard Lewis, Uriel Heyd and Amnon Cohen and other distinguished scholars should be recalled.

The unusual sympathy, friendliness and protection shown toward the Jews by the Ottoman Turks were not simply the outcome of the well-known Turkish hospitality and compassion for the people in distress, or of certain idyllic feelings. The major question to be answered by the historian is to explain why, in a particular period of time Ottomans showed an unusual sympathy and interest in European Jewry, which was indeed unprecedented and unparalleled in Islamic history.

The motivation behind the remarkable tolerance and good will of the Turks toward the Jews already had a long history before 1492. It is actually due to a combination of circumstances in the second half of the fifteenth century. To explain the historical conjunction which led the Ottomans to show a particular interest in the predicament of the Jews expelled from Spain, we must recall that crusading fervor that had then reached a climax in Europe with the Ottoman conquest of Constantinople and the Spanish Reconquista against the Muslims of al-Andalus. In 1492 the fall of Granada was celebrated in religious processions throughout Europe. Then, the Pope invited all the Christian nations to send their delegates to Rome to discuss a full-fledged crusade against the Ottoman empire, with the intent of using the Conqueror's son Djem Sultan, then a captive of the Vatican, as its center piece. The attempts of the Andulusian and north-African Muslims to attract the attention of the Ottoman Sultan to their imminent conquest by the crusaders already had started in 1477, when a delegation visited Mehmed the Conqueror and solicited his aid and protection. Soon after the fall of Granada in 1492, the Algerians, fearing the same fate would befall them, sought Ottoman protection, and in 1519 they sent the venerated scholar, Sayyid Abu al- Abbas, to Istanbul. As a matter of fact, the Muslims and Jews of Spain, who were living together for centuries in such a harmonious and prosperous society, had a common fate before the rising national monarchy of a united Spain. No nation is immune to the excesses of intense nationalism and religious bigotry and intolerance. Spain, then, pursuing the *reconquista* drive and struggling to achieve its territorial and national unity, was determined to take drastic measures not only against the Jews but also against Muslims. Ottomans did not make a distinction between the Andalusian Muslims and Jews. Both communities solicited Ottoman aid and protection. In other words, victims shared the same fate in Ottoman eyes and aid and relief was to be extended to the oppressed against the common enemy.

The Jewish immigration to the lands conquered by the Ottomans was a century-long movement going back to the fourteenth century. Ever since the year 1360 when the Hungarian King Louis the Great issued a decree of expulsion to Jews, European Jews had looked to the Ottoman territories as a place of sanctuary. Salo Baron states that the Jewry of Central Europe may have been aware of the favorable conditions for the Jews in Ottoman territories in the Balkans prior to 1453, although he says, this general sentiment did not occasion a Jewish exodus into the Ottoman dominions in that period. However, Ottoman sources testify that there were growing and prosperous Jewish communities in Balkan cities such as Edirne and Salonica already before the year 1453.

The Ottoman sultans, particularly after the conquest of Constantinople, came forward as the protector of the Jews. In fact, Ottoman protection of the Jews was a rational and deliberate policy on the part of the Ottomans in response to a crusading Europe wherein increasing religious intolerance and persecution was encouraged against the Jews. Mehmed the Conqueror must have been aware of the plight of the Jews in Europe for he encouraged them to take sanctuary in his own territories. This attitude corresponds to the general policies of the Sultan, who was most concerned with the settlement of Jews to improve economy in his depopulated and ruined capital.

Thus, the well-known circular of Isaac Sarfati gains credit when placed in this context. Incidentally, I believe the circular belongs to the Conqueror's time although Salo Baron is inclined to trace it back to the reign of Murad II. A refugee himself from Germany, Sarfati in his pamphlet vigorously encourages the Jews of Swabia, the Rhineland, Styria, Moravia and Hungary to immigrate to Turkey where "every man may dwell at peace under his own vine and fig- tree.... O Israel, wherefore sleepest thou? Leave your accursed land for ever." In view of the circumstances after the conquest of Constantinopole it is plausible that the Sultan himself had Sarfati send out such a circular to European Jewry.

The Conqueror wanted to bring and settle as many Jews as possible in his new capital city. The Venetians were eliminated and the trade depots of other Latin nations in the port area completely destroyed. These trading nations had formerly been in control of, and responsible for, the economic prosperity of the Byzantine capital. The Conqueror's first and principal concern was to repopulate and restore the economic activities in the city. The well-to-do people in Bursa and other Anatolian cities did not respond to the Conqueror's order to come and settle in Istanbul. Also, as the Ottoman census of 1455 reveal many Turkish settlers had soon returned to their original home in Anatolia and Rumili. For the reconstruction of the city the Conqueror realized that he needed first people with mercantile skills and capital. The same census shows that many abandoned houses and districts were now occupied by Jewish settlers from Balkan and Anatolian towns. Driven from their homes under the Ottoman *sürgün* system, many of Jews were settled in the port area from Çifut-Kapı or the gate of the Jews to the Zindan Kapı, which was the business center of the city, formerly occupied principally by the Venetians. The Sultan needed to have the Jewish businessmen and traders there to replace Venetians whose return was forbidden. However, it is interesting to add that the Conqueror demanded the Doge of Venice to let Venetian Jews return, who had fled to Venice from the Istanbul port district before and during the siege. At any rate, the Ottoman survey of 1477 records 1647 Jewish households in Istanbul but no Jews in Galata while in the census of 1455 we find a group of 44 Jewish families, many of them quite wealthy. After the census of 1477 a new census made in 1492 reveals that 380 new families joined Istanbul Jewry. The Conqueror's attitude toward the Jews indicates that he considered the Jews, even those Venetian Jews who fled during the hostilities, as trustworthy and he believed that they were indispensable for the economic development of his new imperial capital.

His successors' policy toward the Jews, the Sephardic Jews in particular, would be based on the same assumptions. We believe these are the reasons why the Ottoman bureaucracy had a particular sympathy toward Jews just before the Sephardic mass immigration into the Ottoman dominions began. Of course, along with these historical circumstances of the period, we have to take into account established rules of the Islamic *Sharī'a* pertaining to the religious minorities, the so-called *ahl al-dhimma.* In return for payment a poll-tax, the *djizya,* the Islamic state assumes the responsibility of providing the same protection for its non-Muslim subjects as for Muslims. It was a strict religious duty for a Muslim ruler to abide by this basic rule. True, under the Islamic tradition restrictions such as the obligation not to dress as Muslims, prohibition of mounting a horse, or owning a slave, practicing religious ceremonies in a way not to offend Muslims, etc., were all designed to indicate the social inferiority of non-Muslims. But ordinarily such restrictions were overlooked by the authorities. We learn this from the imperial Ottoman orders issued on occasions when popular feelings against non-Muslims exploded as a result of a defeat at the hands of the Christian powers. Wealthy Jews are described in such documents as indistinguishable from the Muslim elite with their costly caftans, richly harnassed horses and their slave attendants. In brief, Islamic Law and state accepted non-Muslim communities including the Jews as part of the larger Islamic society.

On the other hand it is a fact that Turkish state tradition practiced Islamic Law on *dhimmīs* in its broadest interpretation and even went beyond it. From the time when, in the eleventh century the Seljuk Turks took control of Islamic lands in the east, they introduced a new concept of state and law in the Islamic world. In the Turkish states down to the Ottoman empire, political power and state law jealously retained its independence in the face of the Islamic Law and *ulema.* The Ottoman sultans went so far as to issue their own, imperial law-codes. The transcendent character of public authority and law in a muslim Turkish state must actually originate from the central Asiatic *törü* or *yasa* tradition. As a kind of constitutional law, *törü* or *yasa* governed the imperial organization under a charismatic Kaghan. In the steppe empires, all those elements which provided information, skills and wealth for the empire, particularly travelling merchants, were given special attention and protection. These people filling the Kaghan's treasury, their bringing of luxury goods and information was believed to be indispensable for the ruler's power. Ottoman Sultans, like the Turco-Mongol kaghans in Central Asia, were most concerned with this function of protection which was considered something involving directly their own state interests and power.

In sum, special historical circumstances in the second half of the fifteenth century produced solidarity and cooperation between European Jewry and the Ottomans in the face of a crusading Europe. Moreover the Turkish state tradition of Central Asia favored those dependent subjects who possessed skill and capital. Finally Islam's constitutional *dhimma* law providing guarantees for religious minorities made it possible for the Jews of Europe to immigrate, settle and give rise to prosperous Jewish communities in the Ottoman empire.

As noted earlier the Conqueror resorted to forced Jewish resettlement from Balkan and Anatolian towns to Istanbul, and it soon became evident that the measure caused disruption in the economic well-being of these towns. But the opportunity now arose to settle these towns with new Jewish communities from Spain. According to a cautious estimate made by Loeb, out of a total of 165,000 Jews who emigrated from the Iberian peninsula in 1492 and after, approximately 90,000 came to settle in the Ottoman dominions. These immigrants were settled in Istanbul, Salonica, Avlona and other cities in the empire.

Once in Ottoman territory, the Sephardic Jews first formed *djemā'ats* (communities) in urban centers on the basis of their towns of origin before they were, over time, integrated into the already existing Jewish quarters or formed separate quarters around a synagogue of their own. The Ottoman government let them maintain their traditional community organization and autonomy in communal affairs. Under the guarantees provided by Islamic Law and Ottoman state *ḳānūns,* as well as a vigilant central bureaucracy ready to act against frauds and oppression against minorities, the Jewish communities prospered and had a freedom and protection enjoyed by other sections of the city. The situation is well recorded by the vast Jewish responsa literature and travelers' accounts as discussed by the panelists in this conference.

To demonstrate the Ottoman government's sensitiveness and energetic action for the protection of the Jews against the false accusations against them made by the scum of the urban populance, let me illustrate with the following case. One of the most hideous forms of anti-semitism was libelous accusation of ritual murder, the allegation that Jews would kill a person and have ritual bread baked with his blood. This libel was widespread in Christian Europe. Amnon Cohen[1] finds a relationship between the spread of such accusations against the Jews in the Ottoman empire and the growing influence and presence of Europeans there in the nineteenth century. In the previous centuries there were sporadic cases, and the Ottoman government took a decisive attitude against such false accusations. A circular order of the sultan to the judges in Arab lands said: "There were some vicious people in the territories under their jurisdiction, who have perpetrated various kinds of injustice and oppression against the Jewish community. They fabricated lies, saying, 'you have killed a man and you have had bread baked with

1 His article in *Journal of Turkish Studies* (Harvard), X (1986).

his blood.' In order to extort money they said (to the Jews): 'you have cursed our religion and our tongue.' There is no permission to interfere with [them] in contradiction to the true Sharia and the old Ottoman law.... So I have ordered that you should not hear their claims altogether. You should not allow [others] to commit injustice and oppression against the Jewish community with such pretexts. If there is anyone of the vicious people who openly follow falsification and deceit like this under your government ... you should not hide [his identity] but you should write down the details of their deceits that they committed and let it be known in my exalted Porte."

Obviously, Amnon Cohen adds, in these early centuries certain local Christian traditions filtered into the Muslim population in urban centers. The empire's administrators were alert against such criminal acts against the Jews.

As Ottomans anticipated Jewish contribution to the Ottoman economy, finances and urban development proved to be most substantial as several speakers in this conference have discussed. Here to emphasize this unusual contribution to the Ottoman civilization I would like to add some particular cases.

Against the Venetian and Genoese domination and exploitation in the Levant Ottomans showed a conscious and systematic policy of favor and protection toward the native Ottoman minorities including Greeks, Armenians and Jews. Having become a part of an important segment in Ottoman society, the Jewish community became particularly active in tax-farming as well as in interregional and international trade from the earliest times. Here skipping over the spectacular improvement the Sephardic Jews brought in the empire's industries, for example the flourishing woolen industries in Salonica, Safad and Istanbul, I shall concentrate on tax farming and trade.

In the fifteenth and sixteenth centuries, Ottoman Jews, Turks and Greeks were competing for tax-farm contracts, and Jews were particularly active in the business. Tax-farming, extensively applied in the Ottoman empire even at this early stage, was a big business for those who had accumulated cash capital. Short of regular cash resources for its immediate needs, and lacking the expensive and complex tax collection system of a modern state, the Ottoman government encouraged commercial capitalists to take an interest in tax farming- Registers of tax-farming, the so-called *muqāṭaʿa defterleri* of the second half of the fifteenth century, contain many names of Turkish, Greek, and Jewish "capitalists" serving as tax-farmers.

We find Jews undertaking all kinds of tax farms everywhere in the empire particularly in the big cities, important sea ports, and towns of Rumelia and Anatolia. At the auctions of tax-farms, there was keen competition between bidders. For example, in 1483 a Jew, Sabbetay, son of Avraham, offered 1,200,000 akçe and outbid all competitors on the tax-farm of the saltworks of Thrace (Hrishna, Gömüldjine, and Karasu).

In October 1477, offering an increase of 400,000 akçe, a partnership of the Jew Altina, the Turk Seyyidi Küçük of Edirne, and an Italian by the name of Nikiroz undertook the collection of the customs dues of the ports in the Istanbul customs zone for 20,400,000 akçe (45 akçe was worth one gold ducat at this time). They thus outbid the previous offer made by a partnership of the Greek Palaeologos of Istanbul, Palaeologus Kassandros, and Lefteri Galyanos of Trebizond. Anyone who engaged in tax-farming had to find at least two sureties with assets large enough to meet the debt in case of default. In our records, the sureties designated by the Jewish bidders are all from the Jewish community, but as seen in the above example, Jews also joined in partnerships with Muslim Turks. In this connection one should not forget that the latter group included many Jewish, Greek, or Italian converts.

In view of its incomparable importance for state finances, the customs house of Istanbul bestowed a very influential position upon its tax farmer, and during the fifteenth and sixteenth centuries this position was quite often held by a Jew. Jews also farmed other *muqāṭaʿāt* of Istanbul. Besides rich merchants and money changers, there were also enterprising Jews who put together small savings or inherited money and such people became quite prominent in taxfarming and were found engaged in the business for a long time. We may call them professional tax-farmers. They were assisted by Jewish scribes and financial experts.[2]

In the second half of the sixteenth century, Jewish bankers and tax farmers gained a predominant place in Ottoman finances and long distance trade.

The most spectacular case of Jewish enterprise in the Ottoman empire is that of the Marrano-Jewish family of Mendès in the mid-sixteenth century. The Marrano Jews, victims of the inquisition in Catholic countries, decided to immigrate to the Ottoman empire. Controlling the spice trade in Europe, the Marrano banking house of Mendés moved to and settled in Istanbul in 1552. Under the protection of Sultan Suleyman the Magnificent, the head of the family, Doña Gracia Mendès, arrived in Istanbul. Her relative and partner, Don Joseph Nasi, became the most prominent member of the family. Initially his spectacular rise was due to his financial services to Prince Selim who had made him one of his intimates, a *müteferriḳa* (distinguished attendant) in his provincial palace. When, in 1566, Selim acceded to the Ottoman throne he appointed Don Joseph "the Duke of Naxos" (Nakşa Dukası), which comprised the Cyclade archipelago, a group of islands producing rare wines for export. This appointment must be related to Joseph being the tax-farmer of wine exports to the northern Black Sea countries, and to Poland in particular. The tax-farm from the Dukedom was fixed in the amount of 6000 gold pieces. Joseph's control of this trade was a loss for Venice. Previously, the Duke of Naxos had been a Venetian who did not give up his claim and harassed Don Joseph afterwards. Customs dues on the wine exported from the Aegean and from Venetian Crete to Poland came under Joseph's actual monopoly of the wine trade, since under the Ottoman tax-farm system the government controlled the traffic to enable the tax-farmer to prevent smuggling and to realize the maximum amount of revenue. Joseph

2 H. İnalcık, "Jews in Ottoman Economy and Finances," C. E. Bosworth *el alia*, eds. *The Islamic World*, Princeton 1988, 513-550.

Nasi's annual revenue from the monopoly on the export of Cretan wine was estimated at 15,000 ducats a year. Around 1575 it is reported that one thousand casks of wine were exported from Crete alone. Don Joseph's influence on Ottoman policy against Venice regarding Cyprus, which was another center of wine production comes to us in the form of a tale. In fact, considered an expert in European affairs, Don Joseph became one of the most trusted counselors to the Sultan at this time. Evidently Nasi was one of the supporters of vizir Lala Mustafa's plan to conquer Cyprus in opposition to Grand vizir, Sokollu Mehmed, who was against the plan and wanted to continue the war in the north against Muscovy. The plan to colonize the conquered island with Jewish settlers is also worth noting in this context. The conquest of Cyprus leading to the Christian Holy League in the Mediterranean resulted in the Ottoman disaster of Lepanto in 1571. However, Don Joseph continued to keep the sultan's favor.

Later, in 1588, Alvaro Mendès, like Joseph Nasi, an arch-enemy of King Phillip II of Spain, came to settle in Istanbul bringing with him reportedly 850 thousand gold ducats, and he received the same favors once enjoyed by Don Joseph. Esther Kyra, a Jewish favorite of the ladies in the palace and a liaison between them and Jewish interests outside, became involved in tax farming and trade undertakings and amassed a large fortune during her long connection with the Seraglio. She had a tragic end at the hands of the *Sipahis* who hated her for her monopoly of the poll-tax farm for her Jewish relatives. Her fortune at the time of her death was reported to have amounted to fifty million akçe or 300 thousand gold ducats.

It is suggested that the Marrano-Jews introduced into the Ottoman Empire the techniques of European capitalism, banking and even the mercantilist concept of state economy.

International trade and banking operations were inseparable and the family operations were carried on through a network of agents in the principal centers of Europe. Thus, the Mendès family controlled a large portion of the commerce between the Empire and

Europe which consisted of the exchange largely of European woolens for wheat, pepper and raw wool. Also investments by merchants in the treasury's tax-farms seem to have been quite high. In 1555 when Pope Paul IV confiscated the possessions of Jews in the Papal territory, the sultan protested saying that many Jews of Salonica and Istanbul had gone bankrupt and were unable to meet their payment obligations to the treasury to the sum of 400 thousand gold ducats. Under the management of Doña Gracia (d. 1568 or 1569), a Jewish bank or *dolab* appears to have involved Ottoman finances and capital investments within European markets. Gracia's son-in-law, Don Joseph, became a big creditor for the kings in Europe. His large loans to the king of Poland procured for him various commercial concessions. Under the sultan's protection, he obtained a monopoly on beeswax exported from Poland. Also in 1555, when the French King Henri II was pressed for money, Don Joseph floated a loan in France in which the interest increased from 12 to 16 percent. Little wonder that many Turks invested money in the loan through Don Joseph.

Jews played a crucial role in the relations of the Ottoman empire with Western Europe. In the beginnings of Ottoman-Dutch relations, for example, Joseph Nasi played a decisive role. Since he was active in the Antwerp banking house of Mendès before he came to settle in Istanbul the Prince of Orange, William I, sent a secret envoy to Nasi seeking Ottoman support in the Dutch revolt against Philip II. There were even talks of a Dutch alliance with the Ottomans. In a letter to the "Lutherans" in Flanders and other Spanish provinces, the Sultan promised to send troops to their aid at a time to be determined by them.[3] Indeed, against the Catholic front in the Mediterranean, the Ottomans took the initiative in establishing an agreement with this Protestant country which had a powerful navy.

A little known case of how the Jewish spirit of enterprise became responsible for the economic development of the empire is that of the Jews of the Adriatic. Under the protection of the Ot-

3 Ferīdūn, *Munsheāt' us-Selāṭin*, vol. II, Istanbul 1275/1859, 542-543.

toman government, Jews promoted their trade and legal status in Venice throughout the sixteenth century. The Ottoman government protected the Sephardic Jews settled in Adriatic ports during the period of 1492-1520, and these Jews emerged as the most active partners and rivals of Dubrovnik in regional trade. Avlona was one of the important sea ports where the Ottomans settled Jews expelled from Spain in 1492, from Portugal in 1497 and from Italy, 1510-1511. They constituted one third of the population of Avlona, with a community of 527 households by 1520. The Jews appear to have had a dominant position over the Christians and had a great freedom of action as the court records demonstrate.[4]

The Jews of Avlona were principally engaged in long distance trade. They dominated the city's trade with Venice as attested by Venetian insurance documents. In the register of insurance covering the years 1592-1609, there were 16 Jews of Avlona resident in Venice.

Avlona's role in Adriatic trade declined in favor of new ports closer to Venice. Many Jews moved to Dubrovnik during the Ottoman-Venetian war of 1570-73 when woolen cloth imports from Venice shifted to this neutral port. Meanwhile, the Ottomans deported and settled a great number of Sephardic Jews to Nova (Herzegnovi) when it was reconquered in 1570. Many Ottoman Jews, chiefly those engaged in the cloth trade, settled in Venice or moved to Split in the last decades of the sixteenth century. Clearly there had been large scale Jewish emigration from Avlona to northern Adriatic ports. In Avlona the Ottoman tax registers of 1583 reveal 212 Jews but only 50 in 1597.

In the wake of the Ottoman-Venetian peace of 1573, an enterprising Jewish merchant, Daniel Rodriguez, proposed to develop Split into a free port by improving its facilities and abolishing or reducing customs dues. Venice was hesitant; then Ottoman Jews approached the council of Dubrovnik and obtained a privileged tariff for a time. In the end, with the support of Ottoman Jews residing

4 See *An Economic and Social History of the Ottoman Empire*, Cambridge 1994, 213-215.

in Venice and the active involvement of the pasha of Bosnia, the Venetian Senate finally decided to go ahead with Rodriguez's plan. On June 20, 1590, it was decided that Split would become a free port, that customs dues on the imports from Ottoman dominions through Split to Venice would be reduced by half, and that dues on the export of soap, rice and some other goods would be totally abolished. Ottoman Jews who arrived in Venice would not be subject to any resident tax and could settle in the old Jewish quarter. Rodriguez's plan can be seen as part of the Jewish attempt to organize an international trading complex under Ottoman auspices. At Split Venetian-Ottoman trade based mainly on the export of wax, moroccos, timber, silk, mohair and hides from the Ottoman lands rapidly flourished. From 1590 onward Split superseded Dubrovnik and Avlona in Ottoman trade with Venice and assumed a very important role in the overall Venetian commerce.

VII

THE TURKISH IMPACT ON THE DEVELOPMENT OF MODERN EUROPE

SINCE A Euro-centric view of history in the West began to be replaced by a true world history concept, the history of the Ottoman Empire, which lasted in a very important part of the world for over five centuries, is attracting new interest. A number of contributions recently made in Europe and America on the problem of the place of the Ottoman Empire in European history can be considered as a sign of this growing interest. Although some of these new studies were still not free of certain biases, mainly because they did not make use of the Ottoman evidence, they, however, explored new ideas and had new orientations.

Under the light of these publications we are now able, for instance, to speak of how the Ottoman state became an important factor in the balance of power of European politics. Even during the first stage of the Italian wars from 1494 to 1525 the Ottoman state was an important part in Italian diplomacy. Fr. Babinger and J. Kissling in their studies based on the Italian archival material, and S. Fisher, Pfefferman, Schwoebel, D. Vaughan in their more general treatment of the subject showed how the Italian courts maintained diplomatic relations with the Ottoman Sultan. It is true that the Western archives do not yield much on the subject, for political and military matters were concealed in such negotiations and never put in writing. But sometimes even if an Ottoman military intervention was not really desired the rumor of a secret alliance was used as an intimidation. Hard-pressed Italian states used as a last measure the threat of calling on the Ottomans. In 1525, the French followed actually this Italian policy when their king was made prisoner by the Emperor. The Ottomans welcomed this opportunity to invade Hungary in 1526 and open a sea front against the Emperor in the Mediterranean in 1532 just as in the past they had exploited the situation in Italy against Venice. From 1480 onwards the Ottomans always thought of an invasion of Italy. Two factors made them hesitate for a decisive move, the possibility of resistance of a Europe united under the Pope and Emperor, and their own naval weakness to open an overseas front. In 1537, however, Süleyman thought it was the time for such a move. As early as 1531 the Venetian ambassador was writing to the doge, "Sultan Süleyman says, 'To Rome, to Rome,' and he detests the Emperor for his title of *Kayser* (Caesar), he, the Turk, causing himself to be called Caesar." Ottoman attempts to capture from the Venetians strongholds along the Adriatic coast and the isle of Corfu in 1537 and 1538 were in fact a preparation for the invasion of Italy. France was then an ally of the Ottomans. They were reinforced by the French navy at the siege of Corfu. But the King and Emperor saw the great danger for the whole of Christendom in Europe. In July 1538, Francis made peace with Charles V at Aigues-Mortes and what is more he promised to take part in a crusade against the Ottomans. Two months later Barbarossa, Grand Admiral of the Sultan, succeeded in routing a powerful crusading fleet at Prevesa. Then, this victory became useless without French alliance.

What I am trying to emphasize is that the Ottomans became an active part in the second stage of the Italian wars and there was a moment when the Western contenders for Italy saw that the balance of power was lost in favor of the Sultan. It must be added that the Ottomans fully appreciated the value of the French alliance and also supported the King financially. In 1533, the Sultan sent Francis a sum of one hundred thousand gold pieces to enable him to form a coalition with England and German princes against Charles V. Two years later the French King asked the Sultan to send him a subsidy of one million ducats. Later on, in 1555 the French King Henri II, pressed for money, floated a loan in France with the interest increased from 12 to 16 percent, and at this time many Turks, pashas among them, found it profitable to invest in this loan. The King borrowed 150,000 scudos from Joseph Nasi, Jewish tax farmer of the Sultan. On his part the French king appreciated the Ottoman Alliance as the principal power to check the Habsburg supremacy in Europe. In 1532 Francis I admitted to the Venetian ambassador that he saw in the Ottoman Empire the only force guaranteeing the continued existence of the states of Europe against Charles V.

In brief one can say that the Ottoman Empire played an important role in the balance of power in Europe in the sixteenth century and consequently in the rise of the nation-states in the West. This role continued with the Ottoman support and encouragement to the English and Dutch in the period after 1580 when these nations proved to be the champions of European resistance to the Habsburg attempts at supremacy.

In the sixteenth and seventeenth centuries support for Protestants and Calvinists was one of the fundamental principles of Ottoman policy in Europe. Already in 1552 Süleyman tried to incite the Protestant princes in Germany against the Pope and Emperor. He said in his letter to them that he himself was about to embark on a campaign and promised on oath that they would not be harmed when he entered Germany. Melanchton was directly in touch with the Patriarch of Istanbul, who was in effect an official of the Sultan. Later on, in a letter to Lutheran princes in the Low Countries and in other lands subject to Spain, the Sultan offered military help and saw them as standing close to him, since they did not worship idols, believed in one God and fought against the Pope and Emperor. Under Ottoman rule, Calvinism was propagated freely in Hungary and Transylvania, which became a Calvinist and Unitarian stronghold in the seventeenth century. It is convincingly argued that Ottoman pressure on the Habsburgs was an important factor in the extension of Protestantism in Europe.

Further, it should be pointed out that the Ottomans contributed to the rise of Muscovy by supporting, as a great power in the politics of Eastern Europe, the Muscovy-Crimean alliance against the Jagellons and the Golden Horde, which then tried to establish or restore their hegemony in the region. When the Ottomans realized the danger for their Black Sea and Caucasian interests in the Muscovite supremacy and expansion in the middle of the sixteenth century it was too late.

Now, I would like to deal in a more detailed way with the economic relations of the Ottoman Empire with Europe.

Speaking of the Ottoman economy one can certainly not ignore the attitude of the Ottoman ruling class towards the productive classes and the problem of its economic policy in general.

At the outset, it must be emphasized that the Ottoman state was not a nomadic empire, the models of which could be found in the Euro-Asian steppes. It was a typical Middle East empire with all its age-old administrative principles and institutions. It was concerned primarily with the protection of the settled populations under its rule and promotion of their agricultural and commercial interests. It should be added that this policy was not based on purely economic reasoning but mainly on the financial ends of the state. Even if in the thirteenth century nomadic elements in the Ottoman frontier society played a certain role, the Ottoman state had soon become a typical Islamic sultanate with the basic structure of a Middle East state. Its legislation and actions leave no room for doubt on this point. We know, for instance, that the longest internal struggle the Ottoman state had to make in the fifteenth and sixteenth centuries stemmed from the basic fact that it endeavoured in the interests of the settled population to take under control the semi-nomads of the *Uzun-Yayla* in Inner Anatolia and of the Taurus range from the Euphrates to Western Anatolia.

The economic system of the Ottoman Empire and its basic economic principles derived from a traditional view of state and society which had prevailed since antiquity in the empires of the Middle East. These principles, since they determined the attitude and policy of the administrators, were of considerable practical importance.

In the Muslim state, as in earlier states in the Middle East, all classes of society and all sources of wealth were regarded as being obliged to preserve and promote the power of the ruler. Hence all political and social institutions and all types of economic activity were regulated by the state in order to achieve this goal. The populace was regarded as forming two main groups -those who represented the ruler's authority (the administrators, the troops, the men of religion), and the ordinary subjects, *re'āyā*. The former were not concerned with production and paid no taxes, while the latter were the producers and tax-payers. A main concern of the state was to ensure that each individual remained in his own class; this was regarded as the basic requisite for politico-social order and harmony.

To increase revenue from taxation, the governments of Near East States appreciated the necessity of developing economic activity and promoting the greatest possible increase in production from all classes of the *re'āyā*. It was recommended that cultivated land should be increased by the digging of canals and that trade between different regions should be promoted by the construction of roads, bridges and caravanserais, and by ensuring the safety of travelers.

Within the class of the producers, the tillers of the soil and craftsmen were subject to a code of regulations distinct from that of merchants; the methods of production and profit margins of the former were under strict state control, since, in this view of society, they were the classes who produced the essential necessities of life and whose labors therefore were most intimately connected with the preservation of social and political order. That a peasant or a craftsman should freely change the methods of production was not countenanced; his activities were permitted only within the limits of the ordinances laid down by the state. In Near East society, it was only the merchants who enjoyed conditions allowing them to become capitalists. "Merchant," *tüjjar,* in this context, means the big businessmen who engaged in interregional trade or in the sale of goods imported from afar. Craftsmen who in the cities sold goods manufactured by themselves and trades-people who sold these goods secondhand fell outside the category of "merchant." The merchant class was not subject to the regulations of the *hisba*, that is, rules of the religious law to ensure fair deal in the market.

In an Ottoman Mirror for Princes, Sinan Pasha's *Ma'ārifnāme* written in the second half on the fifteenth century, the ruler is advised:

> Look with favor on the merchants in the land; always care for them; let no one harass them; let no one order them about, for through their trading the land becomes prosperous, and by their wares cheapness abounds in the world; through them the excellent fame of the Sultan is carried to surrounding lands, and by them the wealth within the land is increased.

Going through the state papers issued by the Ottoman Chancery one is struck by the fact that the administration was always most concerned in applying the principles summarized above.

The Ottoman government's concern for promoting commerce and protecting the interests of the merchant class found its expression in various ways.

It was mainly with the purpose of encouraging trade that the Sultans granted capitulations to the foreigners. It should be emphasized that a capitulation had never been considered as a contractual bilateral document and it maintained its character of a grant of concession by the Sultans until the eighteenth century when they had to give the same privileges to the Habsburgs and Russia. Before this actual change the Sultan retained the authority to decide unilaterally when the pledge of friendship on the opposite side was broken and the capitulation rendered void.

Once its nature as a concession granted by the Sultan is established a capitulation was, however, granted with certain political, financial and economic expectations. The determining factors were usually the opportunities of acquiring a political ally within Christendom, of obtaining scarce goods such as woolen cloth, tin, steel and paper, and especially bullion and increasing customs revenues, the principal source of hard cash for the imperial treasury.

The Ottoman Empire was not self-sufficient economically as it is sometimes claimed. It was vitally important for its economy and finances to import western silver. Its import was encouraged by tax exemption and measures were taken to hinder its flow to the Eastern countries where gold was cheaper. The Europeans knew well that the Ottomans were dependent on their commerce in the Levant and when they had to bargain for a special privilege in the capitulations their chief weapon was to use the threat that they were going to boycott the Ottoman ports.

A new period in the economic history of the Ottoman Empire started with the annexation of the Arab countries between 1516 and 1550 which actually gave it the control of the trade routes between the Mediterranean and Indian Ocean. It is now commonplace knowledge that the Near East continued to receive spices directly from India and Southeast Asia throughout the sixteenth century. According to the Ottoman records, in 1562 customs levied on spices transported from Mecca to Damascus alone amounted to 110 thousand gold ducats. What is interesting to note is that most of the spices imported there went to Bursa and Istanbul to be shipped further north. To give an interesting example, in 1547 we find a Hungarian merchant in Bursa selling kersey and buying a great quantity of spices.

In this period the newly rising nation-states of the West, France, England and the Netherlands, became most anxious to get trade privileges in the Ottoman Empire. The belief was that the Levant was, as in the past, the most promising field for economic growth. It was not solely on religious grounds that the Marrano family of Mendes, then controlling the spice trade in Europe, came to settle in the Ottoman capital in the 1550s.

The Ottomans had always favoured the rival nations, first the Genoese, then the Ragusans and Florentines against the Venetian dominance in the Levant trade in the fifteenth century.

As to the Western nations, the French made their first progress in Syria and Egypt after Selim's renewal of the Mamluk capitulations in 1517. But they really began to replace the Venetians in the Levant trade only after the Ottoman-Venetian war in 1570-73. Incidentally, the so-called French capitulations of 1536 had never been concluded. The first official Ottoman capitulation to the French is dated 1569. The other Western nations were then to sail and trade under the French flag. At the beginning of the seventeenth century, the volume of French trade in the Levant rose to thirty million French livres, making up one half of France's total trade at that time. Later on, when the English and Dutch proved to be even stronger rivals of the Habsburg power than the French, the Ottomans did not hesitate to favor these nations too by granting them capitulations, to the English in 1580, and the Dutch in 1612. Except during the civil war between 1642 and 1660, the English had the lead in the Levant trade in the seventeenth century. According to a contemporary source, the Levant market for the English cloth which was the main article for export, expanded by one-third and was one-fourth of all English manufactures exported to the Levant. As W. Sombart put it, without recognizing the significance of the Levant trade for Western economic expansion it is difficult to comprehend the rise of Western capitalism.

The capitulatory privileges were gradually extended so much that Paul Masson and R. Mantran, two French specialists on the Levant trade, could unanimously assert that in the seventeenth century there was no other state in the world practicing a more liberal policy than the Ottoman empire towards foreign merchants.

The Ottomans had then no idea of the balance of trade, an idea that we find for the first time in a clearly defined form only in the mercantilist England of the sixteenth century. Originated from an age-old tradition in the Middle East, the Ottoman trade policy was that the state had to be concerned above all with the volume of goods in the internal market so that people and craftsmen in the cities in particular would not suffer a shortage of necessities and raw material. Consequently, imports were always welcomed and encouraged and exports discouraged. Hence sometimes we find higher customs rates for exports and even prohibition of the export of such goods as wheat, cotton, hides and beeswax. As for silver and gold, no customs dues were levied to encourage their importation and every step was taken to discourage exportation. The Ottomans were definitely bullionists, a stage preceding true mercantilism in the West. The difference with the mercantilist nations of the West was that the Ottomans clung to the guild system as the mainstay of the state and society while Europeans saw in the export of manufactured goods a principal means of getting bullion from outside. In order to achieve a favourable balance of trade they intervened in domestic industries and trade organizations to develop them on capitalistic lines and to export more and more goods and conquer more and more overseas markets. Incidentally, one might speculate that the increasingly unfavourable balance of trade of the West in the fifteenth century pushed them perhaps in this direction and caused a mercantilistic policy to develop, since they had no important commodities other than cloths and minerals to export to the East. The capitulations were complementary to this pattern and it is noteworthy that the mercantilistic nations of the West had been concerned in the first place to found their Levant companies and obtain capitulations. Unwittingly the Ottomans became a part of a European economic system which gave rise to modern capitalism.

VIII

POLITICAL MODERNIZATION IN TURKEY

We can best describe the original features of Ottoman-Turkish traditional society by going back to the times of Süleyman I (1520-1566). In the period, immediately before the political modernization of the nineteenth century, we find only more or less degenerate forms of the original Ottoman institutions, and new social and political developments threatening the basis of those institutions. The generation of reformers confronting the period of decline after the sixteenth century avowedly sought to restore the Golden Age of Süleyman. Under the impact of the defeats in Hungary between 1683 and 1699, the Ottoman Turks first became aware of the superiority of the West; the reforms thereafter increasingly acknowledged Western influences, first in the military field and then, in the nineteenth century, in administration. The decisive modernization movement, accompanied by a basic change in the concept of state and society, began with the national revolution after the World War I.

The hesitations and delays in the Turkish modernization process were due to the fact that, until the twentieth century, Turkey was an empire comprising nations of different cultures and that the dynasty became at a certain time the only focus of common loyalty. On the other hand, the political and social superstructure of the empire was still based on the *sharia* (Turkish: *şeriat),* the unalterable religious law of Islam, and this politico-religious structure culminated in the office of the sultan-caliph.

The position of this Ottoman ruler and the developments which reduced his power and ultimately led to modernization will constitute the main theme of this essay.

The Ottoman Ruler and Ottoman Society

Tursun Beg, Ottoman statesman and historian of the late fifteenth century, stressed that harmony among men living in society was achieved only by statecraft, which kept each individual in his proper place as determined by his ability. As the instrument of social order, statecraft possessed two aspects or sanctions: the authority and power of the ruler and the divine reason or *sharia.* Insofar as the rules instituted by the ruler did not have a perpetual character, he should always be present in a human society. He should have absolute power to determine the place of each man in the social scheme. Always seeking to strengthen his position by expanding his revenues and his armies, he should serve society as a whole by consolidating public security and order. Tursun Beg's rational arguments were manifestly designed to prove that every society must have one ruler with absolute power and with the authority of issuing regulations and laws outside the religious law. The values which this ruler was to conserve were social order and security under justice. These ideas constituted the basic political philosophy of the Ottomans.

The absolute power of the Ottoman ruler found further support in the old Oriental maxim that a ruler can have no power without soldiers, no soldiers without money, no money without the well-being of his subjects, and no popular well-being without justice. Repeated in Turkish political literature from *Kutadgu Bilig* in the eleventh century to the *Gülhane* Rescript of 1839, this formula was regarded as the summation of practical statesmanship. Kâtib Çelebi in the seventeenth century particularly stressed the central position of the sultan in the state. Though absolute power was ascribed to the caliph in the Islamic community, the theorists stressed that absolute power was simply a means of implementing the religious law.

The Ottoman rulers first made this theoretical absolutism a reality by establishing a type of administration that concentrated power in their persons. They achieved this notably by eliminating all kinds of aristocracies in the conquered lands, by entrusting executive functions only to slaves trained in the court (*kuls*), and by enlisting the *'ulema* in their service. The sultan's slaves were entrusted with executive power and the *'ulema* with the administration of law, including the supervision of all legal and financial matters. Both of these branches of administration were attached to the central government but each was independent of the other. A governor had no authority to give orders to a local judge (*kadı*) appointed by the sultan. If a conflict arose between the branches, it was appealed directly to the central government. The same judges administered both the *sharia* and the subsidiary laws and regulations directly issued by the sultan. On the other hand, the *Şeyhülislam,* the highest authority in formulating opinions on points concerning the *sharia,* had no right to interfere directly in the government or in legal administration. Once, when *Şeyhülislam* Ali Cemali came over to the seat of the government to protest against a decision of sultan Selim I (1512-1520) which he thought contrary to the *sharia,* the sultan denounced him as interfering in state affairs. But in the eighteenth century it became established practice to seek the *Şeyhülislam's* opinion on every governmental matter of importance. The limitations so imposed on the government by the *sharia* and by religious authority in the period of decline made the application of reforms especially difficult. The all-embracing *sharia* became the stronghold of traditionalism in Ottoman government and society - introducing, as we may note in passing, a major difference between the Turkish and the Japanese modernization processes.

Ottoman social policy conformed closely to the traditional view that for the sake of social peace and order the state should keep each man in his appropriate social position. In the first place, Ottoman society was divided into two major classes. The first one, called *askerī,* literally the "military," included those to whom the sultan had delegated religious or executive power through an imperial diploma, namely, officers of the court and the army, civil servants, and *'ulema*. The second included the *re'āyā*, comprising all Muslim and non-Muslim subjects who paid taxes but who had no part in the government. It was a fundamental rule of the empire to exclude its subjects from the privileges of the "military." Only those among them who were actual fighters on the frontiers and those who had entered the *'ulema* class after a regular course of study in a religious seminary could obtain the sultan's diploma and thus become members of the "military" class. It was, in fact, the sultan's will alone that decided a man's status in society. In the period of decline, Koçi Beg and others asserted that a major cause of the disorganization of the empire was the abandonment of this fundamental rule in favor of letting subjects become Janissaries of fief (*tīmār*) holders.

The subjects in turn were divided into Muslims and non-Muslims, townspeople and peasants, sedentaries and nomads, each with a different status, as reflected in their tax obligations. Taxation was indeed the most important factor in determining the subject's status. Those who were granted certain tax immunities in return for public service actually constituted an intermediate group between the simple subjects and the "military," who were wholly tax- exempt. Living for the most part on state-owned lands as tenants, the peasantry was subject to special taxes and was divided into groups according to the taxes they paid, the status of each being individually recorded at regular intervals. Peasants were not allowed to leave their lands, nor could they settle in towns.

These laws reflect a rigid social organization imposed by the will of the Ottoman ruler. But in the late sixteenth century, a profound transformation took place which may be attributed ultimately to economic and military changes in Western Europe. During this period, for example, in order to resist German infantrymen, the Ottomans discarded their *tīmār* cavalry in the provinces and increased the force of Janissaries, who were by this time equipped with firearms. This neglect of the fief holders within the army was followed by the disorganization of the land and taxation system upon which their status had been based. Simultaneously, the shift of international trade routes to the Atlantic Ocean and the invasion of the markets of the Levant by American silver resulted in the disorganization of the rigid Ottoman fiscal and economic structure.

Already during this period of "decline", the sultan and his bureaucracy, who sensed immediate danger to the state from outside, adopted the idea of reform, although they thought of it as reform along traditional lines. The Japanese, at a much later date, experienced the same challenge from outside and their emperor, too, personified the idea of reform. But the Japanese reform movement found national support at least among some leading classes in the society, while in the Ottoman Empire the major ruling classes took a reactionary stance. In the Ottoman Empire reform remained a concern of the sultan and his immediate collaborators alone. *ʿulema* and a rising semi-feudal landed aristocracy in the provinces, called the *aʿyān,* resisted any innovation that might disturb their vested interests.

The Decline of the Sultan's Power: The Janissaries, the *ʿUlema,* and the Rise of the *Aʿyān*

In the capital of the empire, the politically influential groups were the military corps at the sultan's Porte, particularly the Janissaries, constituting the "military" proper, and the *ʿulema,* the learned in Islamic sciences, who were vested with authority to express and apply the commands of the *sharia.* In the provinces, too, the *ʿulema* and the Janissaries at one time possessed commanding power, but in the eighteenth century the *aʿyān,* a group of provincial magnates, came to be the most powerful class throughout the empire.

The Janissary corps constituted the original foundation of the centralist government and the principal support of the sultan's absolute power. It formed a standing army at the Porte, which was directly attached to the person of the sultan and which he could use at any time to strike at an internal or external foe. In addition, Janissary garrisons were stationed in the main strongholds in the provinces. In the large cities, they occupied the forts, which no one else, not even a governor, was allowed to enter. In the period when central authority grew weaker, these Janissaries took over the actual control of the government in such distant parts of the empire as North Africa, Baghdad, and Belgrade. In the capital, they determined who would wield control. As early as 1446, Murad II had accepted the throne only after obtaining their consent in a public meeting. In the first half of the seventeenth century, they strengthened their grip on the government. In 1628, for the first time, a former commander of the Janissary corps was appointed Grand Vizier with the support of the *Şeyhülislam,* the head of the *'ulema.* In the 1630s Koçi Beg complained that the balance established earlier between the power of the Janissaries and that of the provincial forces was gone and that the Janissaries invaded all sectors of the empire. The viziers, courtiers, and heirs to the throne all sought their aid to attain power. The Janissaries furthermore obtained for themselves additional privileges, among them that of engaging in trade. Hence many of them joined the class of small shopkeepers and were thus affected by the government's financial policy as was the rest of the Istanbul population.

Let us observe also how the *a'yān,* a powerful class of magnates, rose in the provinces. Traditionally the Ottomans granted the craftsmen and merchants in the towns a distinct and honorable status and recognized the most influential and wealthy among them as their natural leaders. Organized in so-called *ahi* unions, the craftsmen had played a major social and political role in Anatolia from the thirteenth century onward; their leaders, the *ahi*s, acquired control of the administration in many Anatolian towns. Under the centralist government of the Ottomans, they were gradually reduced to simple guild masters, but each guild continued to elect its own master, called *kāhyā,* to supervise the application of the guild's rules and to act as its representative before the authorities.

Above the guild masters were the *a'yān* (notables) and the *eşrāf* the most influential residents of the city whom the government always addressed on matters directly concerning the town population. We find these *a'yān* and *eşrāf* present even in fourteenth-century Ottoman cities. Whenever an imperial order was to be communicated to the townsmen, the local judge convoked the *a'yān, eşrāf,* guild masters, and *imāms* (district clerics) of the town, because "these were," our source adds, "the agents and representatives of the people, who did what they said to do." Among the population, *kāhyās* were elected as representatives of each district of the town and, from very early times, a town *kāhyā,* represented the whole municipality. The local *eşrāf* included the head of the descendants of the Prophet in the town, the head of the local *'ulema,* and the mufti, the local agent of the *Şeyhülislam.* Though their influence derived originally from religious services, the *eşrāf* were usually among the well-to-do citizens.

The *a'yān* were the most influential and wealthy citizens in a town except for the *eşrāf.* Most of them came from humble origins, many being minor local officials or Janissary officers who had risen by exploiting their official position.

As pointed out earlier, the tax and land-tenure system of the empire underwent a transformation during the upheavals between 1595 and 1610. The new conditions enabled the *a'yān* to become feudal lords in the provinces, replacing the fief holders in the state-owned lands as lessees or tax collectors. In the meetings of *a'yān* and *eşrāf* under the judge, the most important issue was usually the distribution among the people of the total tax assessment of the district. After the decline of the earlier *tīmār*iote army, the central government, in increasing need of money to support the enlarged Janissary army, resorted more and more to extraordinary assessments, which were allotted to the counties. These special taxes and the assessments for local expenses were farmed out to individual persons by the council of *a'yān* and *eşrāf,* who often used these responsibilities to increase their own wealth and influence. They usually added to the assessment books items for themselves, or collected additional dues for their services. They often neglected to send the assessment books to the central government for inspection, and thus levied taxes without government control. In 1705 in Manisa, a city in western Anatolia, the populace became outraged by such abuses, and invaded the judge's court where the *a'yān* and *eşrāf* were sitting.

But usually the *a'yān* managed to show themselves to the people as their protectors. They occasionally sent the sultan petitions for tax exemptions, which bore their own signatures though they were confirmed by the judge. They contended with oppressive government officials sent by the sultan. They were so influential in their areas, all in all, that the sultan's governor and judge often became simple tools in their hands. Without their cooperation, the authorities could not collect taxes, levy troops, or maintain public security.

The *a'yān* gained their wealth and power through leasing state-owned lands as well as by tax farming. The larger part of such lands ceased to be assigned to fief (*tīmār*) holders and were leased by the state to local notables, *a'yān* and *ağa*s (*a'yān* usually had the title of *ağa*s, but *ağa*s mentioned together with *a'yān* meant lesser *a'yān* in the provinces), and more than fifty percent of agricultural lands in the empire were state-owned leaseholds. Large areas of endowed land and land assigned to officials and favorites were similarly exploited. The *a'yān*'s influence on, and close cooperation with local authorities, favored them in these leasing operations. Later, in the eighteenth century, the leases were made for lifetime and priority rights to the leases were granted to the sons of lessees.

Tax farming, too, was extended after the dissolution of the old *tīmār* system near the end of the sixteenth century, and local notables benefited from their involvement in this profitable business.

In the period of decline, the sultan's governors themselves employed the *a'yān* as their local agents in financial and administrative matters under such various titles as *mütesellim, voyvoda,* and *subaşı*. Increasingly in need of new troops for its prolonged wars, furthermore, the state encouraged the *a'yān* to equip forces at their own expense under their direct command. Thus, in the eighteenth century the groundwork had been laid for the rise of a powerful semi-feudal aristocracy in the provinces of Anatolia and in the Balkans. Many of the *a'yān* families were able to maintain their position for several generations and founded local dynasties. Actual clashes sometimes occurred among rival *a'yān* seeking to extend the area of their leasehold. Some of the most powerful among them even forced the government to confer upon them the official titles of vizier or pasha, thereby consolidating their control of the provinces in which they held their estates and becoming able in time to challenge the sultan's authority. The latter tried in his weakness to play one *a'yān* against another, but often only with the result of making his ally excessively powerful. Tepedelenli Ali Pasha, actual ruler of southern Albania and northern Greece, was the most famous example of a pasha of *a'yān* origin.

The Revolutions of 1807 and 1808: The Struggle for Power among Janissaries, *'Ulema,* and *A'yān*

A brief account of the revolutions of 1807 and 1808 will illustrate the part which the Janissaries, *'ulema,* and *a'yān* played in political developments in the Ottoman Empire at the turn of the nineteenth century.

Selim III (1789-1807) has been regarded as the father of Ottoman-Turkish Westernization and as an exponent of general reform in the state. He was indeed interested in Western civilization in its various aspects. Ebu Bekir Ratib, his envoy to Vienna in 1791, brought him a detailed report not only of the military and administrative establishments but also of technology and social advances as embodied in such institutions as the postal system and hospitals. Selim gave positive instructions to his newly appointed ambassadors to Western capitals to study the administrative as well as the military institutions of those states and encouraged the staffs at the embassies to learn Western languages and observe all the things that they considered useful. At home before he began his reform he invited the foreign officers in his service, among whom was a French officer in the Ottoman army, to submit appropriate reform proposals. But Selim's main motive for reform was his determination to restore the military power of the empire and throw back the Russians, who had recently conquered the Muslim-inhabited lands north of the Black Sea and now threatened Istanbul itself. His state philosophy was not very different from that of his predecessors. He reasoned, that there could be no power without an army, no army without sufficient sources of revenue, and no revenue without justice and prosperity among his subjects. In his decrees introducing military reforms he pointed out that his ancestors had given him guidance and that the *sharia* permitted Muslims to use "the enemies' tricks to overcome them." What was new and anti-traditional in his measures was the introduction not only of European weapons but also of the sciences, training procedures and uniforms of Europe. Western scientific thought challenged traditional Muslim thought, and the European uniforms challenged traditional symbols.

He also issued reform decrees on governorship, *a'yān* leases of the domains, currency, and the status of the *'ulema,* but all these followed absolutely traditional lines.

Despite his personal conservatism, Selim III created in Ottoman society a trend toward Westernization and a sense of the necessity for rapid and progressive change. The *'ulema,* representing religiously sanctioned traditions, opposed him for the most part. The reforms found support only among some of the higher *'ulema* who either sought the favor of the sultan or considered the reforms necessary to the ultimate interests of Islam and caliphate. These supporters, too, appealed to the *sharia* to justify their position.

The true reasons for the opposition to Selim were to be found in the social situation. His efforts to create a regular army under his direct command threatened the dominant position in the state of the Janissaries, on the one hand, and of the *a'yān,* on the other. In addition, his financial measures created widespread discontent in the country and turned public opinion and the *'ulema* against him.

To finance the new army, Selim created a treasury of the "New Order" (*Nizam-ı Cedid*) and allotted to it the revenues of an important part of the domain leaseholds. To find additional resources he also raised the rates of the various dues. Since the dues paid for the imperial diplomas conferring an office, immunity, or fief were among these, he thereby alienated a number of influential people. The first reaction came from the *a'yān.* When the sultan in 1806 planned to extend the military reform to the Balkans by a transfer of "new troops" from Anatolia, the *a'yān* in the Balkans gathered together in Edirne and opposed his further advance. Selim retreated, and this marked the beginning of his fall. The conservatives at once seized power under the leadership of Hilmi Pasha, the new Grand Vizier who had once been the commander of the Janissaries, and *Şeyhülislam* Ata'ullah, a fanatic supported by the reactionaries. The opposition of the Janissaries to the New Order was understandable enough: it was no less than an instrument of their own destruction. They also rallied the populace of Istanbul, who were afflicted by the new taxes and by the inflation following Selim's debasing of the currency. The sultan's price-fixing and terrible threats against profiteers had proved useless. The abolition of Janissary pensions in the possession of non-military persons had also affected a number of people in the capital. Finally, Selim had let a group of favorites draw up his reform plans and control their application. Exploiting his ambition to restore the power of the sultanate, many of these favorites in fact set out to gain wealth and power for themselves. The responsible government officials hated them and in time turned against the sultan himself. In their eyes, the reformist sultan had merely brought back the arbitrary rule of a handful of favorites.

In brief, the population of Istanbul was, as our analyst says, split into two camps, partisans of the New Order, and its enemies. Finally, in 1807 the Janissary *yamak*s rose against the reformist sultan. All the Janissaries, *'ulema,* and the populace of Istanbul joined them, seeking the abolition of the New Order and of the treasury created for it, and the execution of the favorites. The head of the *'ulema,* Ata'ullah, gave a formal opinion (*fetva*) for the deposition of Selim III, in which he said that Selim was unfit for the caliphate because he had let irresponsible men usurp power and use it against the Muslim population. The rebels made an agreement with the new sultan, Mustafa IV, providing that they would not be prosecuted for their past actions; in return they themselves promised not to interfere in state affairs any more. Our analyst notes that such a pledge on the part of the sultan was unheard of in Ottoman history. The Janissaries and their conservative allies were now in control of the whole government and busy with the purge of Selim's partisans. Mustafa's authority was not heeded outside the walls of his court.

The *a'yān* were quick to seize power from the hands of the Janissaries. The *a'yān* of Rumelia under the leadership of Alemdar Mustafa Pasha, formerly an *a'yān* of Rusçuk (Russe), marched against the capital together with the imperial army then on the Danube. Alemdar seized Istanbul, suppressed the Janissary leaders, and demanded Selim's restoration to the throne. When it turned out that Selim had been put to death in the meantime, Alemdar made Mahmud II sultan and became himself Grand Vizier and dictator. In his diploma of appointment to the Grand Vizirate it was stressed that he should be most careful to act in accordance with the *sharia* in all state affairs, to cooperate with the Janissary corps and *'ulema,* and enforce the ancient laws of the Ottoman sultans. Under Alemdar, nevertheless, there was a violent reaction against the enemies of the New Order, about one thousand of whom were executed in two months.

Previously the *a'yān* had not made a united front against the Janissary corps. In 1806, those in Rumelia had cooperated with the Janissaries while some powerful *a'yān* in Anatolia supported Selim's New Order. But now the *a'yān* of Rumelia and Anatolia united against the reactionaries, less out of sympathy for the reforms than from a desire to control the central government and guarantee their position in the provinces. Soon the joint forces of the *a'yān* flocked into the capital with their armies, terrifying the Janissaries and the court.

Following the example of the Janissaries, they, too, made the sultan sign an agreement called *Sened-i İttifak* (Covenant of Union). In the introduction of this document, it was emphasized that the division and conflicts within the government and among the *a'yān* in the provinces were the main causes of the desperate situation of the empire and that this covenant proposed to revive the empire. The main provisions were as follows: viziers, *ʿulema,* high officials, "dynasties" of major *aʿyān* in the provinces, and military corps in the capital promised always to respect the sovereign authority of the sultan and the orders of the Grand Vizier, who represented in his person the sultan's absolute power, and to take united action against any rebellion. The important article 5 declared that just as the signatories promised collectively to safeguard the person and authority of the sultan and the order and security of the state, so the security of the provincial "dynasties" was to be protected by joint action of the signatories in the event that any law-abiding "dynasty" was assailed by the "state" or by viziers in the provinces. The "dynasties" further undertook not to punish any lesser *aʿyān* under their own authority without first consulting the central government. Each "dynasty" was to respect the boundaries of the other's area of control, and all were to take joint action against any transgressor. In article 2, the "dynasties" and lesser provincial notables sanctioned a state army and promised to conscript soldiers for it in the face of any opposition, including opposition from the military corps in the capital. In the same article, they promised to cooperate in the collection of state taxes for the sultan in the provinces. They further pledged themselves to protect the population under their authority and observe carefully the tax regulations agreed upon among the state, ministers and provincial *aʿyān* (article 7).

The document was drawn up in the form of a regular contract according to the *sharia,* the parties being the state and its officials, *ʿulema,* generals of the military corps in the capital, and representatives of the provincial "dynasties." It will be noted that the "state" but not the sultan himself was mentioned as a party in the document. He took no oath as the others did, but for confirmation put his imperial seal upon the covenant, even though he had been warned by his closest advisers that it would severely limit his absolute power. The several "dynasties" stood surety for each other. In the postscript, it was made clear that the covenant was to be the perpetual and unalterable basis for the regeneration of the empire. As such it was to be signed by every Grand Vizier and *Şeyhülislam* upon his accession to office, and these were to see that it was observed in every detail. A copy of it was also to be deposited with the sultan, who would see in person that it remained in force forever.

This important document has been interpreted in very different ways, often without sufficient recognition of its historical meaning and background. Like Magna Carta, it was a limitation upon the king's power imposed by local magnates; it was not, like Magna Carta of popular conception, a basis for liberal-democratic development. It clearly indicates the diminution of the sultan's power and the rise of the provincial magnates. In it, the "dynasties" acknowledged many traditional rights of the sultanate: the supreme authority of the sultan, the independence of his government, and the rights of the state to conscript soldiers and collect taxes directly in the provinces (articles 1-4). At the same time, it clearly stated that as long as the "dynasties" did not infringe upon the central authority, the government had to respect their status and their established rights. The "dynasties" and grandees of the empire, furthermore, were arrogating the right to take common action against anyone, including members of the sultan's government, who violated the provisions of the document. Article 4 provided that if the Grand Vizier violated the laws and fell into corrupt practices, it was the duty of all to sue him and check the abuses. But the document did not constitute any special organization which might carry out such a suit. What the "dynasties" wanted, in fact, was precisely to assure themselves of a degree of autonomy incompatible with a centralist and progressive government.

The Restoration of the Sultan's Power in the Empire: His Bureaucracy Takes the Lead in Modernizing the State

The rule of the *a'yān* did not last long. The court and members of Ottoman bureaucracy as well as the population of Istanbul were in a state of terror and rather welcomed the counter-attack of the Janissaries which put an end to *a'yān* rule. To reestablish his authority in the provinces, Mahmud II (1808-1839) could only rely on the Janissaries, who now become more disobedient than ever. In 1812, nevertheless, immediately after the conclusion of the peace treaty with Russia, Mahmud began to suppress the principal *a'yān* in the provinces. He crushed some of those who resisted him by sending into their territories troops commanded by the neighboring governor. Others he was able directly to deprive of their titles and leases so that they themselves were forced to submit and their sons to accept humbler positions. But in 1821 Tepedelenli Ali Pasha, the most powerful among the pashas of *a'yān* origin, raised truly massive resistance. The Greek insurrection followed his revolt.

Mahmud's war against the refractory *a'yān* resulted in the dispossession of many of them and restored much of the sultan's authority in the provinces. Yet hundreds of these notables remained at the head of local administrations and in possession of large leaseholds. Still constituting the most influential class in the provinces, they often appeared to the passive local populations in the guise of protectors against oppressive governors and an arbitrary central authority. Later, when the masses were given the opportunity to participate in political life, men of this class were to play a major part in political leadership.

In 1826, during the most critical period of the Greek insurrection, Mahmud II at last made the fateful decision to get rid of the Janissaries. Having done away with these as well as the rebellious *a'yān* in the provinces, he would then possess unlimited power to reorganize the empire as the conditions of the time required.

Before the destruction of the Janissaries, Halet Efendi, a favorite whom they had supported, had been virtual master of the state. Thereafter, Hüsrev, a reformer left over from Selim's time, was given the task of creating a new army and became the major force in the empire for fifteen years. He was a product of the old Ottoman *kul* (imperial slave) system. This institution, established to provide wholly reliable instruments for the exercise of the sultan's absolute power, had been clearly defined by Kemal Pasha-zade at the beginning of the sixteenth century. Hüsrev, its last great representative, had himself trained many slaves who became generals and governors of the empire. It would remain, of course, for westernized diplomat-bureaucrats to introduce truly modern reforms in the Ottoman state.

Muhammed Ali, who had become pasha of Egypt in the manner of pashas of *a'yān* origin, proved more dangerous than Tepedelenli. From 1833 on, he threatened to extend his power to all Asiatic provinces of the empire. His influence was felt even in Anatolia, where the *a'yān* and conservative masses hostile to Mahmud's reforms were sympathetic to him. He defeated Mahmud's new armies in 1833 and 1839. It was during this critical period that a new generation of reformers, of whom Mustafa Reşid Pasha was typical, emerged to save the empire from total destruction. Differing wholly from the military reformers like Hüsrev, these men were chiefly diplomats who had become acquainted with international conditions and with the structure of Western states during service in European capitals. They came out of the age-old bureaucracy which formed the third class of Ottoman state functionaries, the other classes being the *'ulema* and the military. Their training was a practical one in the state bureaus, differing from that of the military, who were mostly trained under the *kul* system, and more markedly still from that of the *'ulema,* who came from the rigidly formal religious seminaries. Thanks to their services in diplomacy and finance, the bureaucrats gained an increasing influence in the administration from the eighteenth century on. Devoted exclusively to the secular interests of the state and free from formalism and the bonds of tradition, they were ready to become faithful instruments of radical administrative reform. In 1821 when the Ottoman government had to replace the Greek interpreters with Turks, a Translation Office was created at the Sublime Porte, and Western languages were taught there, the first teacher being a professor from the military engineering school. This Translation Office, like the embassies which Selim III had established in Western capitals, became an educational center for a new generation of Westernized administrators and intellectuals. Âli Pasha, future Grand Vizier and reformer, and Fuad Pasha, collaborator of Reşid, received their first education in these centers.

Confronted with the disaster at Navarino in 1827 and Muhammed Ali's starling successes, Mahmud II heeded the advice of his reformist diplomats who saw the necessity of gaining the sympathy and confidence of Western powers and modernizing the Ottoman administration. Accordingly, he introduced, between 1831 and 1838, some administrative and social reforms which can be regarded as the first decisive steps toward Westernization. Principal among these were the creation of state departments and of a council of ministers with a prime minister, the establishment of two high councils for military and civil reform, the use in the administration of civil servants with fixed salaries, the founding of a modern postal service and of secular professional schools, and modernization in clothing and state protocol. But Mahmud's most significant achievement remained the restoration of the sultan's power in the provinces and in all branches of administration.

After his success on a diplomatic mission to London in 1838, when war was pending with Muhammed Ali of Egypt, Reşid Pasha gained an increasing influence over Mahmud II and was able to persuade him that the disposition of Egypt would finally be decided in Western capitals. The very survival of the Ottoman state, in his view, was dependent on a modernization of its administration which would enable it to enter the concert of European states. The Ottoman defeat at Nizib in 1839 was followed by the death of Mahmud II, and thereafter everyone, including his great opponent, Hüsrev, looked to Reşid for salvation and became receptive to his reform projects. The most radical Turkish decisions to reform, we observe, were almost always made in time of crisis.

On November 3, 1839, an imperial rescript, read by Reşid Pasha at *Gülhane*, initiated the era of reform called *Tanzimat* in Turkish history. That document said in summary: The empire had been declining for one hundred and fifty years because the religious law and imperial laws had been disregarded. In order to restore its prosperity and strength, new legislation was required which should be based on the principle of securing the life, honor, and property of all subjects. Taxation and conscription laws would be revised in accordance with the demands of justice. The tax farming system would be abolished and each citizen taxed in proportion to his means. Every accused person should be publicly judged. These guarantees should be extended to all subjects of whatever religion or sect.

A high council of reforms *(Meclis-i Vālā-yi Ahkām-i Adliye)* would devise, after free debate, bills fulfilling the purposes agreed upon, and those in turn would be submitted to the sultan to be confirmed and published. Since all the bills would be drawn up for the sake of resuscitating Islam, the state, and the empire, the sultan promised to take an oath not to disregard them. The *'ulema* and grandees of the empire were to take oaths to the same effect, and those who broke their word were to be punished without respect of rank and position according to the provisions of a penal code. These dispositions, finally, were to be made public throughout the empire and communicated officially to all the ambassadors of friendly powers resident at Istanbul.

In this rescript the main features of the European constitutions of the 1830s are quite skillfully combined with traditional Ottoman institutions and with practical necessities. A number of references to the *sharia* obscured from conservatives the revolutionary content of the document, and indeed the traditional state philosophy was genuinely apparent in it: The rescript said that the state needed armed forces which in turn required money, that state finances could remain in good order only if the subjects were protected against injustices, and so on. The basic principle of legislation, also, was discovered not in natural rights but in the practical necessity of resuscitating the empire. In brief, state power remained the ultimate goal as before; the people were still regarded as mere subjects of the state.

It should be remembered that in classical Islamic thought, no principles of law could exist apart from the *sharia.* But with the Ottomans there had always in fact been an independent category of laws called imperial laws or *kānūns* which were derived directly from the sovereign will of the ruler. For their justification, it was asserted that, though applying to situations not covered by the *sharia,* they were necessary for the well-being of the Islamic community. The Ottoman sultans had promulgated hundreds of such *kānūns* concerning public law, state finances, taxation, economic life, and criminal law. The *Gülhane* rescript was promulgated on the same principle, the legislation which it envisaged being thought necessary to regenerate the state. The document itself was rendered in the form of a decree.

When all this is said, it remains nevertheless clear that the rescript introduced revolutionary ideas and institutions into Ottoman society. Among them was the sultan's promise, confirmed by an oath, to respect the laws to be made pursuant to its principles and the establishment of a council for legislative activities with the guarantee of freedom of debate.

When he composed the decree, Reşid had intended to impose limits on the despotic power of the sultan. In his letter to Palmerston, dated August 12, 1839, he confessed this intention: "Les puissances de l'Europe," he wrote, "savent à quel degré était progressivement parvenue la tyrannie des Empereurs ottomans depuis la destruction des Janissaires.... Lorque malgré la considération, si forte du voisinage, l'Autriche et la Russie, quelqu'en soit le motif, permettent à la Walachie et à la Servie, d'adopter une constitution, auune puissance ne sauraitelle jamais vouloir empêcher que les populations musulmans obtiennent rien que de simples sûretés pour leur [sic] vies et pour leur fortune."[1]

A further revolutionary element in the document was the extension of the guarantees in it to all subjects. Later, in 1846, the sultan could confirm these principles in a speech saying: "The differences of

1 F. E. Bailey, *British Policy and the Turkish Reform Movement,* Cambridge, Mass., 1942, 275.

religion and sect among the subjects is something concerning only their persons and not affecting their rights of citizenship. As we are living all in the same country under the same government, it is wrong to make discriminations among us." The revolt of the Greeks and the European crusade for Greek independence had taught a severe lesson to the Ottomans. Now, possessing equality before the law, the non-Muslim subjects would, it was expected, no longer feel that they were a segregated and oppressed element in the state and would no longer strive for independence from it. The Western powers, too, would appreciate this change in favor of the Christians in the empire. It must be noted that with their demands for equality, freedom, home rule, reforms in taxation, and land ownership the non-Muslim subjects were contributing to the Westernization of the Ottoman-Turkish state. Perceiving their peculiar position and the intervention of the West on their behalf, the sultan was moved increasingly to secularize public institutions. As sultan-caliph, he began to distinguish as best he could between his offices as ruler of all Ottoman citizens equally and his office as caliph of only the Muslims in accordance with the *sharia.* The significant concession made to the non-Muslims caused apprehensions among the Muslims in general, who regarded it as the destruction of the caliphate and denounced the Westernization movement as a whole. The fanatical ones stigmatized it as apostasy. The division thereby brought into focus between Westernizers with chiefly secular views and conservatives attached to the rule of the *sharia* remained for many years the principal schism in Turkish political life.

In brief, equality before the law and the securing of life, honor, and property for all subjects were the revolutionary ideas in the rescript. Reşid himself asserted that the *Tanzimat,* the reforms introduced with the rescript, would change the imperial regime completely. The change in the concept of the state was further visible in the various decrees in which the sultan announced that the laws were made solely for the subjects' benefit.

We can ascertain the sincerity of Reşid's professions when we study the measures by which he undertook to put into effect the principles proclaimed in the rescript. Reşid showed his zeal to make the rule of law a reality by the haste with which he published a penal code.

In the provinces, administrative councils were established, the members of which were the governor, his two secretaries, the local judge, the mufti, the local military commander, four notables, and, if there was a Christian community in the province, the metropolit and two Christian notables. The notables were to be elected by the people. The provincial councils and smaller councils in the dependent towns were to discuss freely all administrative matters and were to sit as criminal courts. The High Council of Reforms in the capital constituted a court of appeal for them. With the establishment of the provincial councils, Ottoman subjects, non-Muslims in particular, may be said to have received for the first time a voice in the local administration, though in actual fact these councils were composed of the local high officials, *ʿulema*, and notables, and differed little from the old councils of notables under the judge. Sometimes, paradoxically enough, the local *aʿyān* and *eşrāf* used their new positions in local administration to obstruct the *Tanzimat* and incite the conservative masses against it.

Introduced with the intention of protecting both the peasants and the public treasury, financial reforms followed soon after the proclamation of the rescript. To secure greater justice in taxation, Reşid abolished the tax immunities and exemptions affecting such influential groups as *aʿyān*, *ağa*s, *ʿulema*, and the military, as well as the exemptions connected with religious endowments. The affected groups started an intense propaganda campaign against the reforms. The survey and census embarked upon for purposes of the reform gave them an opportunity to incite the conservative masses, and they spread rumors variously that the government had determined to double the taxes or to abolish them altogether. The abolition of tax farming affected the large group of tax farmers and credit agents and the substantial number of officials profiting from it in dubious ways. It must be recalled that most of the tax farmers were local notables who had gained wealth and influence through this activity. Again, in order to extend the state's protection over the peasantry, Reşid abolished forced labor and usury. One of the first decisions of the High Council of Reforms read: "In the Balkans most of the notables used to think that the peasants were their serfs, and employed them for their own services without any compensation. Also, they did not permit them to leave their estates to work elsewhere and they interfered even in their marriages. Now the sultan has never accepted such abuses, and those who oppose this order [abolishing them] will be punished according to the provisions of the penal code recently published." Another decree pointed out that the usurers were getting twenty percent per month for the money they lent to the peasants. Never able to pay their debts, they were eventually deprived of all their possessions. The usurers also used to appropriate the peasants' crops at below market prices. Now the government reduced the rates of interest and permitted the peasantry to pay their accumulated debts in installments.

The government had ordered the officials in the provinces to explain to the people in mass meetings the principles embodied in the Rescript of *Gülhane*. In some areas in the Balkans, the peasants became so impatient to see the results of the reforms that they attempted desperate actions. Seeing that the *Tanzimat* had not brought any immediate relief in their tax burden, for example, and that they were still subject to forced labor, the Bulgarian peasants around Nish rose up under their own lesser notables. Further uprisings in 1849 and 1850 in the Vidin area were even more serious. Most of the agricultural lands in this area were originally state-owned. But local Muslim *ağa*s had the exclusive rights to lease them and in fact possessed them as their own estates. Rejecting the popular demands and organizing a local militia *(başıbozuks),* the *ağa*s fell upon the rebels, and it required regular government forces to end the struggle. The High Council of Reforms in Istanbul decided first to abolish the existing administrative council and granted the Christian peasants the right to lease the state-owned lands themselves. These radical decisions proved impracticable, however, and the situation did not change much subsequently. Similar reactions occurred in Anatolia.

The *aʿyān* of Bala near Ankara, for example, was prosecuted before the High Council of Reforms for evading tax payments, subjecting the peasants to forced labor, inciting people to rise against the government. The difference here was that the Muslim population, under the influence of the local *ʿulema* and *aʿyān,* were extremely conservative, whereas the Christian subjects in the Balkan, under the influence of nationalist leaders, were in a mood to rebel.

These examples indicate how difficult it was for Reşid to affect his reforms and how various were the social forces arrayed against him. The privileged classes of the old regime, especially *ağa*s in collaboration with the *ʿulema,* were asserting that the grant of civil equality to the non-Muslims and the "indifel" was pure disregard of the *sharia* and would ruin the state and religion. To control them, Reşid had hastily published his penal code so that he might legally prosecute offenders against the government's reform measures. Many reactionaries in the capital as well as in the provinces, including even old Hüsrev, were punished. In Ankara, a mufti, member of the administrative council, was condemned for inciting people to rebel against the reforms.

In line with his efforts to introduce a Western system of administration, Reşid decided to entrust public service in the provinces exclusively to salaried civil servants appointed by the central government and to abolish all forms of dues and bribes which the *aʿyān* and officials of all degrees had been accustomed to accept. In seeking to create a corps of civil servants to implement the reforms. Reşid was directly threatening the position of the provincial *aʿyān* who, as agents of the governors-general, then occupied most of the local administrative posts in Anatolia. Reşid was intent on changing those features of the organization of the empire which were inherited from feudalism. His administrative reform meant, in the last analysis, profound social reform. One of his radical measures after the abolition of tax farming was to appoint revenue collectors *(muhassıls)* in the provinces who were attached directly to the central government. But he failed to find enough civil servants trained for the job and was forced after all to employ local notables, who often followed the old practices.

It was later decided to found special secular schools to supply the civil servants so urgently needed. In these schools and in the military academies a body of Westernized officials were trained who were destined to play a decisive part in the modernization of Turkey. The resistance to Reşid's reforms caused his fall in 1841 (he was then foreign minister). The newly introduced institutions had not worked well; the new system of tax collection especially was a failure. Reşid had relied solely on the sultan's favor, which he had gained through his services in solving the Egyptian question. His successor in power was Rıza Pasha, the Minister of War, who like many old-type reformers believed chiefly in military reorganization as a means of resuscitating the empire. Tax farming came back with him, and radical reforms in the administration generally were judged to have been ill-timed. When in 1845 Reşid came back to power he gave priority to training the bureaucrats needed to implement his reforms; to his end, he created a High Council of Public Education and projected the foundation of a university.

In the same year, the government took the bold step of asking each province to elect two delegates and send them to Istanbul to consult on the reforms to be undertaken. These delegates were "elected from among the prominent and respected people." The assembly seemed in concert as simply an extension of the provincial administrative councils. Yet it remains the first representative assembly ever convoked in the Ottoman capital. Though the *a'yān* who appeared at the sultan's Porte had enough and soon returned home, the conservatives were appalled. Serasker Said Pasha went so far as to denounce Reşid for intending to proclaim a republic. Perhaps more significant in its consequence was the promulgation of a commercial code borrowed from France which established tribunals of commerce, the first secular tribunals of the Ottoman state.

For two principal reasons the bold steps taken by Reşid remained without effect. In the first place, the current severe economic depression was identified in the popular mind with the West and its ways, not improperly, since the cheap and plentiful products of Western industry, invading the Turkish market under the capitulatory regime, were ruining the native industries. Contemporary consular reports give us vivid descriptions of these happenings. In the second place, disgruntled persons were accusing the reformist Sultan Abdülmecid (1839-1861) of letting Reşid abuse the power of the sultanate. The highly centralist and authoritarian system of government espoused by Reşid and his followers became the particular target of the rising Ottoman-Turkish intelligentsia, who saw in it a despotism harmful to the empire. Organized as the secret society of the Young Ottomans in 1867, these intellectuals embraced the romantic nationalism then prevalent in Europe and advocated a constitutional regime which would introduce elements of Western civilization while preserving traditional Islamic-Turkish culture. For the first time, we find a group of progressives acting independently of the government and opposing the official reform program. The Young Ottomans were the real forerunners of the nationalist and democratic movement in Turkey.

The major characteristics of modernization in this early period can be succinctly summarized.

A program of modernization was first adopted by the state as a measure of self-defense against an aggressive and imperialistic Europe. The superiority of European military techniques and organization was recognized as early as the end of the seventeenth century. This perception was a necessary psychological preparation for the later cultural borrowings from the West.

Second, systematic modernization started with military reforms in the eighteenth century, especially under Selim III. From 1830 on, the process was extended to administration and public institutions, a trend which culminated in the proclamation of the Ottoman constitution of 1876.

Third, the state was the initiator of the modernization movement and changes were imposed from above, the sultan using his absolute power to create the bureaucratic machinery necessary to effect changes.

Fourth, the masses, the great majority of whom were living in a closed rural economy, were generally dependent on the *a'yān, ağa*s, and clerics, who were vitally interested in keeping them attached to the traditional institutions. Even in the period between 1800 and 1850 these groups actively resisted the reforms imposed by the state; the Turkish-Muslim population of the empire remained indifferent or even refractory in the face of change in general.

Fifth, a desire to satisfy non-Muslim subjects and the Western powers definitely encouraged the Ottoman state to adopt secular laws and institutions. The Western powers were interested in furnishing the empire with liberal institutions, which they thought would guarantee at once the integrity of the empire and their own economic interests in it.

Sixth, around 1860 a small group of Turkish patriots with a Western outlook emerged and carried out, in the newly introduced press and in a number of literary periodicals, a vigorous campaign against the sultan's absolutism. His reform measures were, they believed, both arbitrary and contrary to the real interests of the Turkish-Muslim population.

In the Turkish modernization movement, finally, the principal difficulties stemmed from the religious basis of the traditional society and state. In general, the *Tanzimat* reformers and intellectuals, though wanting to Westernize the administration and to borrow modern techniques, believed it desirable to preserve such basic traditional institutions as the *sharia,* religious courts, and religious schools. It was thought that these might be taken out of public affairs and relegated to their own sphere. Later, radicals who wanted wholesale Westernization and national sovereignty like that of European states were to blame the failure of the *Tanzimat* upon this dualism. But no concept of the nation-state was in fact realized until Atatürk called the Turkish Republic into being after the dissolution of the empire in 1919.

IX

TURKEY BETWEEN EUROPE AND THE MIDDLE EAST

Within the Islamic community of peoples Turks have had a special state tradition from the time they entered and controlled the Islamic world in the eleventh century. Originated in the steppe empires, this tradition can be defined as recognition of the state's absolute independence of action and upholding the state's absolute right to legislate on public matters. Thus, in Turkish states in the Islamic world, *töru, yasa* or *kanun,* that is, a body of laws and regulations, existed independently from the Islamic Law and led public life in the highest interests of the state and community, giving elasticity in formulating state policies and interpreting the stipulations of the Islamic Law in the most liberal manner. The *kanun* regime was also instrumental in introducing reforms and innovations as required by the circumstances.[1] The Ottoman *ulema* ingeniously interpreted the state's independent action and legislation within the canonical principle of *istihsan* or *maslaha.* This principle said: What is necessary for the well-being of the Islamic community is to be preferred. It is to be added that more strict commentators of the religious law contended that this liberal attitude leads to heresy and state laws approved by the liberal *ulema* were in fact innovations against the Islamic Law. This contention gave rise to a prolonged struggle between the "official" or bureaucratic *ulema* supporting the state's legislative power and the "popular" *ulema* acting as a

1 See Halil İnalcık, "Ḳānūn", *Encyclopaedia of Islam*, 2nd ed., IV, 556-562; Halil İnalcık, "Ḳānunnāme", *Encyclopaedia of Islam*, 2nd ed., IV, 562-566.

mouth-piece of the populace against the privileged. The Friday sermons in the mosques offered a strong propaganda base for the latter. In other words, liberal or strict interpretation of the divine law gave rise to a political, cultural and social contention in the Ottoman-Turkish society since the middle of the sixteenth century and can be viewed as the initial phase of fierce struggle between modernists and reactionaries in the nineteenth and twentieth century when the modernization process gained momentum.

In Turkish states the ruling elite constituted, and had the consciousness of being, a separate, privileged governing body above the tax paying productive classes or *reaya.* The ruling elite, however, did not make up a caste with hereditary rights, except the Ottoman dynasty. The ruler chose and introduced into the ruling elite anyone whom he considered of use to serve and enhance the state interests and the institution. Within the ruling elite, the central bureaucracy occupied an absolutely special position. Composed of state secretaries so to speak, it was the nerve center of the whole state organization and formulated all the decrees and laws as required by the state interests. In one word, it was this group which really embodied the state and its independent policies. It shared the Sultan's absolutism.

For the topic under discussion, this traditional bureaucratic despotism is of extreme importance. Motivated by the idea of the state interests, the central bureaucracy was responsible for the introduction of modernizing reforms and became the origin and ardent defender of all the movements leading to reforms, secularism and westernization in the Ottoman state. It naturally rallied military and religious bureaucrats around. It should be added that thus, the ruling elite, headed by the central bureaucracy, formed a powerful group with obvious class interests.

During the nineteenth century, the ruling elite played a key role in promoting westernization, and alliance and identification with the West as the best policy for "the state". For the integrity of the empire or for the preservation of the imperial political and social system the central bureaucracy decided that westernization and western alliance were the only way out. The immediate danger posed by the military imperialism of the rival empires of the Habsburgs and Romanovs always served as the incentive and excuse for the intensification of the westernization process introduced by the reformer bureaucrats.

On the other hand, it has rightly been observed that the civilian and military bureaucrats emerged at the moment of the collapse of the imperial system as the champions of the independence of the Turkish nation and culture. At the footsteps of the nineteenth century reformer bureaucrats, they espoused again, in a most radical fashion, the western ideals – this time ideals of nationalism and democracy – the preliminary forms of which were introduced already in the Tanzimat period. Westernism was a rooted tradition with the elite during the Young Turk revolution of 1908 and the independence war of 1919- 1922.

If Turkey emerged as an independent state, developing its own identity and national culture in the modern world, that became possible only as a result of ideological zeal and consecration of the great leaders who emerged from the ranks of the Ottoman bureaucrats. In other words, the independent national state of Turkey owes its existence and development primarily to this group who tried in the decades after the national victory a complete westernization of the state and society. The point will be well illustrated when we recall the landmarks in the western alliance – trends which proved to be of determinant import in creating the modern Turkish nation-state and democracy.

Westernization of the Ottoman state passed through several stages with different orientations. From the earliest times of the Ottoman state, the bureaucrats were alert in borrowing weapons and tools of Christian Europe– including naval construction and seamanship, gunnery and tactics which made the Ottoman military power a match of its western enemies, and superior to its eastern rivals. From the religious point of view, the bureaucrat *ulema* thought there was no stipulation prohibiting such technical borrowings and subscribed to them mainly on the basis of the Prophet's saying that in fighting it is permissible to use the enemy's tricks.

Generous remuneration of such skills was so well known in Renaissance Italy that several famous masters were attracted to Turkey. A project by Leonardo da Vinci to construct a bridge on the Golden Horn was discovered in the Seraglio archives and published by Franz Babinger.[2] Thousands of Jews expelled from Spain and Italy settled in several cities in the Ottoman empire and were responsible for the promotion of various arts, in particular woolen cloth manufacture in Salonica and Safad. It can safely be said that among the countries of non-western cultures, Ottoman Turkey was the first to come into close cultural relations with the rising western civilization. Various means of contact through war, trade, captives and converts, refugees, port cities with European communities such as Pera, Salonica and Beirut made these close relations and interactions possible.

At this stage, however, Ottoman westernization was limited to borrowing cultural objects and imitation. The second stage was reached in the eighteenth century when the Ottomans opened military schools where western sciences in military and related fields were taught by European experts, and the printing press was introduced to publish books in technical subjects. Thus, the Ottoman mind was for the first time stimulated by western science in a systematic way. Already in the seventeenth century, the intellectual curiosity of Ottoman bureaucrats had given rise to some kind of clubs in the *konaks* of Istanbul where Greeks educated in Padua and Ottoman bureaucrats came together to discuss, in the most liberal fashion, subjects in philosophy, politics and ethics.[3]

An atheist and mundane view of the world spread among these literati in this period which can be considered a prelude to the secularist trend in Ottoman- Turkish thinking. What was most

2 "Vier Bauvorschläge Leonardo da Vincis an Sultan Bayezid II (1502-1503)," Nachr. der Akademie der Wissens in Göttingen, Phil-Hist. KI., no. 1.

3 "Eastern and Western Cultures in Dimitrie Cantemir's Work," H. İnalcık, *The Middle East and the Balkans under the Ottoman Empire*, Bloomington: Indiana University Turkish Studies 1993, 412- 416.

significant in this was the new attitude of the Turks towards western civilization – an attitude of admiration and desire to understand, which is the first condition of a real acculturation. However, it should be noted that this first Ottoman enlightenment was linked to the growing sense of political and economic dependence of the Ottoman empire to the West and recruited its adherents among the small circle of reform-minded bureaucrats.

The third stage in Ottoman westernization came with the borrowing of western administrative and political institutions with the aim of re-organizing the Ottoman state on this basis. Still this was interpreted and defended by the bureaucrats of liberal thought as technical means used for the good of the Islamic community. This radical move was explained and justified as necessary for the survival of the empire at a critical moment in 1839. During this period of liberal reforms, known as Tanzimat (1839-1877), the administrative reforms were coupled with the translation from French and enactment of dozens of state regulations. Basically these reforms aimed at creating a centralist bureaucratic state on the model of European monarchies.

In fact, the Ottoman reforms were partly imposed by the Western capitalist nations, to serve their expanding market needs by introducing a most liberal regime in trade, and administrative and judicial safeguards for their nationals with extensive guarantees for non-Muslim subjects of the empire in a partially secularised system of government.

The liberal reforms of the Tanzimat culminated in the proclamation of the first Ottoman constitution in 1876. The short-lived Ottoman experience of parliamentary government was quite successful as judged by a student of the event, Professor Devereux. Let me, however, point out that the ballot system at the elections was so incomprehensible for the voters that the government resorted to quite an awkward regulation at the elections. At any rate, one of the first constitutions outside Europe, the Ottoman constitution is an important step paving the way to the Turkish Republic of 1923.

The half a century of experience under the Republic proved that the democratic system of government, a direct product of the Ottoman liberal movement in the nineteenth century, is an irrevocable reality in Turkey's political life. No government can survive in Turkey today outside the popular vote since Turkish citizens of every walk of life are accustomed to and want to exercise the power to elect their own government.

Westernizing reforms led to a dualism in the Ottoman Turkish state and society. To give a particularly illustrative example of the dualism and conflict in Turkish state and society, I thought I should summarize here the process of secularization of the judicial system which I recently studied in detail. In the period prior to the nineteenth century, the *cadi's* court was much more than an ordinary judicial court. It was at the same time a town meeting place where the city notables, representatives of the craft guilds, and *imams* of the districts got together for various occasions such as allotment of certain taxes among the local population, formulation of complaints to the Sultan, or price fixing. During the Tanzimat period first such community affairs were shifted to the provincial councils which assumed more extensive administrative responsibilities. At the same time, the *Shar'î mahkama* areas of jurisdiction were increasingly restricted, and, the section of the religious law concerning obligations, as well as administrative law, began to be dealt with by newly created non-religious courts. It is interesting that the need for the new courts emerged first in the sphere of commercial transactions which began to assume increasingly complex forms under the impact of the commercial revolution of the eighteenth century. By the end of the eighteenth century the state recognized the establishment of a special court for the merchants with the authority to solve business disputes arising among themselves, and in 1850 a commercial code based on French law was proclaimed, and new commercial courts instituted in 1860 were composed of members appointed by the state and elected by the merchant community.

The commercial and criminal courts, called collectively *nizâmiyye* courts were secular courts side by side with the *Shar'î* courts. The introduction of a dual system in law and its court administration led to a serious confusion over jurisdiction. The newly-established courts were not permitted to pass any decision in conflict with the *Shar'îa,* and for subjects clearly within the jurisdiction of the Islamic Law they had to obtain a *fatwâ* from the *muftî* who was appointed to these secular courts.

During the height of the Tanzimat between 1864 and 1876 the whole Ottoman judicial system was re-organized on the French model with the formation of the ministry of justice and the publication of various secular law codes for the use of the new courts. The adoption of the western judicial system during the Tanzimat period, especially the projects for introducing the French civil code, aroused deep concern among the Ottoman *ulema* as is reflected in comments in Cevdet Paşa's memoirs.[4]

As a result of the reaction, the section of the *Shari'îa* Law dealing with *muâmelât,* obligations, was codified under a new system of classification by a special committee, and, published between 1855 and 1869. For the first time, a single Islamic Law code, *Macalla,* was declared as the sole official text to be implemented in both the *shar'î* and *nizâmî* courts. Now judicial decrees of the courts were to be sent to the office of the *Şeyhulislâm.* But the *Macalla* failed to meet all the needs of Ottoman society's increasingly complex commercial relations and to save the shaky position of the *Shar'î* courts.

However, as the Constitution of 1876 confirmed later on, the Ottoman state declared its adherence, as an Islamic state, to the principle of the supremacy of Islamic Law over all other legislation. The conservative Muslim masses had looked with suspicion on the introduction of western judicial institutions. Thus, the Ottoman ulema continued their efforts to maintain their position by introducing reforms in the Islamic system itself as well. Already in 1855 a regulation was passed on the training and selection of the

4 "Tezâkir", ed. C. Baysun, vol. I-IV, Ankara: Türk Tarih Kurumu, 1986.

nâ'ibs, deputy-judges in the courts. Other regulations on the issuing of shar'î documents were also published. Finally, in 1915, a procedural law for Shar'î courts was introduced. During the Union and Progress administration, which advocated the unity of judicial power under state control, the secularization movement gained in intensity, and in 1914, all religious courts were taken away from the control of the *Şeyhulislam* and put under the ministry of justice like all other courts. But the decision was reversed upon the fall from power of the Union and Progress party in 1919, and the *shar'î* courts were returned to the control of the *Şeyhulislâm.*

The radical secularization was effected only under the Republic in 1924 when the *shar'î* courts or *Şerî'at mahkemeleri* were abolished, and the *Macalla* was replaced by new secular codes of civil law, criminal law and commercial law, based respectively on the corresponding Swiss, Italian and German codes.

The story of the Ottoman judicial system is repeated in every facet of Turkish life, not only in such institutionally regulated areas as education, but also in social life, ethics, manners and art. The common characteristics of all these changes were a dualism and a conflict between secular western institutions imposed or supported from above by bureaucrats, and traditional Islamic institutions sustained by the religious groups and supported largely by masses clinging to the traditional value system of the Turkish society. The conflict found its expression in the sharp discussions during the Tanzimat period led by the Young Ottomans, notably by Namık Kemal and Ziya Paşa in the 1860's and 1870's, and later in a more analytical way in the sociological writings of Ziya Gökalp.[5]

Namık Kemal and Ziya criticised vehemently westernization as inspired or imposed from outside with shattering effects on the traditional socio-economic set-up as well as on the traditional value system.[6] They identified westernization with bureaucratic

5 Ziya Gökalp, *Turkish Nationalism and Western Civilisation*, ed. and trans. N. Berkes, London 1959.

6 İhsan Sungu, "Yeni Osmanlılar," *Tanzimat*, I, Istanbul 1940.

despotism, and, thus expressed popular reaction to the government of the masses which saw in westernization the ruin of the traditional crafts and unemployment and the concomitant erosion of the Islamic traditional value system.

Namık Kemal and Ziya Paşa formulated clearly the problems and views of the Turkish populace at large as follows: 1. The westernizing reforms were imposed by a bureaucracy working in alliance with Western Europe. They thought this meant relinquishing the search for a solution to national problems to the foreign powers who were only concerned with their own interests. 2. The bureaucrats used westernization as a way to consolidate their own despotic power. Kemal and Ziya advocated a constitution and parliamentary government in order to modify this situation. 3. Ziya and Kemal were keenly conscious that the fundamental problem was an economic one. They bitterly observed that the dumping of machine-made textiles of the West, imported under capitulatory privileges, killed the native crafts in the country, and, since there was no native industrial enterprise capable of being substituted to the traditional crafts, unemployment became widespread. 4. The economic exploitation of the West was a well-known fact at the time. In 1869, Namık Kemal wrote "we finally were able to renew the commercial treaty with England (of 1838). But how? The late Lord Palmerston, considering the disastrous state of our finances, had sympathy and agreed to make some changes in our favor... The question is whether the Sublime Porte can demonstrate to the European powers, by skillful diplomacy, the unjust conditions imposed under the capitulations and make them recognize our rightful position... If the Ottomans open a new war (against Russia) and are defeated, the Great Powers are well aware of the grave consequences for the civilized world of such a disaster." Kemal held the Tanzimat's liberal policy responsible for the economic ruin of the country. He advocated internal development projects and exploitation of natural resources by the Ottomans. 5. Criticizing dependency on the West and the imposed reforms, the Young Ottomans were also vigorously critical of the imitation of the West in culture, ethics, and manners. They were against the adoption of European laws. They made a clear distinction between culture and civilization, and while they advocated the adoption of western methods in industrialization, commerce and other material skills they rejected identification in culture and life style.

They linked to the Islamic principles their program of a constitutional government and an administration based on absolute rule of law. They demanded that in preparing a constitution each provision should be examined by the *müftî* and his opinion adhered to. They vigorously denied the idea that Islam was the source of the ills in Islamic society. It was, they argued, on the contrary, the failure of the complete implementation of Islamic Law and the maintenance of a dualistic judicial system that caused disorder and decline. In sum, the Young Ottoman movement of the 1860's is described as the first clear expression in Turkey of the popular protest against the unchecked exploitation of western capitalism and their bureaucratic ally in the country. It was directed against westernization and the centralist autocratic form of government. What is most interesting, the whole movement found its emotional core in Islam and its value system.

Rejecting the dualistic view of modernization, Atatürk led westernization to its most radical forms. In the new nation-state of Turkey, the logical revolutionary step was complete secularization of the state. Though opposed by fundamentalists as contrary to the basic tenets of Islam, Atatürk's secularism became the essential issue throughout the contemporary Islamic world. Atatürk made a far-reaching revolution in Islam though he never intended or wished to be a religious reformer, Secularism was to solve many complex problems in Turkish society. First of all, the modernization process could advance in an unchecked and unconditional fashion to lead the modernizing moves to their logical ends in a nation-state.

This was particularly significant in an Islamic society in which Islam demanded to control all acts of Muslims, private and public, for the sake of their salvation in the next world. In a more practical way, secularism would accommodate all creeds and sects within the state on an equal footing, and remove religious causes of conflict. By that I am referring in particular to the upsurge of dangerous events between the shiites and sunnites in recent years when the secular principle was often ignored by politicians. Atatürk confessed that his bureaucratic reforms from above were revolutionary methods intended to ultimately terminate the bureaucratic autocracy in the Turkish state. In its worst interpretation, the bureaucracy was thought of as the monopoly of state power for the exclusive interests of those implementing this power and this was basically what was inherited from the Ottoman state concept and practice.

Atatürk's most efficient method in his modernization program was to be the secular educational system in which no place was given to Islamic teaching. He believed that a new generation brought up under such a system would be the guarantee of his secular nation-state. But what has actually happened was a profound cultural cleavage between the educated and the uneducated in the Turkish society. The cultural division cutting across the social classes appears to prove the fact that the cultural problem is the overriding one in Turkish society today.

Atatürk was also keenly concerned with making Turkey a full and equal member of the western community of nations and his nation-state program was aimed at this goal. It must be admitted that it was not easy to overcome the age old biases in the Christian West. Europe continued to identify modern Turkey with the Ottoman state, or a backward Islamic country, despite the emphatic assertion of Atatürk that Turkey is just one of those modern nation-states born out of the collapse of the medieval empire of the Ottomans. But we have to recognize the fact that today, in terms of historical identity and cultural orientation, Ottomanism is somewhat revived in Turkey itself. As a substitute for the Islamic identity, Atatürk was keenly seeking to give the Turkish youth a sense of historical identity with the Hittites of Anatolia and pre-Islamic Turks of Central Asia. Again, as a most recent development, Islamic identity increased vigorously throughout the country, mainly as a result of deep disappointment with the social and economic development expected from a secular westernizing policy.

I think the convulsions modern Turkey is experiencing today are symptomatic of the basic demographic, economic and social problems to which a dynamic, developing society gave rise, and, rendered its expression in a culture crisis. The prescription Atatürk and İsmet İnönü strove to enforce for the solutions of a modernized Turkey is widely questioned or flatly ignored by large groups in Turkey today. Paradoxically enough, the Islamic reaction which started in the 1950's under the Demokrat Parti regime was at the same time a reaction against the age-old patronage of a bureaucracy which used to prescribe and impose reforms from above, but its failure in economic and social spheres gave momentum to the protest of the masses which used popular elections to assert themselves.

Though differing among themselves in their attitude toward Islamic identity, the conservative popular front's outlook closely resembles that of the Young Ottomans of the nineteenth century. From the 1960's on, a more radical group of socialist intellectuals have been advocating a new program for the solutions of Turkey's problems, again mostly ignoring Atatürk's principles for a national state. The socialists in Turkey basically believe that the capitalist West is by nature of its economic system uncontrollably exploitative of the underdeveloped societies, regardless of the politicians' assertions of good will and aid. Furthermore, given the restricted resources for development and social welfare, they think, a complete planning and control of the economy is a necessity. While a larger group of the socialists confess loyalty to democratic methods, a revolutionary minority group affirms that the Western system of government is totally unsuited for real development.

To conclude, the struggle in the middle of which Turkey finds itself today is actually the outcome of a long historical process bringing newly emerging forces and movements in clash with its traditional set up and expressing them differently according to the value systems the interested groups or classes find themselves associated with. One can easily see that there is a steady development towards an increasingly differentiated society in which there is no longer a place for the bureaucratic patronage system of the medieval Ottoman past.

X

THE CALIPHATE AND ATATÜRK'S *İNKİLÂB*

My focus in this paper will be on how Atatürk's *inkilâbs* or "revolutions" actually constituted one total revolution during which the events occurred in sequence as links of one whole historical process. I believe most of the historians of Atatürk's revolution are often too dependent on his historic speech, *Büyük Nutuk,* which he delivered after the major *inkilâb* was already completed in 1927. The *Nutuk* is one and undoubtedly the most important source for the period. But basically, it was delivered before a party convention for explanation and justification of the *inkilâb* and the tactics used for its victory.

It will be seen that historically the separation of the Caliphate from the Sultanate and the abolition of the latter set off a sequence of events and movements which led to the major *inkilâb*s including the abolition of the Caliphate and other secularizing reforms in the period 1922-1927.

The most urgent problem subsequent to victory over the Greek army was to make the allied powers recognize the objectives of the Independence War in a formal treaty. This in turn raised the fundamental question of the country's regime: who was going to represent the Turkish state in the coming peace conference. The claim of the Sultan's government to this effect triggered the great *inkilâb.* Mustafa Kemal reacted by declaring that absolute sovereignty of the Turkish state is embodied in the Grand National Assembly (GNA). Only three days after the Sultan's claim, Kemal proposed to the GNA the separation of the Caliphate from the Sultanate and the abolition of the latter (November 1, 1922). A fortnight later, the Sultan Vahideddin fled aboard an English warship, still claiming to be the Caliph of the Muslims of the world. A new Caliph, Abdülmecid Efendi, was elected by the GNA. Then the question came up whether the new Caliph was to be considered the head of state and would enjoy political power in the Turkish state. The question was asked by many deputies including the *hocas*, Muslim clerics, and the most influential nationalist leaders and companions of Kemal, Rauf, and Refet. At the GNA, Kemal stressed that the Turkish nation now replaced the state of Osman in sovereignty and took its destiny in its own hands. "National sultanate and sovereignty," he said,[1] "is embodied only in the GNA composed of the representatives of the nation. As to the question of the future of the Caliphate, history provides examples of the Caliphate continuing side by side with the Sultanate. Now that the Sultanate is gone the Caliphate will stay as the spiritual and religious center of the whole Muslim world. The Sultanate now is replaced by the powerful body of the delegates of the nation and from now on it will be able to take care of the nation's affairs towards a modern prosperous society." In these words, Kemal declared the fundamental revolutionary change in the regime of the country and summarized its future policy. There was no place for the Caliphate in the new Turkish state. The expression, "national sultanate" was chosen by him to argue that sultanate meant secular sovereignty and now it was assumed by the nation. The Caliph's position in the Islamic community was interpreted in a quite unusual way. It was presented as a purely spiritual dignity as in Christendom. And actually, those who tried to support Kemal in the press compared the Caliph to the Pope.

Before the GNA proceeded to elect a new Caliph, Kemal saw to it that the candidate to the post, Abdülmecid, son of Sultan Abdülaziz, vowed by signature that he agreed to this interpretation.

---

1 *Atatürk'ün Söylev ve Demeçleri*, vol. I-III, Istanbul, 1945, 270; *Hilâfet ve Millî Hâkimiyet, hilâfet ve millî hakimiyet mesâili hakkında muhtelif zevâtın makâlât ve mütâliâtından mürekkep bir risâledir.* Ankara, 1339/1923, 216

The document signed contained the following points: Abdülmecid shall bear the title of Caliph of all Muslims. The manifesto that he was going to publish to the Muslim world was instructed to him emphasizing the fact that the election was duly made by the representatives of the nation, that is, by the GNA.[2] Thanking the Muslims all over the world for their support to the Turkish nation in its struggle for independence and to the Ottoman dynasty which he said had always been the defender of Islam he added that "the high office of the Caliphate and in particular the exalted duty of the *imâmet,* which is a trust by God, asked for their continued support. He signed the manifesto as *Halîfe-i Muslimîn,* the Caliph of the Muslims and *Khâdim al-Haramayn al-Sharîfayn,* the Servant of the Two Holy Cities of Islam.[3] In a message to the press he asserted that "the Caliphate is a trust (without mentioning whose trust) and would be happy to perform thereby a service to the nation" like other citizens.[4] Although the idea *of imâmet* and that of God's trusteeship could not easily be reconciled with the nationalist interpretation of the Caliphate, in his letter to the GNA the newly elected Caliph agreed that the election was made "in accordance with the Constitution which guarantees absolute sovereignty of the Turkish nation."[5] Contradiction was apparent and both sides, the *inkilâbcı*s and *hoca*s began a heated controversy on the question as to whether the Caliph could remain as a simple spiritual dignitary in Islam, whether he could receive his authority from a community or from a group, and whether the acts of the GNA could be valid without his ratification. All these points were raised in a treatise published by Hoca Şükrü Efendi, deputy of Karaḥisar. He claimed that according to Islamic principles the Caliph should be the head of the Islamic state or the head of the GNA, and that his ratification was necessary to make the acts of the GNA valid laws for the community or

2 Gazi Mustafa Kemal Atatürk, *Nutuk*, II, Istanbul, 1961, 696; U. Kocatürk, *Atatürk ve Türk Devrimi Kronolojisi,* Ankara, 1973, 238.

3 *Hilâfet ve Millî Hâkimiyet,* 211-12.

4 *Ibid.*, 214-15.

5 *Ibid.*, 215.

nation.[6] However, some other *hocas* supported the nationalist interpretation an *inkilâbcıs* joined them in using as an argument Islamic law and history.[7] Ağaoğlu Ahmed, referring to the Islamic sources, *hadîth* and *siyar* and recognized authorities on Islamic sciences, said that the prophet himself made a clear distinction between worldly affairs and religion, and that, in early Islam, under the first four rightly guided Caliphs, between 632 and 661 A.D., the Caliphate was elective and the affairs of the Islamic community were taken care of by consultative bodies as in a republican government and that a republican government conforms best to the spirit of Islam. In brief, Ağaoğlu found all the principles of the Kemalist revolution in early Islam-republicanism, national sovereignty, liberty, equality and brotherhood, and even populism. He identified national sovereignty with *icmâ-i ümmet,* consensus of the community. He asserted that the Caliphate belongs originally to the *umma,* Islamic community as a whole, and the Caliph has to be elected by its delegates. The concept of divine monarchy, he argued, comes from Persian tradition, and is totally foreign to the original Islamic spirit and practice.[8] Rasih Efendi, a *hoca,* Muslim scholar and GNA deputy, emphasizing the important place of social action in Islam, asserted that exercise of political power is to be entrusted as a trust *(emânet)* to the most capable person or body for the good and salvation of the Islamic community. The most important issue was to defend and maintain the independence of the Muslims. Islam, he said, is incompatible with bondage. Islam is based on the absolute equality of Muslims. Brotherhood and equality are the foundations of the Islamic community. Islam commands management of their affairs in *shûrâ,* that is in consultation. Citing verses from the Qur'an in his article, he asserts that government by a body elected by Muslims is the only valid form of government based on Islamic foundations.[9]

---

6 F. C. "Hoca Şükrü Efendiye Cevap", *Hilâfet ve Millî Hâkimiyet,* 177-85.

7 Hoca Ubeydullâh, "İslâm'da Hilâfet", *ibid.,* 186-90.

8 Ağaoglu Ahmed, "Tarihî Celse", *ibid.,* 11-32.

9 Hoca Rasih Efendi, "İslâm'da Hâkimiyet ve Te'sîs-i Hükûmet", *ibid.,* 33-49.

Many *hoca*s using exclusively Islamic arguments supported Hoca Rasih's view.[10] Later Mustafa Kemal was going to use all the Islamic arguments to defend absolute sovereignty of the nation as represented at the GNA against those who advocated sovereign rights of the Caliph in the Islamic state.[11] Rasih Efendi's emphasis on independence of the Muslims was particularly important in support of Mustafa Kemal's authority, and Islamic leaders in India would wholeheartedly espouse these Islamic arguments of the nationalists. It should be noted that later Kemal sent a delegation under Rasih Efendi to India.

It is almost needless to add that Islamic arguments for modernization were not new in Turkey or in the Islamic world in general. The so-called modernists had been advocating, on the same basis, reforms in Islamic state and society such as constitutionalism for more than half a century.[12] The movement had gained momentum among the Turkish *'ulema* and intellectuals during the second constitutional period.[13]

Ziya Gökalp, the spiritual father of Turkish nationalism, joined in the controversy over the Caliphate. Sociologically, he said.[14] national consciousness is a higher stage in social evolution and basic social reality is nationality while the *umma,* the religious community embracing many nations, confers an additional identity to the individual. Turkey reached to the stage of national consciousness during the war of independence. The Caliph as the head of the religious community, he continued, has to be exclusively a religious authority and spiritual guide. His claim to have a political authority in a nation-state can only lead to conflicts detrimental to both nation and religion. As Islam and *umma,* he argued, are also social and religious realities, a Caliph as their head and symbol is necessary

10 Hoca Ubeydullâh, "Hilâfet-i Sahîha", *ibid.,* 50-54.

11 *Atatürk'ün Söylev ve Demeçleri,* 62-3, 37, 144-46.

12 H. A. R. Gibb, *Modern Trends in Islam,* Chicago, 1947; "Islâh" *EI*², vol. IV, 141-71; Fazlur Rahman, *Islam,* New York, 1968, 237-315.

13 H. Z. Ülken, *Türk Düşünce Tarihi.*

14 "Hilâfetin Hakiki Mâhiyeti", *Hilafet ve Millî Hâkimiyet,* 1-10

for the unity of Islam. In his earlier writings[15] Gökalp had warmly advocated "the re-opening of the gate of *idjtihâd*" for modernizing the Islamic community as far as worldly affairs were concerned. At any rate, Gökalp had exerted strong influence on the *inkilâbcı* concept of a secular state and law. *Hoca*s as well as *inkilâbcı*s writers were concerned with keeping the Caliphate in the custody of the Turkish nation during this period because the England were trying to assume the role of the protector of the Caliphate and were in favor of the idea of recognizing Sherif Husayn of Mecca, a descendant of the Prophet, as the supreme Caliph of the Islamic world. Against this plan the Turkish press argued that the Caliphate can exist and survive only with the support of an independent and strong Islamic state. Islamic leaders in India, notably Maulana Mehmed Ali, Amir Ali and the Agha Khan publicly supported the Turkish nationalist view that only the GNA of Turkey had the right to elect the Caliph, and denounced the English plan as an interference in the internal affairs of Muslims.[16]

The question of the Caliphate was further complicated by becoming an issue of power politics among the nationalist leaders. According to the report given in Atatürk's speech in 1927, Rauf then prime minister told him that "it is difficult for us to make ourselves masters of the general situation; this can be secured by a higher office and the sublime dignity which everybody generally considers to be unapproachable. This office, this dignity and the attempt to substitute it by a body of a different character would lead to disappointment and disaster. This is not to be thought of."[17] The attitude which Rauf Refet, Kâzım Karabekir and others were going to take later on clearly showed that what they really wanted was to prevent Kemal's taking over the control of all state power. Collective leadership of the Independence War was going to split up over the issue

15 Z. Gökalp, *Turkish Nationalism and Western Civilization,* ed. and trans. N. Berkes, London, 1959.

16 *Hilâfet ve Millî Hakimiyet,* 129-64.

17 Mustafa Kemal Atatürk, *A Speech,* Leipzig, 1929, 573.

of the political form which the country was going to take. Now Kemal created an inner circle around him with his closest comrades İsmet, Fevzi and Kâzım (Özalp) to further the *inkilâb.* Incidentally, the word *inkilâb* chosen by Kemal for the revolution he was leading originally meant transformation or radical change without violence. In carrying out the revolutionary changes Kemal's tactic was to introduce them through acts of the GNA which, he always asserted, was the only and absolute holder of national sovereignty. Actually, this was his only source of legitimate power and support in using state power first against foreign adversaries during the Independence War and then against his opponents during the revolution in the period 1922-1924. In 1923, when he encountered potential opposition in the GNA, including from some of the army generals, on the issue of the powers of the Caliph, he decided to create a political party and to gather the nation around himself as *halâskâr ghâzî,* the saviour of the fatherland.[18] Rauf and other generals had reminded him that at the beginning of the Independence War they had declared before the nation that they were fighting to deliver the Caliphate from captivity. Now Kemal was going directly to the nation to seek its support for the *inkilâb.* Kemal's political campaign in western and central Anatolia in January-March 1923 was designed to back up the Turkish delegation at the Lausanne peace conference as well as "to exchange views," Kemal said, "with people on the questions concerning the present and the future."[19] This campaign was to have a tremendous significance for the events to come in Turkey in the following years.[20]

In İzmit, he rejected the idea that the Caliph should be considered as the head of state or a dignitary bearing political responsibility. He argued that since the greater part of the Muslim world was at

---

18 The most important source: Atatürk, *A Speech,* 570-90; A. H. F. Cebesoy, *Milli Mücadele Hatıraları,* Istanbul, 1953; *Siyasî Hatıralar,* 2 vols, Istanbul, 1957, 1960; M. Gologlu, *Devrim ve Tepkileri, 1924-1930,* Ankara, 1972, 57-84.

19 *Söylev ve Demeçler,* II, Ankara 1959, 49-50.

20 *Ibid.*, 50-164.

the moment under foreign domination, the GNA took the Caliphate under its protection until the time when other Muslim countries became independent and gave a definitive form to the Caliphate. In the meantime, he said, the new Caliph Abdülmecid will be wise enough to realize his real position and cautious enough not to cause a crisis by inappropriate action or behavior. All along the campaign he addressed himself to two different groups separately, the *halk,* common people, artisans, peasants, landowners and farmers on the one hand, and, on the other, youth or *münevverân,* that is students and the intellectual elite. But this cleavage between two sections of the Turkish nation he observed had to be remedied; the intellectuals should go to people and try to eliminate the alienation by evaluating popular national culture[21] an idea that will give rise in later years to the *Halk-evleri,* that is people's houses and other populist movements in Turkey. He saw that this cleavage between *halk* and *münevver* could be fateful for the entire *inkilâb* and for the changes he was planning to introduce in the future. Later, in 1924, by suppressing religious schools along with the Caliphate and establishing one secular educational system he believed that he would create one Turkish nation. In the meetings in every city he visited the *hoca*s, clerics came forward as the spokesmen of the *halk,* people, a function established in the traditional Ottoman society. Questions posed by both groups centered around the position of the Caliph and Islam within the new state. Since Kemal's opponents claimed that the Caliphate could not be separated from the state and the new Caliph had to assume real responsibility in the state, the future of the Caliphate had become the most fundamental and emotional issue across the country.

In his answers to *hoca*s, Kemal used the religious arguments forwarded by the Islamic modernists saying that Islam originally depended on consultative government, and the community's sovereignty was an essential principle in early Islam.[22] He said also that sovereignty was later usurped by despots with a theory totally foreign to the orig-

21 Ibid., 140.

22 Ibid., 63.

inal Islamic precepts and thus the exercise of absolute sovereignty by the GNA only means the reestablishment of this right.[23] But on the other hand, Kemal must have been aware that the use of Islam for the *inkilâb* was contradictory. The *hoca*s were using it confidently against the *inkilâb* before a religious mass ready to listen. On this platform, no real agreement was possible, for the reactionary *hoca*s were talking about the Islamic *umma,* or community ruled by the Religious Law and its administrator the Caliph, while the *inkilâbcıs* were considering the people as a nation whose government was based on the national will. In the press, at the same period, Ağaoğlu Ahmed was severely criticized and ridiculed by the conservative *hocas* for defending the *inkilâb* based on the same Islamic sources.[24] In his speeches, Kemal carefully distinguished the modernist *hoca*s by calling them "the enlightened *'ulema*" while he accused the conservatives of following the example of those *'ulema* who served despotic Caliphs for their own personal interests. Kemal talked about conservative *hoca*s as a class with vested interests in defense of the traditional order.[25] Many of them actually made up part of the powerful body of notables in the provinces. He denounced them as enemies of the nation fomenting against the *inkilab* which had restored the nation's sovereign rights. Thus, the question of the Caliphate became a cover for the power struggle between the *hoca*s who were the spokesmen of the old regime and the *inkilâbcı*s who were determined to change the Turkish state and society towards a modern nation-state.

Kemal emerged as a radical revolutionary when he was speaking to the youth and *münevver*s, an elite with secular and professional education, during the campaign. In Konya, a city known traditionally as being unsympathetic to the Ottoman dynasty, in an emotional speech Kemal declared that "if they (the supporters of the Caliphate) make a wrong move he shall consider it not only an opposition against his personal beliefs and goals but a conspiracy

23 Ibid., 145; Ağaoğlu Ahmed, 11-32.

24 *Hilâfet ve Milli Hâkimiyet,* 191-207.

25 *Söylev ve Demeçler,* 144.

and a deadly danger against the life and existence of his nation. When this happens the only thing that he and his comrades who shared his ideals have to do is to act and fight until their total destruction."[26] This speech was published in the official newspaper, *Hâkimiyet-i Milliye* (26 March 1923). This was a declaration of war against those who hoped to create a movement against the *inkilâb*. Confrontation was inevitable. But it was also essential to save the country from an internal struggle at a time when debates crucial for the future of the nation were being carried on at the Lausanne peace conference. This was the purpose of the political campaign and Kemal used every argument to win over public opinion for his cause. In addition to the notion of the supremacy of national sovereignty he opened an intense campaign to discredit the Ottoman dynasty and history. He reminded people how he Sultan-Caliph had then organized "the armies of the Caliphate" against the national movement and used Greek aircraft to drop *fetwâs* on the nationalist forces condemning nationalist leaders as rebels. Historically the Ottoman Sultan-Caliphs, he said, had always acted as despots and, abusing the good faith of the Turkish people they had wasted Turkish blood across remote frontiers for their vanity."[27]

With a personality combining the idealist and statesman, Kemal was at the same time a strategist, and a pragmatic politician. He asserted in his speeches to the youth that the *inkilâbci*s definitely were going to win the struggle. The assurance came from the fact that he had full control of the armed forces. What distinguished Turkey at the time from other Islamic countries was that a westernized military elite trained in the professional secular schools took the leadership of the radical modernization process, and the Independence War had produced a leader with incomparable charisma and ability. Leadership of the military elite for modernization had become a tradition in Turkey since Süleyman Pasha's coup of 1876 and particularly the second constitutional revolution in 1908. At the beginning of his campaign

26 Ibid., 146.

27 Ibid., 100-106, 121.

on January 18, 1923 at İzmit he warned his opponents. "Those who achieved the *inkilâb*", he declared, "have all the necessary power to crush the reaction... It should be clearly understood that the moment a dangerous situation is caused by a dignitary or a person, then, theory stops and action starts."[28] During the same campaign he promised to the reserve and regular army officers as well as to the professional elite that the government shall take measures to improve their welfare.[29]

When he was back in Ankara from the tour he had the GNA pass a law to the effect that anyone acting contrary to the GNA's decision on the abolition of the Sultanate and the legality of the acts of the GNA shall be sued under the law of treason to the country.[30]

Kemal's political campaign in early 1923 is of crucial significance not only for his major *inkilâb* with the radical changes in the political order of the country, but also for publicly expressing the changes Kemal and his *inkilâbcı* companions were planning for the future. First and above all he made it perfectly clear that the GNA representing national sovereignty was the only source of political power in Turkey and no political responsibility was going to be accorded to a member of the Ottoman dynasty under whatever name or office. He declared the Ottoman state dead and replaced by a new Turkish state. This declaration would logically lead to the promulgation of the republic and the abolition of the Caliphate. On January 16, 1923 in an interview with newsmen he declared that "in order to lead the nation and the country to the level of modern civilization and human progress the government and people have to make rapid and long advances." He spoke of equal rights for women, use of simple Turkish by the preachers at the mosques, and having a modern appearance in attire. At Bursa in a talk with people he said, "any nation claiming to be a civilized, progressive and developed nation is definitely to make statues" and there is nothing, he asserted, religiously wrong in this.[31]

---

28 Ibid., 64.

29 Ibid.

30 Kocatürk, 252.

31 *Söylev ve Demeçler*, 127, 133, 151.

The reason for the Prophet to prohibit making statues, he further argued, was necessary in those days to fight idolatry. Today, he said, "I cannot imagine any Muslim Turk looking at a statue as an idol. Our nation shall make beautiful statues and this will not make them less Muslim".[32] Kemal found justification and impetus for his plans of the most radical legal reforms when the allied powers at Lausanne stubbornly resisted the abolition of the capitulations on the grounds that Turkey was a backward country and still under Islamic Law. Kemal immediately set up a committee for legal reforms and the Turkish delegation declared that Turkey was under way to adopt European laws in civil matters soon".[33] The convocation of a conference in Izmir on national economy also coincided with the claims of economic independence of Turkey and abolition of capitulatory ties.[34] It is very interesting to observe the parallelism between Turkish claims to be a fully independent modern nation-state and as such to ask for equal treatment at Lausanne, and Kemal's promises of taking radical measures to modernize Turkey during his Anatolian tour in 1923.

While he rejected the attitude of the western powers toward his nation, he at the same time had come to the realization and deeply felt belief that an independent existence for the nation absolutely depended on complete modernization, and that there is no more fundamental principle than the law of survival in this world. "The law of *inkilâb*" he declared at İzmit, "is above all existing laws."[35] It was impossible for him to subject the nation to a law, even when this law was in the scriptures, if eventually it led to a servile existence in this world. His whole philosophy of life was based on the Darwinian theory of survival. The pragmatic outlook on life with a belief in the decisive role of actual power for survival is the key to understanding Atatürk's personality, and his tactics in politics and *inkilâb.* In his speeches he always stressed that life is struggle, and

32 Ibid., 66.

33 C. Bilsel, *Lozan,* II, Istanbul, 1933, 79-118.

34 *Türkiye İktisat Kongresi, 1923-Izmir, Haberler-Belgeler-Yorumlar,* ed. A. G. Okçün, Ankara, 1968: Atatürk's opening speech, 246, 253.

35 *Söylev ve Demeçler,* 63.

that success in this struggle depends on being prepared for struggle. In 1923 at Akhisar for instance he said, "Every nation in this world wants to survive and survival depends on struggle... this country shall definitely become a modern, progressive and developed one. This is a struggle of survival for us."[36] If we are to define Kemalism in terms of a social doctrine we may find it in social Darwinism.

Representing all the traditional forces in the country, the Caliphate had the potential to become the center of reaction to the *inkilâb* and to the modernizing reforms of the future. Kemal expressed the concern during his campaign that the supporters of the Caliphate had plans to bring back the Sultanate.

Always in his logic of struggle for survival, the reaction to the *inkilâb,* he said, is a conspiracy against the life and existence of the nation and the *inkilâbci*s should use every means to overcome it. The incidents leading to the abolition of the Caliphate in 1924 are well known.

A rather practical matter, the question of *who* actually was the head of the state, came to the fore when the allied powers at Lausanne made it an issue. Conservatives turned their eyes naturally to the Caliph. Subsequently, Abdulmecid's behavior and the attention he was getting in the country and abroad led the *inkilâbci*s to make a revolutionary move although it was as always achieved through the GNA. Seven months after Kemal's tour in Anatolia, and three months after the signing of the peace treaty, the Republic was promulgated by the GNA and Kemal was elected its first president. İsmet became prime minister. This new *inkilâb* further estranged the Rauf group from Kemal, and when the rumours of the Caliph's resignation spread, the opposition beseeched him not to do it because this as Lütfi Fikri, chairman of the Istanbul bar, put it, "would thrust the world into a calamity."

A letter supporting the Caliph written by the Indian Muslim leaders to İsmet Pasha was published in an Istanbul newspaper before it reached the addressee. This as well as Rauf's visit to the Caliph

36 Ibid., 93.

in Istanbul, made Kemal and İsmet decide to make the final move and abolish the Caliphate through the GNA. In the following four years the GNA enacted revolutionary laws designed to complete the secularization of the state and society which actually constituted the logical consequences of the revolutionary *élan* and of the great *inkilâb* which took place in the period 1922-1923. All the pre-requisites for a nation-state were formally enacted and promulgated.[37]

What was accomplished by the abolition of the Caliphate and the immediate measures of secularization was a radical revolution. As Count Ostrorog, a judicial consultant to the Ottoman government and a close observer of the changes in Turkey in 1924 pointed out[38], this was "one of the most considerable events that has happened in the history of the East since the fourteenth century."

The abolition of the Caliphate on March 3, 1924 and the suppression of an insurrection in Eastern Anatolia in the following year marked the final victory of the *inkilâbcı*s over the religious establishment. But secularization introduced by the unification of public instruction under a secular administration and promulgation of the Swiss civil code as Turkey's law in 1926, meant a much more radical revolution for Islam. Free from the intricacies of the Islamic theology and jurisprudence the *inkilâbcı*s went further and asserted that religion is only a matter of the conscience of the individual. In his speech before the abolition of the Caliphate Kemal declared that "For salvation in the next world and happiness in this world of the nation it became imperative to move decisively and without delay to free our consciences and religious beliefs which are sacred and sublime from politics and from all its accretions which have proved to be only an instrument for all kinds of shady and unstable games of interests and ambitions."[39] "The word of Revolution was not pronounced" Count Ostrorog observes,[40] "but activities soon manifested themselves that were indeed not Evolution but

37 Kocatürk, 260-66, and the sources referred to there; and Gologlu, *Ibid.*.
38 Count Léon Ostrorog, *The Angora Reform,* London, 1927,
39 Atatürk, *A Speech,* 576-78; Kocatürk, 266: *Zabıtlar Ceridesi,* Devre II, Vol. VIII,
40 Ostrorog, 70.

such a Revolution as the world of Islam had never seen... what has been done is somewhat more than reform, something that tends to revise fundamental tenets supported by an established doctrine and an ancient observance, not reform but reformation.... It may even become the starting-point for an important renewal of Islamic thought developing on terms of an independent liberal exegesis."

Half a century has passed since Kemal's revolution but Count Ostrorog's hope has not been realized. On the contrary the reaction came in its most fundamental form aiming at subjecting the state and society more than ever to the *Sharia* as established by the great *imâms* of the eighth and ninth centuries. Those governments which followed Kemal's revolution and modernization program even partially have been either totally destroyed or forced to change their policies.

Mustafa Kemal Atatürk was a statesman but above all a revolutionary who believed that rapid modernization was a matter of life and death for his nation, and that could be achieved by revolution legitimized by the modern principle of national will against a concept of divine authority. His modernization pattern can be classified in the terminology of political scientists as a forced one from above by a modernizing leader. "Man" as C. E. Block observes in *The Dynamics of Modernization* (157), "is not a captive of history despite the undeniable persistence of historically evolved traditions... The character of the policies of modernization adopted and the way that they are implemented depend to a considerable degree on leadership." But, he added, "instant modernization is not within the realm of possibility." Modernization is the end result of an historical process of a more or less long period. It was not an accident that Turkey could achieve the most radical revolution in modern Islam, and is today the least affected Muslim nation by the upsurge of Islamic fundamentalism. By revolution and with the strong backing of a group of *inkilâbcı*s as well as with the approval of a large section of the population, Atatürk was able to eliminate the control of a powerful clerical hierarchy and to introduce the legal and political conditions for rapid social development and modernization.

ARTICLE REFERANCES

1. "The Rise of Ottoman Historiography," *Historians of the Middle East*, eds. P. Holt and B. Lewis, London 1962, 152-167.
2. "On the Social Structure of the Ottoman Empire: Paradigms and Research," *From Empire to Republic: Essays on Ottoman and Turkish Social History*, Isis Press, 1995, 17-60.
3. "The Çift-Hane System and Peasant Taxation," Paper read at *Ecole des Hautes études en Sciences Sociales*, Paris, 1992.
4. "Les régions de Kruje et de la Dibra autour de 1467 et 1519," *Studia Albanica*, II (1968), 89-102.
5. "Ottoman Archival Materials on Millets," *Christians and Jews in the Ottoman Empire*, I, eds. B. Braude and B. Lewis, New York 1981, 437-49
6. "Sephardic Jews in the Ottoman Empire," Paper read at the *Conference on Sephardic Jews*, Istanbul, June 4, 1992.
7. "Turkish Impact on the Development of Modern Europe," *The Ottoman State and its Place in World History*, ed. K. Karpat, Leiden: Brill 1974, 51-58.
8. "Political Modernization in Turkey," *Political Modernization in Japan and Turkey*, eds. R. E. Ward and D. A. Rustow, Princeton 1968, 42-63.
9. "Turkey Between Europe and the Middle East," *Foreign Policy*, VIII, 3/4 (1980), 7-31.
10. "The Caliphate and Atatürk's *İnkılab*," *Belleten*, XLVI/182 (1982), 353-365.

INDEX